King Arthur

An Astral King

Owen Knight

LeftHandPress

New Orleans, Louisiana USA

ISBN: 978-0615736143

United States • United Kingdom • Europe

Publisher's Foreword

"Arthur son of Uther Pendragon, son of Custenhin, son of Kynvawr, son of Theoderic the Great, son of Moruawr, son of Urbien, son of Conan, son of Gerenton" the names filled the auto's interior and came pouring out over me as I opened the door. The deluge almost made me spill the remainder of the coffee I had gone into the roadhouse to purchase for our trip.

Owen was reciting a litany of names, markers of obscure and ancient lineages, when I had left the dusty vehicle. They were part of a story he was telling me. He seemed to have continued the recitation while I was busy spilling our coffee on the floor, then counter, then front lot.

I looked at him with some surprise.

"It's the sound that matters." was his simple yet infinitely complex reply.

I nodded knowing that a bard carries much more than news, he carries lineages reaching back into and connecting the worlds of substance and shadow. Sound opens a direct window onto these lineages.

Names are useful things in our arts and Owen's King Arthur could be subtitled a Book of Names. There are subtle conjures here. To know the name of a spirit and withhold your own name is to purchase power over that spirit in a shadowy slave economy of the soul. To reverse the equation is the signature of a faith that can bring the worker to good or ill; witness the unpronounceable Name of God and all those who pay homage to Its power. To exchange names with a spirit can be to bless and burn, die and be reborn in an ecstasy of union. Those who have a practice, reverends, priestesses, and doctors will find much in this book of use in both understanding their experiences and conducting

3

their experiments.

The names in this book dance in the brilliant light of Owen's understanding. They ride like crowns upon the heads of their bearers, their letters as jewels illuminating a manuscript of the soul. They pirouette to tunes played by instruments more subtle than those heard by the rude hammer and anvil of human ear and then spread afar like a cloud of leaves over a Fall land. These are names which contain deeds and tales that rise with the mist then to fall into the neither regions of the evening as their light fails.

It is Owen's assertion that the old tales, now separate, once were one vast diptherama. In his book the tales cross and intersect and once again connect. The beginnings and deeds and endings of men and women and gods and goddesses shake and whirl and pirouette to form vast webs of meaning. Arthur fills a vast space. His comings and goings continue in this and the lands beyond sight.

Owen is my friend and teacher and he is a keeper of these names. In the goodness of time his name and tales will join this splendid company. Honor and Respect to Howerton Owen Knight.

Dr. Louie Martinié
The Witches Ball
On the Feast of All Hollows, 1912
Avenue Saint Charles, New Orleans

Introduction

"As above, so below."

This statement has, in the past, been said by philosophers, and this belief is a major part of the Arthurian Story. Personalities and events in King Arthur's Astral Worlds are reflected from those worlds into this world. Time and time again, there is the occurrence, in material form, in this world, of objects and personalities which have an existence in Arthurian spirit worlds. And these have had a large importance to this world. These have been honoured and the personalities petitioned to give knowledge, justice, charity and other blessings. And this has been especially true of King Arthur himself. King Arthur is thought to continue to give protection and other blessings to his lands. However, as King Arthur and related deities can not be depended on to supply justice, charity and other benefits, it has been considered important for the individuals through out the land to supply these benefits: to be just, generous, charitable.

In lands where King Arthur has been honoured, it has been felt that individuals, including those considered to be deities, have spirit forms which take physical form after physical form. So the history of a person would not have a definite starting and stopping place.

In the histories of King Arthur, an important feature is the use made of the knowledge of the relationship of Earth to the heavens. Many courses of action were taken because of words spoken by those who studied the heavens. And this was true even when the words held little literal meaning. Those words would have been considered things of great value, even when, as with an abstract painting, people for the life of them could not have said what that value was.

The Pendragons

ach personality has an astral form, and this might be united with a physical form in this dimension and in this World. If it is not, it would be in an astral world. In this case, it might be seen in a place in this world, or in more than one place at the same time, but it would not be in the physical place where it seemed to be. It would be in a world which could not be reached by physical movement alone. King Uther and King Arthur have resided, except for brief periods of time, in an astral world.

In the past, a beautiful bear goddess, Kalliste, guarded, along with Thuban, the way to the Underworld, a world filled with deadly forces which could bring disasters to this world. However, not only was the way guarded by Kalliste and Thuban, it was blocked by the mighty Sacred Apple Tree. And Thuban, the mighty judge, was placed to make certain the blocking tree was not disturbed. Thuban was a supreme, unwavering judge, and he had the watchful support of Zeus; however, malicious forces shifted the sacred Apple Tree off the awful hole, and caused Thuban to see wrongly, so that his untrue vision caused him to think all was in place as it should be. But now, the hole unguarded, awful monsters came out of the hole. Typhon came out. And this caused havoc in the world. When order was restored, Gaea brought the King Dragon into the World of the Gods and gave him to Hera. Hera put the Apple Tree back in place; put the King Dragon to guard the tree.

Beside their astral forms, the Dragon King, Uther, and the beautiful Bear Goddess, Kalliste, would take, at times, human form. They were together in human form and their copulation caused Kalliste to become

7

pregnant with Arcas. The land where Arcas lived was called, after Arcas, Arcady. This was a bright, mountainous, happy, peaceful land of song and pastoral activities. It was a land of shepherds, a land where Pan was honoured and Pan is there said to have led the song and dance. And in the middle of the day, there was a quiet, so that no noise would disturb Pan's rest. Arcas was a hunter and his mother had evolved into her bear form. In this form, she was unrecognized by Arcas, her son, and he, while hunting was about to slay her. To prevent this impiety, Zeus put Arcas, as Kalliste was, into bear form and put the two of them into the sky. Not all persons were happy to have them there, as the two of them were now near the sacred Apple Tree which Kalliste was supposed to have been guarding. And her son, Arcas, had now become a form of great power; his spirit, felt to be centered in the Star Arcturus. Poseidon forbade both Kalliste and her son, Arcas, from entering Ocean.

The Spirit of Arcas would, a number of times, have had physical rebirths in Arcady in order to lend force to maintaining the character of the land to which he had given his name. In one age, Arcas had a birth as the grandson of Lycaon who held the spirit of an oak and related to the Spirit of Lightning. When Arcas had lived for nine years, Lycaon slew him and fed his flesh at a dinner which was attended by Zeus. Seeing the flesh, with a flash of lightning, Zeus turned Lycaon and his sons into wolves. Draco, who has the nature to be lusty, and Gaea brought Arcas back to life so Arcas could continue with his civilizing influence.

Later, Arcas had a birth as Artio, and he has been associated with ploughing. In early times, the Plough of Arcas was observed for the learning it provided. Arcas' Plough which was most often observed would have been his plough in its astral existence. Then, the spirit of astral form would invade form in the physical world. This has been seen in great Heavenly Beasts having places on Earth's surface. In Britain, the King Dragon Spirit has been seen to shape land masses such as that at Butleigh. At the coast of Britain, formed by the land, the Guardian Dog of the Underworld is seen. It has been called "The Great Dog of Langport," or "of Logres." It is outlined, in part, by the Parrett River. It guarded the land of apples. Leo, the Lion, was found to be formed by natural boundaries. It's been looked for and not found

8

by the searcher; then, people who were not looking for it have found it suddenly revealed. The Lion holds many powers: courage, health, vigour, the regenerating power of the Sun. The Goat Form was found near the cross formed by the Sun. It gave care to the Old Sun and to the new born Sun. The Round Table was generated by the Round Table of the Stars. Before Uther, the Spirit of the Table would have been seen at a number of gatherings where chiefs sat at a circle of power. The Sacred Cauldron, the Grail, reflected, or was a common spirit, with sacred sky spirits.

The astral forms which are represented by Earth forms might suddenly shift even massive physical forms. The Juggler might transpose a couple of objects, might change a form's direction. One might be on a road which now goes West instead of East, which was once his direction.

Astral personalities take physical form. The upright, authorative Thuban would have taken form as Theodosius. Then again, as Theoderic. He would have been a leader of great integrity who would have maintained order, as the unwavering judge. He organized aid. Magnus Maximus gave the needed power for ridding the lands of disruptive leaders, and a power behind Magnus was Uther. Two large rulers, Valentian and Gratian were disposed of; then, when Magnus Maximus rose to a position of great power and threatened to overbalance the system, Theodosius had him executed. Maximus' son, Victor, left the Earth at this time also and this, at the hand of Arbogast. The demonic Arbogast, with his army, then attacked Uther and Uther was slain.

Uther the Pen Dragon would have been taking a series of forms in this world and in other worlds. He would have had battles with Hercules in this and in otherworlds, and in about half of these he was the victor. In a battle with Cadmus, he was slain. And Uther formed on Earth to influence the stability of large groups of people. He had been a power behind Theodosius: watchful, ever alert, awake, relentless, inflexible, severe. His personality infused land masses. In Britain, Uther formed one of the astral personalities in the area of Glastonbury. The Bull, the Twins, Argo, the Lion, the Virgin with her sheaf of grain, formed around Uther. A form of the Goat protected the new Sun and gave comfort to the old Sun, and the Goat was at the Castle of Venus.

Draco, as people saw him in lands and in physical forms, was at times called the Serpent of Malvern. The Lion, in ground features and other physical form, was called the Lion of Stafford, and it was a challenge to the Serpent. Yet all the time Draco kept an unblinking, unfailing, all seeing eye on the Pole. As it was his duty.

The head of Draco sits at the top of the pyramid, as the Serpent is the Symbol of Wisdom. His tail sits between the Great Bear and the Little Bear.

The Little Bear sits in the pyramid. He has been called the generative force of the world, the God of Generative Powers. The astral form of the Little Bear comes at times into the physical in order to defend his people and to bring them civilization. He has been called Arcus and Artorius when his birthings have occurred. He had a birthing at a time when Gratian and other destructive chiefs threatened to bring disorder, and in this time, became a military leader, routed the army of Gratian, captured Gratian and had him slain. He later died in a battle at the Sare River.

At that time the Polar influence faded as the Great Dragon and the Little Bear withdrew from the scene. With this change, the strongly male rule became diminished. There came confusion: a mad turmoil: a clash of customs and concepts and codes of conduct. This led to conflicts, unreasoned and unreasonable clashes. Warriors walked on the veils which separated this world from the Underworld. Mother Earth made her influence felt. The Great Sow was a dangerous adversary to cross.

There was mad disorder in the land.

The spiritual center of this land would have been likely the Tower on the round hill at Glastonbury. The hill itself is so regular that it seems a glassy green dome on an Underworld temple. There were, however, rises and dips on the green mountain and these made the mountain shimmer on sunny days, and from its top rose a tall, narrow slab of transparent rock, and the last third of its height was a narrow extension which, in sunlight, seemed a ray of fire. And the dome and rock and all might have had an Otherworld connection, as do some of the little blue pools which occur here and there in out of the way places in the land; pools which would be quite there, not infrequently visited; then, one day be gone.

In the warm times of the year, the area around Glastonbury is bright green as if it held the charms of the Sun. And the area around the hill itself is marshy, so blue sky reflects off the still water, and between the water and where the meadows begin their rise are apple trees. And these form white clouds in the spring. The Glastonbury hill is one of a series of hills which swing in a circle. And each hill holds a Star Giant, and coming up into that land is the River Parrett and this, fed by streams and brooks. One of these is the Cam, which flows past Camel Hill. These were names for King Cole, as he was, in some places, known as Camel. And this area was guarded by the Dog. And the Dog was not a Star Giant, but related to the Underworld. He guarded, at Burrow Mump, the way to Logres. And he guarded Langport, or Longborth. And he guarded the Cam, which led to the Gate to the Underworld, which is not under anything, but is another place, and not of this World.

The Cam was the way to the land of King Cole. King Cole was a mighty warrior and he carried a much dreaded sword, but he was usually thought of first for his relation to the arts. He was considered, King of Bards, Lord of Poetry, Master of Song and Chief of all wise men. King Cole, beside his form as an Earthly King, was also a Hazel tree, and this related him to the Kingdom of the Elves over which Gwynn ap Nudd is Lord, as the Hazel rules over magic and wisdom. And as the Hazel is the ninth tree, it is the closest to the inner chambers of the Goddesses of the Underworld. The goddess Creide said that her mate needed to be able to sing a perfect poem in which all the contents of her bedroom were named. There were nine gates to her lands, to her castle, to her bedroom, and each was under the responsibility of a different Tree. As King Cole was responsible for the ninth gate, he came and went as he pleased, so was able to construct the song.

In the World, in those early days, King Cole was not known to be there in human form. However, in the World, there were then many competing forces. Even when there was a king accepted throughout a wide area, there were many local battles and much lawlessness and disorder. When Caswallawn ap Beli was king, he kept the lands free from successful invasions, and he was recognized widely as the great king, though a turmoil of conflicts revolved around him. The little that he got involved in certainly elevated his stature, so that his bigness was taken for granted. When he defeated the Vikings, his victories were celebrated with festivals in highly decorated halls. Fine dress was worn, and sacrifices were made at the shrine of Apollo. Years passed, Caswallawn died. His grand nephew, Cymbeline ap Tenvant, became king.

The land under Cymbeline prospered. He was called wise and just, and Taliesin served as his bard and Taliesin was by many considered to be a wizard. And Cymbeline was considered magical. His lands were held, in part, by a number of magical fortifications. One, Maiden Castle. This, sat on the top of a wide topped hill of an oval shape extending, in length, a thousand yards. This space is covered with a mysterious assortment of walls and entrenchments. This fort was known as the Castle of Strength. And there was Castlerigg Circle at Keswick Carles. Near the fortifications was a thirtyeight stone Druid Circle; the stones, flattened at the northeast. Inside the hundred foot circle, ten stones were set in an oblong. And at the east, there is a hill over which the Sun rises at spring and fall equinoxes. To the southwest, a short distance away, a standing stone marks the direction of the winter sunset. Beautiful mountains stand blue in the distance. All Earth might have opposed transgressions. This might have been felt by those who passed between the huge stones, the megaliths at the north gate of the circle. In some areas Earth would have been an obvious and even at times frightening power. An example, an intimidating installation called Carn Gluze. Under its dark, moss covered roof, an ancient, worn stone stairway circles its way deep into the ground; the stairs, going down between worn, damp stone walls. This was a spooky stairway.

Beside the support of the Goddesses of Earth, King Cymbeline would also have had the support of Lords of the Sky. Cymbeline was able to obtain thunderstones, weapons from the gods which created great roars, and much devastation, when they struck the targets.

Cymbeline was much engaged in trade. Ships came to his ports for wheat, iron and tin. British hunting dogs also brought a fair price. The trade aided in the development of beautiful courts. Especially praised was Cymbeline's court at Colchester. His courts were the envy of many countries overseas and these included some with larger populations.

Cymbeline died and was buried, as Caswallawn had been, near the

Temple of the Sun, in York.

Cymbeline had three sons who had been engaged in the rule of the kingdom: Wither, Arviragus and Ynyr. Wither, the elder, became king after Cymbeline, and he was assisted by his brothers. King Wither was a champion warrior, and was just, but hard and stern. Laws, he said, must be respected. King Claud, believing King Wither was not a well loved king, got a fleet of ships together and invaded that king's lands. However, King Wither, loved or not, was an excellent military commander and more than King Claud could deal with. King Claud attempted to get worthy knights close enough to slay King Wither, but King Wither slew all his enemy who got close to him. So King Claud had a warrior named Hamun dress as a Britain, mingle with the British, slip close to King Wither. Hamun dressed, mingled with the British, stabbed his sword into King Wither's back. Arviragus took his brother's place and the slaughter of King Claud's men continued so that King Claud and his men were forced to flee to their ships, and those captured, they were slit open and their intestines were yanked out. Hamun, who had fled into the forest, was discovered and brought to Arviragus. The lord was kind, but he was just, so he had each arm, each leg, of Hamun tied to a horse, and so, Hamun died.

King Claud returned from oversea with a large army, won a battle, but thought it wise to make peace with King Arviragus. King Claud sent for his family and King Arviragus married Genuis, the daughter of King Claud. King Claud took a noble lady of Port Chester as his mistress and they had a son, Prince Gloi.

The lands then grew prosperous under the wise rule of King Arviragus. After many years, he died and his son, Maurice, became king. King Maurice was a good warrior and was a learned man and the kingdom prospered. He was invaded by a Viking king, Roderic, and King Roderic had joined with him a host of Picts. In a great battle, King Maurice slew King Roderic and after the battle, a peace was made with the Picts. The Picts were given lands and they sent envoys to Eire, to King Gille Caor, requesting him to send warriors who wanted wives to the lands of the Picts, as many Pict warriors had been lost in battle.

King Maurice, after a long life died. His son, Coel, became king, and he, like his father, was a strong man and good leader; however, as he was not young when he became king, his years as king were not many.

His eldest son, Luces, followed him on the throne. His second son, Cenu, wed the granddaughter of King Gloi, and he became ruler of the realm which had been established by King Claud. Cenu was a strong warrior and he kept good order in his lands. And there was not much notice given to his lands by those in other lands. King Luces, on the other hand, had fine cities near the sea, and he was much involved in commerce. It was often to his lands that ships would come. King Luces was wise, well educated, and his people enjoyed good rule. However, in some parts, lords became strong and felt separated from the central authority. King Luces died and his son, Sevarus, became king. At that time there were a good number of kings and lords competing for fame and lands. Three were grandsons of Ynyr: King Cawrdaf, King Ergyng and King Enhinti. And after Cenu was slain in battle his son, Mor became king in the area where there is the city called Gloucester, and ships went to the ports of King Mor with horses and gold in exchange for fine dogs.

Medrawd, the son of King Cawrdaf, was slain and he was replaced by his son, King Dyfnawg. And in the northern hills, King Gerenton ruled. King Sevarus built fortified ditches to keep war minded kings and lords out, but he was attacked by Britons and Picts, who were led by Lord Fulgenes. In a battle, both that lord and King Sevarus were slain; however, the invaders were driven out. King Sevarus had been wise and just, a king of much dignity, and he was buried with honours at York. His sons, halfbrothers, each claimed the crown. The forces of the one fought against the forces of the other, princes Basian against Gezan. Basian slew Gezan and so, became king. Carrais, one of Basian's knights, then went over sea, raised an army, returned and slew King Basian. However, Carrais' rule was short, as warriors led by Lord Allec captured and slew Carrais and Lord Allec was made king.

During this time, a king from Eire had invaded lands of King Gerenton, had been defeated, but that king was slain. His son, Urbien, became king. To his south, King Allec was well liked, as he was generous and just, but his lands were invaded by Lord Asclepidiot and his warriors of Cornwall. King Allec was slain and his son, Prince Angenwit, with many of his warriors, fled the land. Asclepidiot was, of that land, made king. Behind this land, King Moruawr had replaced King Urbien and now ruled lands once ruled by his grandfather, King

14

Gerenton. The sons of King Ergyng, King Pebiew and King Nynniaw, each ruled great sections of land. King Coel had replaced his father, King Mor, and Natanleod had become king in the north. King Asclepidiot was well liked, but in those times, where he lived was dangerous. On one side, Prince Gurgan, the son of King Pebiew; was thought, a force to beware of. To protect against him and others, King Coel increased his own holdings, expanded onto the lands ruled by King Asclepidiot and in a battle, King Coel slew him.

Those lands had been attacked on the other side by King Aeternus, so seemed vulnerable and it did not seem wise to stand idle while others built power in that area. And took wealth from it.

At that time, there were many celebrations which displayed wealth. One: the wedding of Prince Gurgan to Princess Greceilis, who was well known for her beauty. At the wedding, friendships were made between lords and kings, Prince Gurgan was getting more and more a reputation for strength. And his sister, Eurddil, had married the powerful King Dyfrig.

In the north, from over sea, Neol Hangcock, with many warriors, and also many women, landed to establish a colony. As the sons of King Moruawr were gaining reputations for strength and valour, Prince Cunedda, a son of Aeternus, who was widely known for great feats, collected two of them, princess Evdav and the young Casnar, and they went north and drove Neol Hangcock and his people out of the lands and of those lands, Cunedda was made king. The third son of Moruawr, Theoderic, had gone over sea to join King Trahern, the brother King Coel.

At that time, King Coel felt in need of strategic alliances. He and his queen thought it over. He and Queen Stradwawl had two beautiful daughters. One, Gwaw, they negotiated for her to become the wife of Prince Cunedda. The second, Elaine, they gave to Theoderic. This arrangement was promoted by Evdav, which was much to the displeasure of his uncle, Conan, who had desired Elaine for himself.

Then, to add to the troubles of the land, Cerdic, bold son of Elesa, and his son Cynric, came with a force of Vikings and landed on a north shore. They were opposed by Natanleod. King Natanleod was slain at a huge battle at Charford and his forces routed. King Coel sent word to Theoderic. Theoderic came with his family, except for his

15

first son, Kynvawr, who stayed over sea. And with Theoderic came many warriors. But Vikings were coming in boat loads, and they were strong warriors. Stuff and Wihtgar, grandsons of Cerdic, landed with three ships of warriors. After a battle against the Britons, Cynric sent them to the Isle of Wright. Then Cynric fought the Britons at Sarum. Battles continued against Vikings. King Pebiew was now gone, and King Nynniaw was no more to be seen. King Gurgan ruled a large sector of land and was spoken of as Gurgan the Great, was named Gurgan the Great.

Pigs, by many, were considered a troublesome influence. They represented the power of the Mother Goddess, and this challenged male rule. A number of pigs were found to be gods. To honour them, small bronze pigs were made and many of these were found in the winding valley formed by the Tarrant River. King Cunedda came upon a Great Sow at the town of Wells, and he chased it to the Gate to the Underworld at Glastonbury. There, under an apple tree, he caught up with her, but the Sow slipped further on, and as the Great Dog of Glastonbury guarded the gate, Cunedda could go no further. The dog is also called the Great Dog of Langport. It is formed in the ground which borders, in part, the Parrett River. The way Cunedda took became the path which since that time has been known as Sow Way.

As King Coel seemed to have established order and to have a firm hand on his lands, his brothers were content to keep their forces over sea. The brothers: Leonin, Marin and Trahern; all younger than Coel, with Trahern, far the younger. But the situation with King Coel was changing. King Coel had the support of Theoderic and his brothers, Evdav and Casnar, both of whom had become powerful lords. But the Vikings became an increasing trouble. Ceawlin and Cerdic joined together in battles against the Britons. Then a battle, Ceawlin, with Cuthwine, fought the forces of Cunedda. Viking lords Coinmail and Farinmail and King Cunedda were all slain. King Coel rushed to stop the Vikings and Ceawlin was driven out. King Coel chased the Vikings, caught them and Ceawlin was slain.

Cunedda's eldest son, Keredic, became king over Cunedda's lands except for the castles in the north which the second son, Yrth, took charge of, as his queen, Carannog, had her family's holdings there.

Then was King Coel slain by the warriors of Crida. And in that battle was Crida also slain.

There were disputes among the kings and lords and lands fell into disorder. Theoderic, now with his second son, Maurice, and his daughter, Marcel, had his hands full fighting Vikings. He sent for his first son's battle leader, Agricola. Together they kept a step ahead of invaders. A road between Carlisle and Corbridge was called Agricolas Road. Theoderic's brother, Eudav, became ruler over much of the land. This did not please the sons of Cunedda; so, to aid their cause, Coel's brother, Trahern, came from oversea with an army. Trahern, with Lord Yrth and King Keredic, defeated the force of King Eudav and Eudav fled to the lands of King Gunbert, which was over sea. Trahern was made king and many were pleased with his rule. However, large group of warriors, dissatisfied, banded together and refused to come under his rule. A time when King Trahern was on the road with a group of warriors, he came across a group of warriors led by Lord Aldolf, who had been hoping for such an opportunity. King Trahern's small group was defeated and King Trahern caught a spear through his chest. Lord Aldolf sent for King Eudav, then organized an army, and Eudav again became king. Many were not happy with him. However, there was now much confusion in the lands. Gurgan the Great had been slain in a battle against Vikings under Eoppa and Gurgan's son, Gwylffer had been wounded in that battle. His second son, Cynfyn, a mighty warrior, became a power in the north. Cynfyn's sister, Onbrawst, a powerful leader who was considered a witch, in a great wedding, became the wife of Theoderic's son, Maurice, who had become a huge leader throughout a wide area. He was called the Guardian, as he seemed to be where he was needed for protection from raids. His father, Theoderic, had been relied on to keep the Vikings in check. He had defeated the Vikings of King Ida at Cardiff; then he, with Maurice and Marcel, who was as splendid warrior maiden, chased the defeated Viking Force north toward a Viking stronghold. After following a way, they found their road blocked by a force of Vikings. Theoderic held back his major force, sent Marcel with a small force to attack; then, retreat; so as to lead the Viking force away. Marcel worked the ploy to perfection: led the Vikings, set up ambush after ambush; each time, retreating, so that she lost few warriors. Marcel fled first to Llandovery, fought the Vikings; then, to Arianrhod's castle where she lost a few warriors; then, to Whitesands where she fought and lost a few warriors; then, to Porthmawr where she fought and lost a few warriors. Then she fled to the lands of King Coromac and she and her warriors mingled and mixed with the population there and became completely lost to the Vikings. Theoderic had continued up the road to Hayonrye and there, defeated and drove out the force of Vikings.

Soon after she got to King Coromac's lands, Marcel, as a visiting lady, met Prince Anladd, who was a warrior of renown and a much praised leader, and he was much taken with Marcel, and he and she were married with a grand wedding. Marcel brought Prince Anladd to Porthmaur and there they built up the castle overlooking the sea. Then they began work on a castle at Hayonwye.

King Aelle landed with a large force and drove King Teitheyrn from Cymenes.

Powerful lords and kings, as much of the land was unsettled, were establishing sectors for themselves. The Dragon King, King Casnar, and King Edric expanded their lands. King Gwythern and King Aelle were considered, forces to be recognized as having much authority. King Avalach married Gwenn, a daughter of King Keredic. The eldest daughter of King Keredic, Corun, married King Teithfallt, a powerful and influential king. King Teithfallt thus became allied to King Avalach.

Amalasuntha, the second daughter of Theoderic, was stabbed to death while in her bath, and that brought much grief to her family. As Amalasuntha was well liked, it was, by some, thought she had been mistaken for another.

In general, there was a period of peace and orderliness. In the center, Theoderic kept activities under controle, and his son, Maurice, large, fierce and handsome, was right at hand when needed. And his son in law, King Anladd, with Marcel, was in a strategic place near the sea. And King Cynfyn, Maurice's brother in law, kept his sector in order. However, as time went on, discontent flickered among young lords. Rivalries rose up. Some once mighty leaders got to be old and failing in health. And the peoples in the Pict and the Scot areas were becoming restless. King Finbar and King Guinner landed, with many warriors from Eire, and shortly after they landed, Theoderic with his warriors rushed upon them, defeated them and forced them to live by his laws.

Theoderic, now old, retired to a cottage at Tintern Ford, near the banks of the steam. However, when his son, Maurice, was on his way through the area to attack a force of Vikings, Theoderic went along to aid his son. Lord Maurice defeated the Vikings; however, Theoderic was slain. He was buried at Tintern Ford and, the day of the funeral, he led the funeral procession in a fine car which was pulled by two stags. And with no direction, the stags took the car exactly to the grave site and stood until the car was unhitched.

Lord Maurice, with his mysterious queen, Onbrawst, the daughter of King Gurgan and Queen Greceilis, served as a strong leader over a wide area of lands. He was supported by his son, Sir Erbin, who had taken charge of an area along the coast. Lord Maurice's second son, Sir Brochwael, was a mighty warrior and a big help to his father. And he was supported by his nephew, Lord Brychan, a stout warrior and a judicious law giver, and a well respected family man. He and his wife, Lady Erdudvyl, had a new baby daughter: Neffydd.

Near the coast was Glastonbury, a mysterious place ruled by King Avalach, whose wife, Queen Gwenn, was a daughter of King Keredic, who was the eldest son of Cunedda and Gwaw, the daughter of King Coel.

Lord Yrth, the second son of Cunedda, had become a power in the west. And an aggressive young lord, Lord Caw, had, in the north, become a force to be taken into consideration. On the coast, battles continued. King Owen was slain by the Vikings, and Vortigern, Lord of Gewissei, and King Owen's cousin, took charge of the Kingdom of Dimatea, which King Owen had ruled. And he and his family moved into Owen's castle so to more easily supervise the commerce for which he was responsible, and which was of great importance to many peoples over a wide area. His wife was Sevira, a daughter of Lord Macsen. At that time Vortigern had a daughter and four sons, one of which had been newly born.

Flames of strife flickered among the various forces. Some lords felt that the Family of Theoderic was not truly British, so should not rule over the more ancient houses. The families of Lord Caw and King Cynfarch had expressed some such feelings. And the landings of invaders were a threat and that caused problems. Wild tribes out of the dark stretches of land in the north were creating trouble. Even though the coast was somewhat protected by fortifications, Vortigern was worried.

Vortigern had been lord of a back woods country area, an area which had sat sleepily in his family for a great period of time and he was little prepared to rule the busy coast line with its ports. And he had family responsibilities. And unlike the backwoods lands, the lands of King Owen had been attacked time and time again. And, in these attacks, many of King Owen's warriors had been slain, so that many plots which had been farmed had become overgrown with brush. So it was thought food might become short. Or, that areas would go unprotected. And another problem: news had come from Lord Maurice that King Wanis and King Melga had landed in Eire and had made a treaty with King Gillomaur.

Lord Maurice and Queen Onbrawst, seeing that a large area needed to be ruled, decided to send for aid from their relations oversea. For Vortigern, this news was another worry.

Oversea, in Armorica, Theoderic's eldest son, King Kynvawr, was ruler, and he was in good relations with King Eusic, who ruled the kingdom next to his. King Kynvawr and his wife, second daughter of Gurgan the Great, who was Helen of Hosts, so called because she was a battle leader of much force; had two sons. The sons Aldroein, who was the elder, and Custenhin. Lord Maurice sent his chief druid, Guithelinus, oversea in order that he might obtain a ruler. When he got there, he conferred with Prince Aldroein. The prince was then ruling the lands for his father and mother, the king and queen. No, he was not interested in taking the rule of Briton. To him, Briton was a disorganized place full of uncultured, disagreeable people and he wanted no part of it. Beside, his future lay in the lands of his father, and his responsibility for the lands used up his energy and time. But his brother often chose to go out on odd adventures. And he had nothing overly exciting going on where he was. Perhaps he would be interested, suggested Prince Aldroein. Custenhin was asked. Yes, that was the sort of challenge which appealed to him.

Druid Guithelinus was much pleased with Custenhin. He returned to Briton with the good news. On his return, he was informed, there would likely be enough exciting happenings in Briton to satisfy most any adventure seeker: that King Melga and King Wanis had landed in the north with ships full of warriors and had become reinforced by squadrons of Picts and Scots.

Custenhin, with contingents of warriors from Armorica, organized a force for bringing law to Briton. He got together four ships, and these, he filled with warriors. He set sail for Briton and landed at Port Totnes. He was welcomed by Lord Maurice, the family of Lord Maurice and other members of the family of Theoderic. Lord Brochwael was at the landing, and he ruled a large section in the center of the land. And Lord Erbin, an efficient, well organized administrator of an area near the coast, was present at the landing. And he was known as the Lofty Chief. And King Anladd, with Marcel, was there. And also present was King Glywys. Custenhin was made king. Plans were made for getting rid of King Wanis and King Melga, and it was thought, Custenhin should have a queen who would represent the land. Custenhin was introduced to Gwyar, a sister of the mysterious King Avalach. Custenhin, pleased with her, had a family wedding in the halls of Glastonbury.

Custenhin put his capital at York, the place of the Temple of the Sun. This was a spiritual center, a place where many warriors had chosen to be buried. Many decorated graves lay along the road which wound its way toward the lands of the Scots.

From Northumbria, King Ethelfrid attacked Lord Brochwael. Lord Brochwael, even with a smaller force, drove back the invaders. However, even after a successful attack, Lord Brochwael fell back, as King Ethelfrid had many more warriors than had the Lord. Lord Brochwael built up defense positions and reorganized his people

Custenhin's queen, Gwyar, was then expecting.

King Ethelfrid switched his focus from Lord Brochwael; attacked Bangor, marched on King Bledric, defeated him in Cornwall, near the coast.

Queen Gwyar bore Custenhin a son whom he named Custans. Near the time when Custans came into the world; King Bledric, from wounds suffered in a battle with King Ethelfrid's warriors, was going out of it.

King Ethelfrid attacked the forces of King Margadud of Demetrae; defeated his force, but ran into the warriors led by a young lord, Cadvan

21

the Venedoti. King Ethelfrid was wounded and he and his warriors retreated. Peace was made between Cadvan and the king and the king settled his position above the Humber. He parted on good terms with Lord Cadvan and from that lord got word of a happy event: a son, who was named Cadwallon.

Custenhin's warriors had been working on battle skills, and had been coordinating battle plans with the warriors of other kings and lords. This, under the direction of Lord Stilicho, who had come from over sea. Custenhin marched north. Word of the preparations had reached the young King Gillomaur in Eire. Gillomaur, with ships full of warriors, rushed to the support King Wanis and King Melga and their hosts of Scots and Picts.

Custenhin moved deliberately north, as there was no rush. King Melga and King Wanis were not improving fortifications, as it was their custom to fight in open fields. These kings had little use for stone walls, other than as houses built for the pleasures of their gods.

After a long march, with rested horses and men, and many more men than horses, Custenhin's men found themselves in front of the warriors of Melga and Wanis. Thinking the arriving host might likely be tired, Melga and Wanis rushed fiercely at them. Custenhin and his warriors methodically chopped the attackers to bits. King Gillomaur, more cautious than his allied kings, backed off, returned quickly to his ships, and Scots and Picts, in droves, fled away from the battle. King Melga and King Wanis were left on the field among the slain. The law in that area was now Custenhin's law. Custenhin returned to York. A second son was born to his wife: Emrys Aurelius. A celebration was held in honour of the new prince, Emrys.

Custenhin began planning a crowning celebration, and the place for it, he selected Silchester, and kings and lords from far and near were to come and honour him there. Custenhin had Druid Entergynn gather a number of wise druids to have them work on plans for the celebration. He made some suggestions, some inspired by his memory of celebrations over the water. King Kynvawr and Helen of the Hosts, Custenhin's mother and father, came straight away to Silchester, and Queen Helen did not ask who was in charge of the planning: she was. Then King Eusic, with Queen Gwenhaf was there.

Fine tents and pavilions were stretched in rows on the neat grass of a meadow. King Casnar, the ancient Dragon King of Went, he was there; and Lord Cynfyn was there, and his brother, Lord Gwylffyr, was there. King Yrth with his queen, Carannog, was there. King Teithfallt was there with his queen, Corun. Lord Caw was present with his family. The tents began to fill with guests. Lord Brochwael, with his chief knights, arrived to be part of the festival. Erbin, now King Erbin, arrived with his young sons; and King Glywys with Gwerlyn, the daughter of Lord Maurice. Then Lord Maurice was there in his magnificence, and with finely dressed attendants. Lord Athionard and his lady were there. And Prince Anladd and Marcel, in their antique grandeur, were a bright attraction. King Avalach and Queen Gwenn were there in grand state and with them were the elder King Lambord and Lord Seraphe. Lord Guitolin was at the celebration, as was Prince Kyneidd, King Ethelfrid had come with his one time foe, Lord Cadvan. They were now close friends, having much they had in common, and they were now celebrating Lord Cadvan's good fortune in having a fine young son. King Edric, King Margadud, King Vortigern and Prince Bethan were in attendance and were honoured quests. King Meirchiaun, Lord Clydno, Lord Kyner and Lord Tedubre were in attendance and were honoured quests. Sir Dallon son of Gwenddgar was there. The elderly King Conan was there and with him, many knights.

A gracious hostess there, beside Queen Gwyar, was the stately, splendidly handsome, Helen of the Hosts. But at the center of all was King Custenhin, moving with great dignity among the quests, spending not overmuch time with any one quest, but giving good tidings and joy all around, so that it would spread throughout the kingdoms and be an influence toward peace and stability. There were joyous entertainments and many there were favoured with fine gifts. At the crowning ritual, it was said, there could not have been a grander looking king.

Kings and lords returned to their lands and there was a feeling of stability generally felt throughout. Custenhin rode through his lands to be satisfied that all was secure and functioning well, and much respect was shown to him in all the areas which he visited. However, there were areas which troubled Custenhin. The lands of the Picts and Scots were still wild. And King Cynfarch, of Rheged, was not overly welcoming. And Rheged bordered on Gore, a shadowy land which touched areas of the Underworld, and Cynfarch's queen, Neffyn, was from a family of Gore.

Custenhin spent much time, more than he liked, at York, settling disputes, passing judgements, giving advice. Much support was supplied by Lord Maurice, by King Erbin, by Lord Brochwael, and by Lords Cynfyn and, in a way, Caw.

A year after the second son, a third son was born to Custenhin's queen, and he was given the name Uther. Custenhin called for Druid Entergynn. He told the druid he had decided that his first born should be sent to a school for mystical learning. As he was his son, Custenhin said he would certainly be a warrior. But that to be a good ruler, he would need learning.

Prince Custans was sent to a temple to be taught by druids and other masters. Queen Gwyar, who seemed to move in a mysterious, otherworldly atmosphere, to hold an otherworldly aura, had now but two sons to fix her attention on. There were details which she insisted upon being fitted into her specifications. Past her own breast milk, the milk they needed to be fed was the milk from her goats. She mad certain that her sons would have a feel for the Otherworld, would understand their relationship to animals, and would understand their spiritual relationships to other forms in nature.

Custenhin, with his company of warriors, went north to check the intrusions of Picts and Scots. First, the great number of Pictish warriors of King Daire. These liked to battle in woods and on rugged hills, so that getting into battle took time. Then, there was a battle against Scots.

Winter came and Custenhin hied to York. He made certain the Yule Festival would be celebrated in a way in which he approved. And the Yule came. There were games and rituals, and there was masking, which pleased Emrys and Uther.

In the spring, more Viking ships landed and this, in an area in which King Erbin had interests. Custenhin marched, with his warriors, to war against the Vikings and to take charge of that area. Time fled past and Custenhin found himself again at York. Again, it was Yule. Imbolc came and went, and winter passed.

In the spring, it was said, the Vikings had become strong. Custenhin went north. Cuthwine, Cwichelm and Cutha had attacked King

Ethelfrid and been driving his forces toward the South and already his battle leader, Lord Oslaf had been slain. Custenhin put an end to the retreat, slew Cwichelm. The Vikings were driven out. Then, in the summer, Cutha was slain. The battles against the Vikings went on; however, with questionable success. Vikings were difficult to track down, so, Viking raids remained a threat until the coming of winter.

As the Vikings had retired to their strongholds, Custenhin, with his warriors, went to York. Preparations were made for the Yule Celebration. Many lords and ladies gathered and the Yule was celebrated.

During the winter, Picts and Scots moved down further South. King Ecgfrith, a Viking king, with ships of warriors, landed on Eire. As the days lengthened, Custenhin got his warriors in order, went with a force in order to be ready for any threat which might come.

King Ecgfrith, with a great host of Vikings, landed across from Eire. Custenhin drove them back to their ships; then he and his warriors attacked Picts and Scots who had pushed down into his lands. Summer fled away; then, autumn, and Custenhin withdrew his warriors to York. Another Yule was celebrated and the Yule season passed.

Imbolc passed. Vikings landed near London. They were attacked by King Erbin. Custenhin shaped up his warriors, marched to the aid of his cousin. King Vortigern, at this time, was troubled by the movement onto his lands by Scots and other warriors and these, under the direction of King Cynfarch. To Custenhin, it seemed advisable for him to turn his attention that way. He attacked King Cynfarch and drove him and those warriors with Cynfarch back into Rheged; but, on the advice of Druid Eutergynn, he did not follow into that land. He retired to York. Then came Yule.

Then, Vortigern was troubled by raiding Picts which he time and again needed to fight off. Also, the strength of King Erbin was a worry to him. But he had the support of his people. Many of the country peoples, especially in the North, not only looked to Vortigern for protection, but for upholding their values. He was one of them. He had an appreciation of their arts and crafts, the grace of nonrepresentational design. And he supported the ancient customs of the people of his lands. His was a name with which people were familiar, and they rallied around him. And his people were not critical, to any great extent, of his failings. He was indeed lecherous and proud. But he was not cruel, nor was he known for violence. Vortigern had a fleet of ships and these kept his subjects with products which gave them pleasure. However, the wealth attracted invaders who desired to take it.

Picts invaded from the North and it took Vortigern's warriors much effort to drive them out. Then Vortimer, Vortigern's eldest son, went against the Picts and Scots and won a battle against them. Vortimer, in fact, most of Vortigern's family, stayed at the old family castle in the north. At Brecknock, its four sided tower rose up to where the four sides sloped to a point. Around it, flat grassy lands dropped off to steep cliffs.

During this time, Custenhin put a greater order to his situation at York. He supervised construction and reconstruction of towns and fortifications. And he sat in judgement in disputes. The work seemed never to end. Yule came and was celebrated.

A warm spring came and with it, battles from Scots and Picts and Vikings against many of the kings and lords in Custenhin's land. Custenhin assembled his warriors, went first to aid King Tewrig, grandson of King Nynniaw. Scot warriors had moved down and onto King Tewrig's land. Custenhin took charge of all warriors which came under his jurisdiction. The Scots were defeated and driven out. Custenhin then, with his warriors, marched to support Lord Brochwael, to battle against invading Vikings. In support came Lord Maurice with his warriors and the Vikings were driven into the wild northern lands. Autumn came in. Custenhin and his warriors returned to York. Many kings, lords and warriors gathered at York, prepared for a grand Yule celebration. Yule came and was a grand event, and at the center of it was Custenhin; tall, magnificent, looking every bit the part of a king over all. And the young princes had a most fun time taking part in the merriment.

The Yule passed, and Imbolc; then Easter, and word came that King Avalach, in Glastonbury, was being attacked. Custenhin rushed to get his warriors on the road so that he could aid the attacked king.

Custenhin got his men on the road and they began their long and hurried march. They followed the river valley down to the Don, to Hampole, and down to Lichfield. From there, to Avon, then down to

Banbury, to Sodbury; then, down to Calne and on to Bath, a place sacred to Lord Nodens, and there, Nodens had a fine temple at which Custenhin paid his respects. Some of the people there said that Nodens had been seen driving his chariot over the waters.

Custenhin and his warriors went from there to the Temple of Nodens at Lydney, and at Lydney was the statue of a dog. Custenhin paid his respects at the temple. The dog, people said, was The Little Dog of Langborth. The dog seemed to spread his influence over the assembled warriors. The warriors went on and seemed to see the dog on the land on which they walked, on the grassy hills and fields, and it was a confusing way which they followed. And as they tread the Little Dog of Langborth, Custenhin's queen was giving birth to a prince, to Prince Goreu.

Custenhin and his warriors walked through fields made pale by a low mist. Up a rise they walked. Custenhin, from the top of the low hill, looked to the rear. He saw behind him, the high hill of Glastonbury. It stood like a dream hill: terraces set around the hill formed bands of colour, misty blue violets and greens, and on the top, a spiky pillar of shiny stone. Custenhin turned his men and walked toward it. Bands of warriors rode past, but who they were was not knowable. Down in the low fields the Glastonbury hill could no longer be seen.

Custenhin came to a few low, round houses, wattle and daub with thatch rooves, and beyond them, a river. Custenhin had the townsmen ferry them across the river. He was informed he was headed for Pennard, that he could see well from there where he wanted to go. Custenhin continued his march.

Custenhin had the feeling that Earth was a great bull. On he walked until the feeling changed from bull to goat and that, the goat's horn. The goat would be associated with a tall enchantress who led men into copulation. Custenhin walked on. On the right was the finger of a wood. Out of the wood rode some horsemen. When they saw Custenhin and his men, they rode up. They conferred with Custenhin; five horsemen.

No, King Avalach was in no trouble. It had been taken care of. King Avalach was taken from his castle by a whirlwind, while King Tholomer attacked Glastonbury.

King Avalach had gone to Lycoine, then from there to Orcaus. He returned with Lord Seraphe with warriors of Orcaus. Lord Seraphe was a mighty warrior. He slew Manatur, the brother of King Tholomer, and King Tholomer and his warriors were defeated.

King Avalach is fine here. However, the horseman told King Custenhin, you might want to be careful here. King Eoppa and his Vikings have landed near Lyonesse. They could cause King Avalach no trouble, but they are strong and could cause much injury and death.

The five horsemen rode off. A sixth horseman rode up.

He said that King Avalach would want to see him. He said he would explain how to get to the gate of King Avalach's Palace. He and Custenhin rode off together, rode down the hill, down into a grove of beautiful, blooming apple trees. He and Custenhin sat beneath a tree. They talked. The blossoms of the tree were very sweet. Suddenly the horseman rode off. King Custenhin did not rise. His warrior, Aldolf, rode to him.

"He was Eoppa's man," said the king, "some Pict named Cadal."

He died. The king was dead.

King Custenhin was taken to York. He was buried.

The news was sent to the king's and lords who served under Custenhin. King Erbin was busy contending with the warriors of Eoppa, but Lord Brochwael and Lord Brychan had rushed to York, and King Anladd took himself to York. And King Avalach, a short time later, arrived there. Then, the druids; Druid Guithelinus, Druid Eutergynn, Druid Cadfun of the Temple of London and Druid Hoitlon Virgo of Caer Leon Temple. The Temple of York was ruled by Guithelinus. These conferred with Queen Gwyar about the problems of ruling the lands. It was said, Vortigern had expressed the opinion that he had the right, by birth, to be king and planned to claim the throne. Those there all agreed that what they wanted was to hold the crown for Emrys, but as soon as news got out that Emrys was to be king, the land would not be sale for him. Vortigern, if no one else, they thought, would find a way to get him slain. It was said, by Queen Gwyar, that Emrys and Uther should be taken oversea, to King Eusic, to stay with him until they were ready for the duties which they should be doing. Druid Guithelinus took them on a ship to King Eusic, who was newly made king.

Queen Gwyar then went to King Lot.

The Vikings continued to be a problem in King Erbin's area. King Vortigern had problems with Scots and Picts. As winter came on, Vikings retired to their stronghold, however, the Picts and Scots continued to be a problem. Many people looked to Vortigern to give them protection. His chief help was from three of his four sons, Vortimer, Categirn and Pascent. The fourth son, Faustus, Vortigern had sent to a temple to be taught by the druids. Lord Keredig instructed him in things of this world.

Lands which Custenhin had held together began drifting apart. King Yrth, son of Cunedda, and his queen, Carannog, felt that they should, among the kings and lords, be accepted as top authorities. Lord Brochwael thought that position would belong to him. King Cynfyn and King Cynfarch both had thoughts, so it was said, of taking the position which Custenhin had held. It seemed, many were waiting to see where things would go. The year passed. Many had joined Vortigern in his battles with the Scots and Picts, but he was losing warriors, and when his men were defending the kingdoms, they were not tending to the homes, the fields and gardens. And King Erbin, who had driven off the Vikings, was gaining strength. And this was a worry to Vortigern. And Vortigern's queen had died. Vortigern had his complaints. Another year passed and to Vortigern, it seemed the lands were going down hill. Vortigern said that he had the truly British royal family, that Custenhin's family had achieved their status in foreign lands, that he had more right to rule over all the lands than did the sons of Custenhin. But at present, he could not get the other kings and lords to accept him as their leader. He thought, he said, his most power would come from being the power behind the throne; however, this might be a problem if he tried to get the ear of the young Emrys. He might be better if he could get the crown to go to Custans. Not only were Scots and Picts being troubles, but there were invasions from curious, little known, lands to the west. And there were the landings by Vikings. The year passed. The Picts were disorganized, so some of them would hold lands under Vortigern's authority while others would not. But Vortigern had his lords do the best they could to work with the Picts as farms needed to be kept up. Then it seemed the time was right to bring in Custans as king. Winter was passing.

A mild day in early spring, Vortigern with Joram, his chief druid, and a couple of young knights, went to the temple where Custans was being educated. At the temple, the druids were not training Custans to be a king, as it had been planned that they should, but were teaching him with the thought that one day he would be a gifted druid. Druid Joram spoke to the druids of the temple and these were hard to convince that Joram and his associates were there to discuss spiritual matters only, but they permitted a short visit with the prince.

Vortigern with his associates went to the room where Prince Custans was waiting. Vortigern convinced him that he was needed for directing the forces of the land, that people would look up to him as he was the first son of his father, and he should leave that place in the garb of a warrior ready to put on the mantle of rule. Prince Custans changed clothes with one of Vortigern's young warriors, walked passed the guards with Vortigern and his crew and left the temple.

Vortigern with Prince Custans rode to Caer Leon, spread the word that at the Easter celebration there, Prince Custans would accept the duty of being king. The lords in Vortigern's kingdom were pleased and King Erbin, King Anladd, Lord Brychan, Lord Brochwael, King Glywys, Lord Cadvan and King Ethelfrid would all accept Custans as king. Custans was crowned.

King Custans knew little about the job of being king, but he had Vortigern to advise him and this was as Vortigern had planned it. Vortigern was much pleased. However, being an advisor to Custans took much effort. King Custans was little help in supervising his subjects in the upkeep of the land. He said Vortigern might make the rounds in his name as long at the subjects understood Vortigern was acting for King Custans, and that Custans was king and overlord. King Custans had Caer Leon as his center, so he was close to areas where there was much disturbance. Picts were restless and unsettled, and they found much to complain about, and they had trouble following rules and regulations. Vortigern had King Custans appoint a couple of Picts as royal advisors. And these, as other Picts, were difficult to give orders to, but Vortigern felt the Picts being there would please other Picts.

Some areas began making a point in not following the instructions from King Custans. His family was, said some, from across the sea, and what was across the sea they knew not. Many of the land's subjects lived in back woods areas, in mud and wood houses and wore homemade clothes and each person knew little beyond his village. To these people, Vortigern was like a father. He spoke their language. And the Picts liked Vortigern, as Vortigern treated them well and gave them gifts.

If Custans had an ability, it was in, from the throne, passing judgements, young though he was. He was two years short of his twentieth year. Oversea, his brother Uther, two years the younger, was married and his princess had given him, newly born, a daughter, given the name, Anna.

It was said in some quarters, if it were not for King Custans, Vortigern would be king, and some said that Vortigern would be the better of the two as king. Two who said this were the Pict advisors to King Custans. There came a day when, admonished for not doing as they were told, they grabbed King Custans and cut off his head. Thinking King Vortigern would be pleased, they took the head to him. They told the king their problems with King Custans, then said, but now we will have you as king. Vortigern's knights grabbed the Picts, bound them with ropes. On Vortigern's orders, the Picts were taken out into the castle courtyard, their heads chopped off.

Custans was taken to Caernarvon, then at Caer Segeint, near Caernarvon, he was buried, and it was a small, but dignified ritual. Lord Clydno, carried the sacred arc, holding the head, to Caer Segeint.

After the burial, Vortigern felt quite alone. It was whispered about that Vortigern had instigated the Picts into killing Custans. Then, the Picts felt betrayed. They began raids on his subject's farms. And little help he got from any but his own subjects. These thought of him as their father, and they trusted him to do the best that he could. But the Picts and other lawless elements were most difficult to controle. Vortigern did have his fleet and they helped in the defense of his coast ports, but King Erbin had a rival fleet which not only was diverting wealth, but, in a more important way, was leaving his kingdom open to an invasion of his lands by Emrys. He had a dread of Emrys. However, Vortigern was on good terms with Eire and the trade there brought in helpful products. One, Vortigern got from Eire fine horses for his dogs, which he had in good quantity.

Then another problem: Prince Edwin, son of the Viking King

31

Aelle, came with a host of his followers. And with him was Lord Freothogar, and a good number of men were with the Lord. Vortigern gave them a welcome and settled them on vacant, run down farms. And he gave them horses, those of Eire, most handsome horses with long curling manes and curling tails. Prince Edwin's men improved the farms and with interests in common, got on well with their neighbors. They guarded the lands against those who would come on them and cause trouble. Vortigern's lords felt that their king had done a wise thing. Those men raising flowers were not causing trouble. And the Picts were also less trouble, though their boats continued to land on Vortigern's shores.

Many Briton lords and kings objected to the settlement of Vikings, and to Vortigern and his up country manners, but they were not well enough organized, were not united in efforts to be rid of him. So in all the lands the great disorder continued. The young lords were polite to the senior leaders, but were deaf to advice and instruction. There were new invasions of Vikings. The kings and lords began among themselves to say that it was time for Emrys to return, as his youth and vigour were needed.

Three longboats arrived on Vortigern's shore. They landed at Wippidsfleet. And these contained many handsome young warriors, their hair shining bright and golden. When Vortigern was told of the landing, he said that the warriors should be brought to him.

The warriors were taken to Vortigern's castle, old mossy walls of stone which, in places, had fallen into tumbled piles. Beyond it were cliffs overlooking the sea. While the many waited below, the two young leaders from the longboats were taken up a winding mossy stair to where Vortigern waited in a large chamber. It contained, disorganized, some dusty furnishings; these, covered with artistic carvings. Here and there over ragged walls were hangings on which were squiggles which formed beautiful designs. But the hangings were old and worn and covered with dirt.

The two leaders identified themselves as two brothers, Jutes, Hengist and Horsa, sons of Wihtgils, son of Vecta. The reason for being there, Hengist explained, was that his land had an overflow of young men. The way it was the custom to remedy that was for the young men of the land to draw lots to move to some new place, seek new adventures. Said Hengist, in moving to your land, we offer you our service.

Vortigern was pleased. He would most likely need swords to counter attacks. He asked, who were the lords whom they honoured?

"In our land, the great father of us all is Wotan," said Hengist. "Others whom we honour are Apollo, Freya, Tidea, Saturn, Thor, Jupiter, Tervagant, Mercury."

"Some of those are known to me," said Vortigern. "Will you and your men join our forces?"

"If Wotan and Saturn favour it, we will," said Hengist.

Hengist explained that he and his brother had been made leaders of the company in the ships because of their coming from a ruling family.

Vortigern settled the young warriors on the island of Thanet, an island littered with ruined dwellings, and scattered over the island were many graves. And Vortigern gave these new arrivals food, and also, clothes.

Reinforced by these young warriors, Vortigern's patrols drove away one, a second, then a third, boat full of Picts which had attempted to land so that the Picts could cause trouble.

A short time later, King Daire with his army of Picts crossed the Humber thinking to occupy a part of Vortigern's land. Vortigern assembled his force and rushed to meet the invaders. The Picts were astonished to find themselves opposed not only by the Britons, the usual old weapons which showed much wear, the old, ragged clothes; but they faced fierce young warriors who carried shining weapons and who wore beautiful, bright clothes. Many of the Picts fell and the great body of the Pict force withdrew and fled back to their own lands. Vortigern was much pleased with Hengist, Horsa and their men, the help they gave in defeating the Picts. He made Hengist and Horsa, Lords of Lindsay.

Toward the end of that summer, Hengist went to the castle where Vortigern sat, sat looking out, over high rocky cliffs, toward the sea. Hengist went to Vortigern, said:

"O King, I am worried for you. Your subjects hate you. They say you will let the Picts come chop them up. Then, King Erbin will invade and impose his rule. And even if he does not, a tyrant named Emrys will certainly come and make life a misery. You have been fair with me and I want to do right by you, so you too will have joy in life. What I suggest is that you have me get my family, with their warriors, onto these lands so they will protect you. It will be much to your advantage. One thing we would need would be a fort from which we could serve as guard."

"You may certainly bring your family to these lands. That land for a fort, however, I must consider. Much of that is already taken."

"That would be no great thing," said Hengist. "Only an amount of land which I could get into an area surrounded by the hide of a single bull."

That much land Vortigern could spare. Hengist got for this a large bull. He and Horsa skinned it, then from it, created a string so fine it would thread through a needle. Part of the process was watched with dismay by Vortigern. The desired land was measured out and a fort built on it. And the fort, named Thongchester, was made of huge timbers with clay filled in between them. And the family of Hengist, his son Octa, and Ebissa, his pledged friend, and his sister, Hrothwena, came to it to make their home. Hengist and Horsa, in honour of their new home, had a big celebration and Vortigern was invited. It was a fine May evening. Hengist, Horsa and their family were in a mood to celebrate. With them were other fine warriors including Cherdic, a battle leader who had come oversea with Hengist's sister and sons. And Hengist's sister, beautiful she was, with the palest of hair, for which she was named that which translates as White Mane: Hrothwena.

As soon as Vortigern entered the hall where all were celebrating, Hrothwena took a cup of mead to the king, knelt before him, presented the cup, saying:

"This cup, most wonderful king, I give to you alone. Wasshail."

"Thank you, most beautiful maid."

He could hardly take his eyes off the beautiful Hrothwena. Hrothwena returned, said:

"Lord King, Wasshail. I am glad of your coming."

"Drink happy, Maiden Hrothwena. It is you who art most lovely."

He returned the cup.

Hrothwena kissed the king three times. So they were pledged.

Hengist said that now Vortigern was a member of his family, he

34

expected to be treated like the brother he was.

"As now a brother, might he ask a boon?" said Hengist.

"If it is in my power and honour to grant it."

Hengist thought he and his family should be given Kent.

Vortigern was then happy. He had missed his late wife and his desire for sex had made him overly aggressively with women. And he, perhaps, because he was lonely, had gotten the reputation of being grumpy and haughty. Vortigern now had new found pleasure, but the reason for it caused him trouble with his sons. His eldest son was the one most angry with him over his taking a wife from oversea.

Vortimer began raising an army of men who were against those from oversea. More help for his army came from outside his own area than from in it.

Spring came. Vortigern gave over Kent to Hengist and Horsa. Hengist moved onto Prince Kyneidd's lands. Bold was the son of Cian to deny the usurper the land; bold, that man from the stone of Gwyngwn. As Hengist had had improved his position with boatloads of warriors from overseas, Prince Kyneidd, with his warriors, joined with Vortimer.

The situation in the castle in Dimatea had changed. It was now his daughter and his new wife who had the management of it. His three older sons with their followers had in anger, and with hard words, departed for the old castle in the north. Vortigern was then surprised to see his son Pascent walk into the central chamber. Pascent walked up to where he sat.

"Father, it is meet that you should cut my hair and I do request it."

In anger, Vortigern got up and left the room.

Vortigern's castle then seemed a forgotten place. Vortigern's wife and daughter put in the effort to make him happy and comfortable. And the two women got along well together. At the northern castle the war band continued to swell. King Guoyrancgono, with many warriors, arrived and joined with Vortimer. Lord Dallon with many warriors of the lands of Lord Maurice joined with Vortimer. Hengist then was supported by King Edwin and many warriors of the lands of King Aelle. King Wipped joined Hengist and Horsa. Hengist instituted parties of horsemen, flying parties, for scouting patrols.

As the leaves began to turn on the trees, Vortimer and the forces at his command attacked Hengist. Overmatched, at Angelsthrep, Hengist withdrew his forces to Thanet. At Thanet, Hengist augmented his forces, attacked Vortimer who was up along the Darent River. Hengist had been reinforced by many Picts and Scots and they drove Vortimer and his men out of the area. The men of Vortimer retreated up into the northern hills. Vortimer was declared to be king instead of Vortigern.

As many warriors had been slain, and the days were cold, there was a quietness over the land. The Yule was celebrated. From oversea boats came to Thanet. Many of Vortigern's people visited its wooden halls.

In young spring, Vortimer, with his brothers, with the splendid Sir Morien and other battle leaders, stormed down on Hengist. King Teithfallt and King Itheal and their men were with Vortimer, and the two armies met at Epsford. It was a fierce battle and among the slain were Catigirn and Horsa, and the forces of Hengist were driven back to Thanet. To Thanet boats came bringing replacements for those warriors who were lost. The trees filled with leaves and the days got warm. Then fall colours came to the trees. Hengist's warriors marched toward the north. They were attacked by the forces of Vortimer. The forces met near a big stone which was near the seashore. Vortimer then had help from the warriors of King Erbin and these, led by his son, Lord Geraint. Geraint, like a hawk, swooped on the forces of Hengist, and among those slain in that attack was King Wipped. Hengist had been defeated. But Vortimer, badly wounded, was taken to Vortigern's castle. King Erbin and Vortigern signed a truce with Hengist on which Hengist agreed to take his people back oversea. The forces of Hengist had retreated to Thanet.

Vortimer, at this time was getting weak, so he gave burial instructions. He said he should be buried under a pyramid near Big Rock, near the sea. In that way, he said, he could keep those coming ashore from causing harm.

Vortimer died and all those with him said his last request was a bit of foolishness. They took him to the family castle in the north, Brecknock Castle, and he was buried with honours beside Belin's Gate.

King Erbin, with Vortigern, Pascent and King Teithfallt, supervised a large group of Hengist's followers taking boats and heading out to sea. Thanet became a much quieter place. Yule came and Vortigern celebrated it with Hengist and three of his sons, who were Octa, Aesc and Hartwaker; and a daughter, Sardoine.

Vortigern said what they needed was a better relationship with the Britons, so they could be seen as joining together as equals, so the Britons would not feel they were being lorded over by tyrants.

"That is a good suggestion and you are a most wise king. I will plan some events," said Hengist, "which they and we can do together."

Vortigern admitted that his being called wise was a good way to his enthusiastic cooperation in their plans.

In February Vortigern was told that in keeping with his suggestion, a fellowship meeting was planned and would be held May Eve. All noble Briton lords should be there, and that all efforts would be made to see that all who came would be entertained in a splendid way. Vortigern should insist that each lord come to the event.

Much effort was made to get the word to all the Briton lords and May Eve came. Threehundred lords of Briton arrived at a decorated wooden structure near a circle of stones, and many of these lords were of the oldest and most distinguished in Briton. Included among these was King Keredic. It is certain Hengist looked to see who was not there.

Inside, the hall was bright with coloured fabrics. In the center of the hall was a cauldron of fine pale wine. As this was to be a sacred ceremony all weapons were to be left outside the hall. Hengist's warriors, equal in number to the number of Briton Lords, were dressed in fine ritual garb: white, trimmed in gold. Hengist himself wore a white robe bright with gold; and he on his bright hair, wore a wreath: green leaves decorated with golden amber.

Beside Hengist were two ritualists. It was said the featured ritual would take place within the circle of stones. In the hall, in the waving light of torches, the Briton Lords drank pale wine cheerfully served by the hosts. Conical stones were set up and on these, libations were poured. And the young bard, Owen ap Marro, dressed in pure white, sang beautiful song, and the song mixed with the sweet fragrance of the many flowers spaced around the hall. It was said, Owen had a clean knife, meaning he was a man dedicated to peace: clean knife:

emblem of peace.

Hengist rose to give a signal of death. He drew a long sharp knife from under his robe, as did all his warriors. He stabbed Owen in the stomach. At that, each of his warriors tried to stab a Briton Lord. Two warriors grabbed Vortigern. Vortigern cried, struggled to get loose. Eidiol grabbed a ceremonial staff, slew his attacker, then with it, several others on his way to break through the door. Aldolf of Gloucester grabbed a wooden stake, used it as a club, slew an attacking warrior and escaped. Cinric and Cenon, both of Glamorgan, got knives from attackers, fought their way out of the hall, got lost in the darkness. Aldolf jumped on a horse, rode to Gloucester, shut the city gates. Eidiol also made his way to Gloucester. Kyneidd slew several knife wielding warriors, but he never left the hall. After the slaying, little attention was given to Vortigern. Hardly noticed, he left the hall, made his way back to his dwelling, shut himself up in his quarters.

Word of the slayings spread through the lands and notice was sent to Emrys that close to threehundred Briton Lords had been slain. And the word got out that they were slain at an event to which Vortigern had invited them. And that none of Vortigern's people had gone to the event. It was not considered that the reason was that Vortigern's lords had disliked Hengist so much that they would not go. And Pascent and Vortigern were still at odds over the haircut. Some had not gone because a breaker of twigs had foretold misfortune. Semno had warned them.

At the end of summer, Emrys Aurelianus, so called because he wore a golden chain, arrived with Uther and five ships and landed at Totnes. He was met by King Erbin and Lord Maurice and declared to be king. First, said Emrys, he would rid the land of Vortigern, the miserable traitor. Pascent, who had taken the title of King of Builth, had been expecting Emrys' return, so his force had marched to the place of the expected landing. And he went to his father and told Vortigern that their lands were threatened. Vortigern dressed for war and sent heralds to summon all warriors of the land. King Meirchion arrived with many warriors and he was most welcome to Vortigern.

A message came for Vortigern that the flammen Eldadus had properly buried all the dead lords of the May Eve ritual and the news eased his mind on that score. They had been buried at Caer Caradoc.

Vortigern went with his countrymen toward where Emrys, with his force, was coming to meet him, and many of Vortigern's men had no liking for the Britons whom they thought of as London based and owing much to Amorica, and Pascent was one of those who disliked them the most. Emrys' forces met those of Vortigern and Vortigern's forces, being the less skilled, were cut to pieces and those who were left, fled, and the battle became known as the Battle of Wallop.

Vortigern and Pascent, in a mad scramble, left the scene of battle, as did many other. The two of them went to Erging Hill, which overlooked the sea.

"What we need to do," said Pascent, "is go to Eire, get support from a lord there, then get our warriors back together. We will go to Ballybank and to Knockaboy."

"I have different thoughts," said Vortigern. "The reason for their aggression in this direction is their hate for me and me alone. To them, I am the chief traitor and murderer and when they slay me, their interest in this area will fade away."

Pascent said, "But you are neither of those things."

"They do not see how I could not have known. And how could Hengist have done a thing so wicked. It was a disrespect to Lady of Earth to whom the rite had been dedicated. And she demands purity."

"As the king, you did not do well. You should have done better."

"How could I have known? But I will be here alone so none others are associated with my wickedness. I will ask the advisors what place would be most safe. I will steer clear, well clear of Brecknock, so there would be little reason to disturb the family there. And your young son, Riagath, would be there. I will talk with wise men."

Pascent bid farewell to his father, found one of his ships, set sail for Erie.

Emrys and Uther organized their forces. More Briton Lords arrived to join them. Many would like to have chased after Vortigern, but Emrys said that could wait, that the Vikings needed to be dealt with. Uther said, he for one could not be content until he had put his sword into Vortigern's guts.

Vortigern went quickly up to his Castle Radnor, sent for Druid Joram and other wise druids, asked for their advice. The druids threw sticks and studied the problem. Joram looked hard at the sticks. Said he:

"I have a path for you - Go to a remote part of your land, to Mount Eryri. A place among steep cliffs is there. Get workmen to build a strong fort there and it would be a long time before any could get to you there."

Vortigern, his servants and advisors, set out for that mountain, found there a remote crag projecting out over the valley below. He sent out scouts who would find good builders, and he promised good pay. High above, he saw eagles circle and scream.

All the while, Uther was sending out people to find out where Vortigern was hiding. Then cold weather came, and snow, and people took shelter from the cold. The Yule was celebrated.

The weather warmed and a good crew gathered at Mount Reir, designed a fort. Construction began, the stones for walls were placed one on another. In the night the walls fell down. Vortigern saw them in the morning and was dismayed and wondered what could have happened to his walls. The workmen began again, but in the night the stones not only had fallen, but had sunk into the ground. A third day, stones were placed and secured with care, but in the night they were swallowed by the ground. Vortigern gathered his wisemen. Said Joram, the chief druid, it is not unusual for an important building to have, or to cause, trouble. Often, the spirit of the building demands a sacrifice. What I see, the next walls which go up need to be splashed with the blood of a boy who has no father.

Vortigern sent the wisemen out to search for such a boy. The wisemen went from village to village. Two of the wisemen got to a village near the ruins of an ancient castle near the sea: the Castle of Arianrhod. Being tired, they sat on an old wall. By the wall gate were two boys at a game. The wisemen sat and watched. One boy said:

"Dalbut, that was my point."

Said the other, "You have your nerve disputing with me. I am the son of a mother and a father; each, from a noble family, and you have no father at all."

The wise men listened until they heard the second boy called Merlin. At hearing the name, the wise men gave each other a nod, climbed down the rock covered hillside to the worn stones of a narrow street. On asking Eli, the town constable, they were told that Merlin was the son of a lady who lived in an old stone tower which was on the up hill side of the town. To the tower the wisemen went, and they told the lady that she and her son were wanted by the king. When Merlin went home to the tower, he and his mother packed bags and first thing next morning, they, with the wisemen, set off toward where Vortigern was camped. Along the road and over the hills they rode and climbed up to the place of the camp. Vortigern greeted Merlin and his mother kindly, as she identified herself as being from a noble family. Vortigern asked the lady, what man had been responsible for Merlin's birth?

The lady, who identified herself as the daughter of King Conla, said that no man had, before Merlin's birth, been close to her.

"How could that be? There must have been some way beyond your knowing?" said Vortigern.

The lady said that one night she had dreamed she was with a handsome young knight, a golden knight. Then, the next night, a non human being came into her room, did to her what a man does. He was grotesque, but in somewhat human form. The lady said that she then lit hypericum and the smoke chased the being from the room.

Maugant, a wise druid who was there, said that demons did sometimes come to people, and especially young girls were in danger of being attacked. The attackers were often incubuses, and these were Spirits of Air.

Merlin went up to the king:

"What do you intend for my mother and me?"

Vortigern explained his need for a strong castle and – .

"I see," said Merlin, "You would slay me to save you. Show me this place where the walls refuse to stand."

Vortigern walked with Merlin to where the walls had been, and they were followed by all the others.

When Merlin saw the place, he laughed. The others looked at him surprised at the laughter.

"Then are the walls in some way funny?" said Vortigern.

"It is funny no one saw the obvious flaw in the location," said Merlin. "The stones will not stand because Earth is unstable beneath them. Have the workman dig there and you will discover the problem."

Vortigern had the workman dig.

41

At this time, in another part of the land, Uther had sent out scouts to spy out where Vortigern was hiding. And Uther and Emrys, with their forces, were moving in Vortigern's direction.

"Look, there is your problem, an underground lake. And in the lake are two fighting dragons, and these disturbed the land around the lake. And for that, these wise foolish men would have had me slain. All of my blood would not make a whit of difference to those dragons."

Two dragons rose up out of the pool and fought. A white dragon seeming to have the better of a red dragon.

"The pool is a symbol for the land," said Merlin. "The Red Dragon is the Spirit of the People of Briton; the White, the Spirit of the invaders. In Briton's valleys the brooks shall run red with Briton's blood. But I see a future: the Boar of Cornwall shall bring relief from the invaders," said Merlin. "It will trample their necks beneath his feet."

"But what should I do?" said Vortigern.

"As for advice, if I were you, I would pack bags and, with the needed help, head for the most remote, most distant place I could find. Even now, Emrys and Uther are making their way toward this place and they are not far distant. And, have these wise men be on the road and gone. They are less than worthless."

Merlin mounted. He and his mother rode away.

Vortigern stood amazed, then took the advice and with his helpers, less the wise men, packed and left the area.

Long Vortigern wandered. He got into the lands called Erging, went to Rhyvoniawg Castle. Here he was welcomed, and he rested; but knowing he would not be safe here, after a couple of days, he rode on. He got to Cloard; then on, Doward Hill, to the old castle, Genoreu; an ancient fort built on an earthwork, an old ring mound which seemed of itself to have risen from the ground. And it was built over mysterious caves. No one was there. Vortigern made Genoreu his new home. The winter came and the serving people had a time finding enough food to keep them all from hunger.

During this time, Uther, with Emrys, had been moving up the land, searching out the hiding place of Vortigern. He, at last, got the words he wanted. On a spring day, Uther came in sight of Genoreu Castle. He had his warriors completely circle the castle.

Too late Vortigern saw the circle of warriors. He went and got his sword.

"What do you intend to do with that?"

Vortigern looked around and there was Merlin.

"Defend my home. And, perhaps, avoid a death which they have planned for me. They did not come all this way to make that quick: Even should they leave, it would be a lonesome friendless life I would have and this, for the ill I have caused."

"Take those clothes off quickly and put these on. You are now a wandering shepherd. Many men would not make good kings, but do well enough. What do you mean you have no friends? And you are never alone when you are under Father Sky. And there is Uncle Wind. And when you feel alone, reach down, touch Mother Earth. Now walk out in those trees where the shadows are thick; then, come back toward the castle, up between groups of warriors. Here, a bit of soil. Here is your staff. Now walk out."

Merlin watched.

"It is time we go out," said Merlin to the serving people.

Vortigern walked out. When warriors might have looked his way, a flight of quails flew up and distracted them. Vortigern walked around, then down out of the trees, stood between groups of warriors. In front, warriors with huge beams were smashing in the great gate. Dark clouds from the higher hills were sailing over. CRASH: a bolt of lightning hit the castle and a great fire lept up. In a short time, the entire wooden structure was on fire. Vortigern walked back up into the wooded hills.

Emrys organized his forces, moved toward Viking strongholds. Hengist heard of the forces of Emrys moving toward him. He withdrew the majority of his forces over the Humber, and this included many from ships which had newly arrived. With Emrys were the warriors of King Erbin; his sons, Prince Dweyl, Prince Geraint, the Lord or Erbin's fleet, and Prince Ermid; and Lord Gorlois with his warriors; and Lord Brychan with Sir Nevyn and his warriors; and Lord Brochwael with his warriors led by Gwyddiew the Strong, who was his son. And with Emrys also was King Cynfarch, son of Meirchiaun. King Glywys was, with many warriors, there also. This large force moved toward the Humber.

A large force of Vikings, led by Hengist, met the force of Emrys

43

at a short distance past the Humber. There was a wide plane, on either side of which were wooded hills. It was decided, Uther would controle the flanking forces on the hills, while Emrys would hold the center. From Amorica, Emrys had come with a reputation of being a splendid tactician and bringer of victories to warring forces. He seemed unbeatable in single combat. When he had ridden out by himself, many other knights avoided conflicting with him. He and his forces advanced on the Vikings. The Vikings came over the hill and charged on them. The fighting was furious. Hengists' forces retreated, reformed. Emrys had his horsemen, from the left, sweep, on a diagonal at the Vikings; then, on a diagonal from the right. Hengist, with Ebissa and Octa and their forces, stood firm. Gorlois, on one flank, proved a valiant commander. After much fighting, the Vikings retreated from the fields of Maesbeli to Caer Conan and deployed in the fields in front of the castle. To the rear, below rocky cliffs, was the River Done. The two great forces met together at dawn with much slaughter on each side. Emrys' battle leader, Aldolf, showed great strength. Eidyn, a warrior of Emrys, showed great strength, and supported the center of the Briton line. But the Vikings were gaining momentum until Emrys' horsemen charged and put the Vikings into disorder. Gorlois then, with his warrior, Sir Aliduc, took this time to advance. This gave Eidiol, son of Ceidiaw, an opportunity to spot Hengist and rush at him in revenge for May Eve: Hengist who, for strength, few could match. These warriors fought fiercely. Eidiol's helm was split, but he cut off Hengist's hand, grabbed him, threw him down and Hengist was made prisoner. The Viking force, in disorder, retreated. Many of the Vikings lost themselves in the surrounding woodland, but the large body of them fled with Octa to York. Hengist was taken into the town below the castle and, because of the May Eve killings, was taken outside the town and his head was chopped off. By the order of Emrys Aurelianus, Hengist, in that field, was buried in Viking way. In the town, Conisborow, by the healers, care was given to all those there who had been wounded. Three days Emrys spent in burying the dead and in giving care to the wounded, then he marched to York where Octa and Ebissa were, with their warriors, in York Castle.

Emrys, at York, with his many warriors, surrounded the castle holding not only Octa, but many other Viking lords as well. Octa saw the many warriors outside his castle. And he saw the shortness of his food supply. At sundown, he and the lords with him built an omen fire and around it carried a sacrifice. It became plain what they needed to do. The next morning, at sunrise, Octa and the lords who were with him: Ebissa; Aesc, son of Hergist; Cherdic; Cymen, son of Aelle; Cissa, son of Aelle; and Wlencing, son of Aelle, unclothed, and Octa carrying a chain: were directed to Emrys, and to him, they surrendered.

Druid Eldad counseled giving a pardon.

Emrys said that since Eidiol was one of those at the May Eve ritual, he would be the one to judge whether or not to accept the surrender. Eidiol said that that surrender would be accepted.

The Vikings returned to their homes: Aesc, to Kent, where he would now be the chief lord.

Emrys spent time putting York back in shape and making it his chief center. Then he went to Caer Went, had workmen make repairs on that city. The Yule was celebrated and warriors were honoured: Eidiol, Lord of Gloucester, and Aldolf, who was Steward of the lands in the area of Gloucester, and Lord Gorlois, and his war chiefs, Aliduc and Brastias, and Sir Eidyn, and Sir Nevyn, son of Lord Brychan, and Glyddiew the Strong, and King Erbin, and Prince Ermid, and Prince Dweyl. And the names of slain warriors were honoured.

Yule passed and at the Festival of the Sun, Emrys decided to make a fitting burial memorial for the warriors who had fallen in the great battle. He summoned wise men, druids and builders to discuss the matter with him. He had them meet with him at Amesbury. Various suggestions were presented and each in turn was declared by Emrys to fall short. Then a flammen, Tremorion of Caer Leon, said that he had heard King Vortigern had discovered a marvelous boy wizard, and this wizard seemed to know much about building; that he might be the very person to give advice on this matter.

The boy magician was a person whom Emrys was interested in seeing. Yes, he should be found. And then the memorial would be decided on.

When red and gold was beginning to fall from the trees, a couple of wise men, near the Castle of Arianrhod, came on a boy seated on the banks of a pool. After a few questions, they determined he was indeed the boy wizard. Gold and gems they offered the boy if he would

45

go with them to discuss a project with King Emrys. The boy laughed and poopooed their offer of gold and gems, but he agreed to go with them; as, he said, a friendship with King Emrys, sadly, would need to be a short one, but one not to be missed.

This statement worried the druids, but they were glad to have the boy wizard to present to the king.

The three of them sat on the bank. Below them, a round pool beyond a patch of watercress. A hundred yards up the hillside was the path. They sat in silence.

"So. We will depart," said Merlin.

The three climbed toward the path.

"I will ride off and get you a horse," said a druid.

"No need. There will be a horse when one is needed."

When the three of them got to the path, a horse stood ready for Merlin to mount and he was mounted and ready to go before the druids were up on their horses.

The three of them rode the path to a road, then on they rode the long way to York, where preparations were being made for the Yule celebration. Emrys was delighted to see them.

Said Emrys, "I understand you were Vortigern's top wizard."

"I had no such understanding," said Merlin.

"Whatever," said Emrys, "I am ready to see some of your talents."

"I am not an entertainer," said Merlin. "If you have a need for me, one not unworthy of you or myself, I am here."

That was an odd way to address a king and Emrys gave Merlin a different kind of look.

"I do have a need," he said. "Many worthy warriors, and these included the leaders of many peoples, were slain at Conisboro. For peace and prosperity to continue throughout the land, it is important that there be a fitting memorial and burial space for them. I need a design worthy of them."

Nothing more was said of that until after Yule. February came and Emrys, with Merlin and a company of others, set out for the place where Emrys had determined to have his memorial. Merlin turned to the king:

"The most fitting memorial, the one which would last through the years, would be a ring made from the Grants Stones, in Eire, on Mount

Killaraus."

"Most likely," said Emrys with a smile. "However, all the knights and workmen we could gather would not be strong enough to lift a single stone. And these are stones King Gilloman loves more than life itself. We would need to defeat his army. I appreciate humour. But let us have a thing our craftsmen can construct."

"There is nothing ludicrous, or humorous, about my plan," said Merlin. "I will move the stones."

"But how? Have you seen how massive those stones are?" said one of the lords.

"All things are constructed of numbers. Have the number correct, things can be done. And there are numbers above and below which hold moving spaces which can be used. I will need a good ship which will hold a dozen good sized wains," said Merlin.

"You will have them," said the king.

Lord Geraint got the ship ready and a dozen stout farmers had their wains lined up and ready to sail. The king designated Uther to get the stones. With a small group of knights and the wagon drivers and ships crew, Uther and Merlin set sail. Word had preceded them and people came to laugh at the wains and their drivers.

Said King Gilloman, "This confirms my belief that the Britons are very stupid people. Not less than sixty oxen could move a single stone. And it is not far they could move it."

When Uther and the warriors reached the stones, they were awed by the stones' size and the weight of the stones seemed such that no force they knew of could have budged any one of them. The warriors walked around the stones, felt them, pushed on them, pulled on them. Local people stood around, laughed at the warriors.

Merlin then walked around each stone, his hand touching the stone as he walked and his voice causing a vibration in the air. He circled the stones thrice within and thrice without.

"You may put the stones on the wains," said Merlin.

Local people gasped and ran off as the warriors lifted stone after stone, each stone as light as a feather, and put them on the wains. There were few to watch the wains cart them to the ship. The ship sailed over to the bay in front of the Severn. It put to shore. The wains rolled off the ship and were driven to the place where the stones were needed. King Emrys Aurelianus was there with many lords. He watched as Merlin, stone after stone, set the stones in the Magic Ring, a ring around the graves of many of the fallen warriors and near to many others.

Said Merlin, "The stones each has its healing virtues and gives other blessings besides. The circle will be here as long as there are men to honour it."

The men, in great awe, left the circle and Merlin went on his way. A short time later, to honour the circle, Emrys announced a Whitsun festival to be held at Gloucester. Dubric he appointed Flammen of Caer Leon and the flammen to lead Whitsun Fest.

The days moved into summer and with the heat, troubles were stirring in the North and West. Emrys took a force to the north where Rhydderch had attacked King Hussa, and he was supported by King Cynfarch and Lord Clydno. The Viking Kings and Lords were building strength in the north, and this was also a problem. King Cissa and Lord Bernicia, the son of King Ida, had improved the old fortress, Ranscombe, with a ring of dykes overlooking marshy land in front of the river to the south. To the rear were rugged tree covered hills. And another worry: the warriors of King Eoppa. The king was old and desired to be slain in battle. Emrys marched west to connect with King Hussa, a proud, impatient king who was called the Flame Bearer.

Emrys joined with King Hussa, and with Hussa on the right, went forward until at evening he came on a force of unknown size. Cynfarch had spread out his force in separate units spread out over the hills. Emrys camped in front of the warriors of Cynfarch.

At the crack of dawn, Emrys was ready to demolish his enemy. In front, Lord Eidiol with the warriors of Gloucester was the first to attack, and with him, with many warriors, was Sir Aldolf. To the left, Lord Eidyn, with his stout threehundred, attacked. Held to the rear of the forward units was a great unit of stout horsemen, and these, led by Lord Bodloan, the splendid son of King York. And the King with the Golden Chain, Emrys, was every place encouraging and directing the slaughter. And among the forces of Cynfarch and Lord Clydno were units of Vikings. Hill after hill, the warriors of Emrys drove off those of Cynfarch. Then King Cynfarch's warriors would attack out of the dark woods, then quickly withdraw. Emrys horsemen were dismounted, fighting on foot. It seemed Lord Bodloan was every where slaying enemy warriors; at times, two or three at a time. Toward evening, Emrys gave orders that his warriors should assemble and move down to the flats in front of the marsh. A good number of warriors were missing from the muster. Lord Bodloan had not come off the hill. Emrys, with two warriors, went into the woods to search for warriors who were missing. He saw what seemed a shaman tending the wounded. When the cloaked figure had worked his way close to Emrys, he rushed at the king and gave the king a stab wound from a long knife. The one in the cloak was instantly dispatched. Then without his cloak, he was recognized as the old king, Eoppa.

Emrys wound bled through the night. When dawn came, he had left this world.

In the night, a strange bright comet came into the sky. From the comet shot a beam of light, and the beam turned into a dragon. From the dragon's mouth shot two rays of light. From the end of one of the two shot seven rays of light.

Uther saw this display in the sky. He had been up in the night contemplating the battle he had planned for the coming day. He looked up and saw the marvelous sight.

When Emrys took a great body of warriors to the north, King Gilloman took that opportunity to attack Uther because of Uther taking the stones. He joined with Pascent and his warriors, and these included many Vikings, and they sailed to the coast close to where Uther was, at Menive. Many of them saw the star and these woke others and that camp was much disturbed.

Morning came and Uther and his warriors attacked King Gilloman's camp and it seemed to those of Eire that they were attacked by the very dragon which they had seen in the night. Uther wore a helm of burnished bronze and on it, an onion with its bulb and greens. And it seemed, he wore a rainbow for a belt, and the belt seemed to send its toxic light over the camp of his enemy. And he seemed to float on cloud so that all would see the awful tokens of doom. And Uther's warriors were inspired to be ferocious. These included Sir Aliduc, Sir Brastias, Sir Cyon, Lord Gorlois, Sir Ulfin, Sir Jurdan, Lord Geraint and Sir Morien. Uther caught Prince Pascent, pulled his head back and stuck a long sword down Pascent's throat. The warriors from Eire rushed for their ships leaving their king dead on the field.

Uther went to his quarters, called shamans to give help in understanding the meaning of the star. The shamans discussed the forms in the night sky. For gaining more knowledge they threw sticks. But they all admitted that they were mystified. But that there was important meaning, Uther was certain. By himself, he walked up the road in concentrating on the meaning of the sight in the sky. A cloaked figure walked toward him. The figure walked up. It was Merlin. Merlin stopped and spoke:

"King Uther, I have the knowledge you have been wanting."

"Am I then indeed king?"

Emrys Aurelianus died in the night. But the meaning of the Star is more than that and I will tell it to you. The Star and the Dragon formed by the Star is yourself. From the Star shoot two rays. The first, a strong beam who is your son. And he will have a greatness beyond my telling you of. The second beam is a daughter and her offspring shall establish royal lines which shall stretch into the future. And you will rule and be known as the King of Dragons, which you are. You are Uther Pen Dragon.

"First," said Uther, "I will, in a fitting way, put my brother to rest. I will have two dragons made. One, to be put at Caer Went. The other, to be taken from place to place as I wish."

Uther had kings, lords and their warriors meet at the town of Sarum so that a worthy ceremony might be held for King Emrys Aurelianus. To that place King Uther hied, and then, to the great memorial circle of stones. King Uther Pendragon, with many others, stood witness as Emrys Aurelianus was placed in the East End of the great memorial circle.

A crowning ceremony was planned and held at Yule, and for this ceremony, King Uther Pendragon selected Caer Went. From Armorica came Lord Budic and with him, King Uther's daughter, Anna. Prince Anladd and Princess Marcel were there with Lord Brychan and Lady Erduduyl and their son Nevyn and daughters Pystyl, Gutuyl, Bethon, Tudful, Drynwin and Neffydd. Lord Brochwael and his Lady were present, and with them, Sir Gwyddiew. King Erbin, Lord Geraint, Sir Ermid and Sir Dweyl were present. Sir Ulfin and Sir Cyon were there, and Sir Ulfin was named seneschal. Lord Eidiol and Sir Aldolf were there. Sir Eidyn was present, as was Lord Gorlois with many of his knights. Kings Lot and Hussa son of Friduuald were honoured quests, as was King Bagdemagus. King Nentres was there. And Merlin was present at the crowning.

During the winter, Octa and the Vikings had been getting ready to put the lands under their controle. Octa was sending for shiploads of Vikings from oversea.

Uther Pendragon was organizing his rule. Ulfin, his new young seneschal had castle knights well organized, but Uther, to inspire more fellowship decided on a round table. Merlin's advice was asked and Uther said he would want a table that could be moved, so that it could sponsor Fellowship at any place where he chose to be.

Merlin said this was a good suggestion, that such tables with spiritual attributes had been used; some of them, entirely spiritual; that such circles of fellowship were in the heavens and that a section of sky energy could be transferred. Craftsmen made a wonderful table and Merlin brought sky into it. With changes in perspective, it might be any size.

Uther set his marvelous table in the great hall in Caer Went. He demanded that the best knights and lords in the courts under his jurisdiction be with him at his court. This would sponsor a loyalty in the very best to the fellowship and to its king. Lot was at the table. Cyon and Geraint were seated there. Lord Caradoc was invited to take a seat there. Sir Mael Hir was there and Lord Caw and Sir Morien, Sir Nevyn, Sir Glyddiew the Strong, Sir Eidyn, Sir Aldolf and Lord Eidiol were seated at the table. Lord Kyner and Lord Clydno took places. King Budic was given a place at the table. Lord Gornemant of Rica was given a seat and a seat went to Sir Eiddilig. Merlin was asked by the king to assist in finding worthy champions.

Uther got word that Octa had invaded from north of York, so organized his force, marched toward where Octa was advancing with a huge force. The forces met and Uther's men directly in his front were driven up a wooded hill. On the left flank, however, Gorlois held his place and kept the Vikings from going up Mount Dinian and attacking Uther's left flank. Uther observed how well Gorlois had taken charge, had organized his section. The front of Mount Dinian was friendly to the defenders. The way to the top held many jagged rocks and on the top were clumps of hazel and these, in front of a darker wood which held concealment. By sundown Uther held the hill and the Vikings withdrew. In the night Uther had his lords meet with him. Gorlois said they should attack in the dark before dawn. Uther took note when the Plough was revolving the Pole. He took the suggestion of Gorlois and he and his warriors, in the dark, roared off the hill. The Vikings blew their horns and there followed, the terrible clashing of swords and the Vikings were driven back and they retreated, then withdrew back into the northern hills.

Uther Pendragon and Octa were preparing their forces for another confrontation. Merlin sent some mighty warriors to aid Uther, and on the advice of Merlin they were given Round Table seats. The knights awarded seats were Segurant the Brown, Sir Blaes, Sir Petroc, Sir Nasciens and Sir Aron. Then Sir Cadog, Sir Eliwlod and Glewlwyd Mighty Grasp arrived and were given seats.

Uther set his force so that it would repel any Viking advance. And he said he would need to fight off the raids which would be designed to test his strength. A raid on his right was repelled by his warriors.

The summer passed; then, the fall. Winter came and Uther and his lords retired to Caer Went. Sir Glewlwyd was given the responsibility of being Uther's porter. The Yule was celebrated with much pomp and with many elaborate ceremonies.

After Yule, Uther organized a large body of warriors to be an efficient and effective force. Toward the end of winter, Uther took his force north. Octa, with a great force of Vikings, was then headed south. He set his force below Uther. At dawn, Uther's warriors rose from where they had camped, made a furious attack on the Vikings. The new champions were a great addition to the fighting force. Glewlwyd Mighty Grasp and Segurant the Brown were noticed each to be a devastating force by himself. A great number of Vikings were slain and the others fled back into the hills. Uther, with his warriors, withdrew to Alclud, and there Uther planned a victory celebration to be held in London. As this was to be an informal celebration, the Round Table was left in Caer Went, and at the long tables, lords, and ladies could mingle as they chose to do. And the celebration was to be held on Easter and to be filled with light hearted Easter activities. Many handsome ladies in fine bright clothes would be present.

Easter came. It was a fine bright day and handsome men and beautiful ladies were at the tables and the most beautiful of all, thought Uther, was Igerne, the lovely wife of Lord Gorlois, as he was informed. He ordered food which he thought she would like and had it taken to her, and he sent to her golden goblets of wine. He kept up a lively conversation with Igerne, Gorlois, angry at the attention shown to his wife; rose up, collected her and left the table. Uther could not permit this rudeness of one of his lords, so sent after him an order to return so that proper goodbyes could be said. Gorlois refused that order. This caused Uther to say that because of this rudeness, he would, with Gorlois, have physical conflict.

King Uther got his warriors together and marched toward Cornwall. Gorlois put his wife in what he considered, his safest castle, Tintagel, but he went to a different castle, Dameliock, which sat behind three huge circles of banks behind ditches. Uther had his warriors surround Dameliock. He waited a week, then came the knowledge that Igerne was not in Dameliock, but in Tintagel, which stood on craggy cliffs, which were, high above the sea. Uther looked at Tintagel. It seemed unlikely that one could get into that castle. He spoke to his seneschal, Ulfin of Ridcaradoch, about the problem.

Said Ulfin, "I see this: you must not gain the lady by using force. She must be gained by cunning."

"This is a thing for which I need Merlin," said Uther.

Merlin was sent for. Merlin was soon there.

"You have your heart set on Igerne, so you shall have her," said Merlin. "You will ride up to the castle where she is in the very likeness of Lord Gorlois. Sir Ulfin will be with you and he, in the likeness of Sir Jurdan, who might be expected, as he is Lord Gorlois' chamberlain. I will be Sir Britael, another knight likely to be with the lord, as he is Gorlois' steward. We will go there tonight."

The three rode up to Tintagel, were admitted with not even a questioning look. Uther entered the quarters of Igerne, had a night of caressing and copulation.

At Dameliock there was confusion. Leaders and warriors wandered about in trying to discover what was going on. Lord Gorlois; seeing, from high in his castle, the disorder among Uther's warriors, decided to break out of the castle. All went well except that in the break out,

Gorlois was slain. Those who had been Gorlois' warriors felt that they had best surrender the castle - as there seemed no longer a reason to hold it. Uther's warriors took the castle and many of them took valuable things which they found in it. The warriors explained, and not much to the liking of those in the castle, that this was a usual practice.

In the morning, Uther, Merlin and Ulfin rode the half dozen miles back to Dameliock and Uther was sad to find that Gorlois had been slain and he made peace with Gorlois' subjects and three of Gorlois' knights; Sir Jurdan, Sir Brastias and Sir Aliduc, were given seats at the Round Table. Uther had Igerne come to his castle, Caer Went, which had the bright dragons in front of its gate. Uther had King Lot in charge of Lothian and depended on him to keep some order in that section of his lands. Octa and Ebissa had gone by ship to Viking lands, and then returned, landing in the north with a great many Viking warriors and were invading the lands of Lot. Lot had trouble getting a strong force together for blocking the Viking attacks, so Uther got his warriors together and went north. A great body of Viking warriors charged against the warriors of Uther, but again Uther seemed to float above the Vikings in his bright bronze helm with its crest of onion and with his goatskin covered shield.

Uther had with him many fierce warriors of his table. Sir Mael Hir the Tall rode with him, and the Cambrian, King Caradoc, who had left his kingdom in the care of his brother, Griffin; and Glyddiew the Strong and King Budic, and many warriors with them, were riding with Uther, as was Lord Gornemant. And Sir Cyon, and Sir Cinric and Sir Cenon, son Aeron, the Lady of Light. And the great Dragon himself, King Uther, was leading the charge against the Vikings. Ever so many Vikings could not stand against such swords; and before the battle, Uther had been joined by Lot and many warriors of Lothian. Vikings who had not been slain or crippled fled away and into the hills. Among the slain was Cherdic.

As it was expected that there would for a while be a calm; King Lot, the young King of Lothian, returned with Uther and Uther's other warriors to Caer Went. At the castle there was, because of the triumph over the Vikings, a light hearted joy. Uther's daughter, Anna, was there with King Budic, and she was quite lovely, and King Lot was quite taken with her. Uther, seeing this relationship might cause difficulties, took Lot with him to Glastonbury. Igerne had gone there to be with her family, and she took two of her daughters with her; and these: Elaine and Margause. Margause, even a bit younger than Anna, was also beautiful. She, also, was affectionate and charming. For romance, at Glastonbury there was more freedom than there was at Caer Went, so King Lot spent much time in its beautiful gardens with Margause. Uther also took advantage of the beautiful gardens in entertaining Igerne.

Time got close for celebrating the Yule and preparation was made. The celebration was planned for Caerdiff and long tables were set in the great hall. Greens and many other decorations covered the walls. Women were busy with designing clothes and other bright things to wear.

Yule Eve arrived and a great company gathered for a great feast and entertainment. The weather had been mild, so guests had not been detained on account of the weather. Even the most senior members of the court community were punctual in their arrival. Prince Anladd with Queen Marcel, with their daughter, Lady Dwyanedd, and their son, Lord Brychan and their son and daughter's families. And Lord Brochwael and King Erbin were there with their families. King Budic was there and King Bagdemagus. Sir Glewlwyd was at the gate greeting gentlemen and ladies as they arrived. A man walked up to the gate, his clothes so threadbare that Sir Glewlwyd presumed he was a begger.

"The line is down there for those who are seeking handouts," said Sir Glewlwyd.

"I have come as a guest," said the man.

"And what would you be toting in your basket?"

"A gift for the king."

"Ah, if you present him with a gift, he will give you a reward. It's his way. No matter what it is, and from the looks of you, it can not be worth much. I should not let you in, as your looks are too shabby. But I'll tell you what. If you agree to give me one third of what the king gives as reward, I will let you pass. Now how are you called?"

"I am Sir Cleges."

"Then pass, Sir Cleges."

A short way on, a young serving knight blocked his way.

"Pardon, but this is not the place for you," said he.

"I am a guest with a gift for the king," said Sir Cleges.

"Well, I should not let a person dressed as you are remain in this hall, but if you are permitted to stay, will you agree to give me one third of the reward you will get for bringing a gift?"

"I will."

"Then pass on. And remember, I am Sir Lanyel."

Sir Cleges had not gone far when he heard another knight speak to him.

"I say, you can not stay in this hall."

The knight walked to block Sir Cleges' way.

"Indeed, I am an invited guest. And as I have explained, I bring a gift to the king," said Sir Cleges.

"A gift, aye. I'll tell you what. I am Sir Florence. If I let you pass, will you give me one third of the reward you get?"

"I will."

"And who might you be?"

"I am known as Sir Cleges."

"Then pass on, Sir Cleges."

Sir Cleges walked to where King Uther Pendragon sat on a splendid throne. He knelt and spoke.

"Sire, I humbly present this gift in the hope that thou wilt will find it pleasing."

He gave the king the basket of cherries.

"Cherries! I was just last night dreaming of cherries and, as if by magic, they are here. To give cherries in winter, it must be a magical tree. And instead of eating the cherries yourself, you remembered to bring them to your king. Have you thought, what reward you might like?"

"Sire, if it please you, twelve good swats with the horse whip on the bare back. And they to be given this day."

"I think that a foolish thing to wish for. But they can be supplied. If you would, Sir Guitolin, and Sir Cleremond, escort this good man to the courtyard and see that he gets twelve good swats with a horsewhip."

"Thankyou, my lord. However, I might be accused of thievery if I did not say I had agreed to give one third of my reward to your usher,

Sir Lanyel."

"Ahah," said the king.

"Sire, I must admit to having promised one third of the reward to your usher, Sir Florence."

"Is that the truth?"

"It is, Sire, and the last third I promised to your worthy porter."

"I now think," said Uther, "that the reward should be given out in front of my throne. Have the bard come supply music and song about the event. Knight with the reward, how are you called?"

"Sire, I am Sir Cleges."

"Bard, we'll have a song about Sir Cleges."

Sir Cleges got word he was to go with the page to speak with Princess Anna. He went to where she was and was signaled to be seated.

""You must tell me the story of the cherries," said the Princess.

"No great mystery to it," said Sir Cleges. "The tree bloomed out of season. Then, as we have had a mild spell, and as my wife, Clarys, and I kept protecting it, it gave cherries. Then I did not think I would be here, as my clothes are worn to rags, but my wife said I needed to bring the cherries, then perhaps I would be given a place at the castle. I did not think I would, as even our last horse has died, and to bring into the hall a bunch of cherries would make me look foolish, and all I would get was laughs, but you know how wives are. No saying no."

"I think the tree was magical," said the princess. "And now there is a song about you. So people here will want to see you. Well, I will not keep you from your dinner."

Sir Cleges enjoyed the feast. Then he was told to report for duty at the castle.

Yule went past. There was a small surprise. Princess Anna announced she intended to marry King Budic. She and King Budic returned to Amorica to prepare for the wedding, and Uther returned to Caer Went.

Igerne was expecting and Anna was in Amorica, and this left Uther restless; especially as the lands seemed to be resting in peace. He decided it was the time to be exploring his kingdom. He informed his lords, left instructions and rode off. He took with him items a traveller might need, and his table.

The Fellowship of the Round Table would keep order. With this thought, Uther felt at ease as he rode off.

Uther Pendragon, as he rode, held much safety in his appearance. He was a tall man, a head taller than the average knight, and he had a long, mobile face, a face which could give him an otherworldly look, and this look could be frightening. The network of scars on his face did not make him look overly friendly.

Uther rode northwest, rode past Malmesbury, to Uley and out on a finger of land where, past old, wood, stone and clay forts, which were covered with tall weeds, the land past the finger dropped steeply to a valley which was filled with mist. Uther dismounted, led his horse off the finger. He found himself in a bright mist. Shapes went past him as he walked forward. It became light, Uther mounted and rode among tall stones at the bottom of a cliffy hill, then in front of him was a knight half again taller than he was. "You do not belong here," said the giant knight, and the knight raised a club to strike Uther. Uther moved quickly, wrestled the club from the awful giant, smashed in the giant's head. Uther rode on. In the distance, on a low hill, Uther saw a large, square building and to this he made his way.

He rode on toward the building and this, in spite of his seeing it in the distance, took several days' travel on the rocky road before he reached it.

Uther was stopped at the gate, announced, then admitted into a great hall where, at a long table, sat a gigantic lord, a lord with a huge, ferocious looking head. Down along both sides of the table were many monsterish warriors; many, quite large.

"King Uther Pen Dragon, come join us here. Sit you down by me and we can talk. I am Ogrevran."

"Thankyou, Lord. I am much obliged for your hospitality."

"First of all," said the lord, "be generous to yourself with the food. It is in good supply. And we think it, quite good."

Lord Ogrevran had a huge, deep, booming voice, which echoed around the hall, and this and that bit of information gave Uther a greater size and complexity of many lands, including his own. And at the table were great and mysterious kings. Ogrevran introduced King Gwynn, the Son of Nudd, who was King of the Unknown. And he introduced a large, hard looking lord, Lord Echel Bighip. Odgar, the son

58

of King Aedd was introduced, and Rhuawn Bebyr, the son of Dorath, and Lugh Windyhand and Bradwen, the son of Moren Mynawg, and Gwenwynwyn, the son of Naw, and King Manannan, the son of King Lear. This was a table of Kings and champions and King Uther felt at home.

After talking and drinking and laughing together through the evening, Uther got from out his pack, his table, which was now reduced in size to one which fit his pack nicely.

"Lord Ogrevran, this is my Table. It is intended to seat onehundredfifty worthy warriors. I did not find that number to seat at it, but give it to you in the thought that you can do better than I. And my path might not lead back to my hall in Caer Went, as it seems to hold many strange things."

Lord Ogrevran had tables pulled to the side, put the small table down and took joy in watching it expand. Time for retiring then came.

Morning came. After dining, Uther bid his farewells.

"From here, none of the ways are good," said Ogrevran. "However, to the right, there are ways which lead back to your world. You will need a new horse. Will you accept one of ours?"

"It would be most welcome. Thankyou."

Uther accepted a new horse which was brought to him. He headed down the road. There were hills, twisting valleys full of grottos and groves of trees. A long time on the road he was. He came to a fair country, which was Mallerstang. Some of the people welcomed King Uther and some did not. A tyrant and his associates had taken the rule from those whom most of the population had wanted. Uther saw the situation, caught the tyrant and slew him. He slew one, then another, of the tyrants associates. There was then much celebration and the lady of the king whom the tyrant had slain was especially taken with Uther and she pleased him. The land looked to Uther for giving law. And this was a country which was often troubled by otherworldly beings. Where mountains dropped far down to a low land was a round pool. From deep in the pool, which seemed to have no bottom, would, at times, come a fire breathing dragon and the dragon would slay farm animals and what people it could catch, or it would take them with it into the dark pool. Uther made it a point to have his dwelling one which was, of those of that country, closest to the pool.

On a dark night, Uther saw the dragon rising out of the lake. He grabbed his sword and shield, mounted his horse, met the dragon as the dragon came the long way up the cliffy hillside. Uther charged down the hillside onto the dragon. Rushing into fire and claws, Uther gave the dragon a mighty stroke. After slashing and spitting fire and receiving a number of blows, the long, snake like dragon turned and fled and Uther, injured though he was, followed close on the tail of the dragon giving it a blow whenever he was able. A long way he chased the dragon. He caught up with the dragon on top of a hill and there, slew it. A number of farmers were soon on the hill to give wonder and praise to Uther; then, to bring him food. All the while, a trail of blood from the dragon, which the farmers called the Westmorland Dragon; in a stream, was winding its way down the hill. The farmers told Uther that he was in a place called Uffington, and they much admired Uther's wonderful, white horse. But most, the people there were filled with wonder at their king, and they suspected he came from the Otherworld to kill the awful dragon. Then, for a place to rest, the farmers gave Uther the best they had.

Uther Pendragon gave thanks to a farmer and the farmer's wife after they had enjoyed breakfast together, and he set out for Glastonbury, as he wished to be with Igerne. Igerne was most happy to see Uther back home.

"I have news," said Igerne. "I have a son."

"It would be mine."

"So I was told. How can that be?"

Uther told how Merlin had disguised him. He gave a telling of the evening when they were together. When he left in the morning, he said, Gorlois was already dead.

Igerne then told of the child being born, and of the seven blue mist elves coming, bringing presents for the one whom they called Arthur Pendragon. The first gave a helm, the Helm, Goswhit; the second, a shield, Pridwen; the third, a spear, Ron; the fourth, a burnie, made by Witeze, son of Weland the Smith, and its name, Wygar. And Ron was made by the magician Gofan. The fifth elf gave a dagger named White Haft. The sixth elf gave a white mantle which would hold no other colour but pure white. The seventh gave a blue cloth with a gold sun in each corner. Then Merlin came and said he needed to put the gifts in a secure place. And he needed to put Arthur in a secure place, as Arthur would have many enemies, and that having a foster Father was a custom of his own family, and that it was not a bad custom.

"Merlin has much wisdom. Doubtless he will explain all to me," said Uther.

The first thing the next morning, Uther took himself to Caer Went. He rode through the wooded vales, and his trail came out on hills covered sparsely with trees; then went over meadows and, on its hill, to Caer Went. In through the gate he rode, turned his horse over to grooms and entered the great hall. A good number of warriors were seated at long tables. Geraint was there, and his son, Cador. Aldolf, Ulfin, Jurdan and Caradoc were at a table. And Nasiens, and Cleges were there. And Guitolin and Gornemant of Rica. And Glewlwyd he had seen at the gate.

Uther took his place at the head of the table. Those there acknowledged his presence and they were obviously quite glad to see him. Ulfin came up, took the place next to Uther.

"Your son is a year old," said Ulfin.

"So I understand," said the king.

"But less pleasing, the foreigners have occupied much of our land. And in other places, law and order have suffered," said Ulfin.

The king nodded. Food was brought in for him. He ate. He pushed his plate away, spoke in a loud voice.

"Men, gather here and hear what I have to say."

Many of the men whom he knew; some, by face only; some, he hadn't recalled seeing. Sir Naram he saw, and Dywel, a son of King Erbin, and Sir Gorthmol; and Sir Cleremond was among those at the table.

"Men, I hear the foreigners have taken good parts of our land. We can not have that. Get the word out that all are to gather here right now. Prince Dywel, Lord Geraint, have your father get his force together. King Caradoc be certain Lord Caw is informed. Get word to King Tewrig, to Lord Brochwael, to Lord Brychan. Lord Geraint, get word to King Lot."

Uther watched as the warriors left the tables leaving him by himself sipping his mug of ale. He looked up. Merlin was seated where Sir

Ulfin had a short time ago been seated.

"It's been awhile," said Merlin.

"How do you see it," said Uther.

"One does what he does. The Vikings have their virtues. They are a lawless lot. They have come by boat loads and have settled over vast areas. They could be bargained with. But that would not be how it will be."

"Because I am Uther Pendragon."

"Quite so."

"And I am the kingdom. Those would be fine marvelous gifts my son is to have."

"Four from the land of the Elf Queen," said Merlin.

"And one made not far from where we are," said Uther. "From Weyland's Smithy, and that is not far from where I killed the dragon." "Yes, off Icknield Street. Another thing," said Merlin, "Your daughter has a son. He is Prince Howel. Just arrived."

"That is news."

Uther and Merlin chatted until time to retire.

In the days that followed, warriors and their tents and pavilions arrived, by leaps and bounds, increased in number. In the evening, as tents stood, in their bright colours, spread out over the meadows, Uther sat in his hall, which was filled with lords, leaders and knights of the castle. To his right sat Ulfin, Geraint, then King Erbin. To his left, Sir Aldolf, then Sir Brastias.

"In four days time," said King Uther Pendragon, "I will go north."

In the morning, early, Uther rode to Glastonbury. It was a sunny day and as he got close, watching the smooth sides of Glastonbury's hill gave him much pleasure, as it gave beautiful changes as he rode toward it. The short grass on its sides made the hill look as if it was made of green marble.

A wonderful, warm evening came on; the air, filled with the scent of many flowers. Somewhere in the castle, the notes from the harp of a harper came faintly to the garden, a flower filled garden where water fell into a pool.

Near the pool, on a bench, sat Uther with Igerne at his side. On the grass, in front of where Uther sat, sat three of Igerne's sisters: Goleuddydd, Rieinmeth and Dwyanedd; all, seeming young and enchantingly beautiful.

"We could have the harper join us," said Igerne.

"But we will not," said Uther. "I like the sound of it as it is, mixed with the falling water."

The conversation on small happenings and light fun, which the ladies had, which crossed their minds, was a babble which mixed with the falling water.

"I see Lord Oswy is not at home," Uther said.

"No. He would be at your castle worrying with the condition of his men's equipment. Knowing him, that is what he would be doing. He is one for details," said Lady Rieinmeth.

Uther, as night moved on, went to sleeping quarters. Uther was shown to a place where there was a fine bed. Then, early, Uther set out for Caer Went. The day passed. And so, the night.

Then, day four. King Uther Pendragon, on his fine white horse, was having his lines checked, so to see that all were ready to move forward. Riding beside him was the druid Tremorien, and he had an eye for any problem which might have needed fixing. Uther signaled for a move forward. He looked back at the golden metal dragons on either side of his gate. The knight who was the guide, Sir Cleremond, raised the Dragon Pennant; then, the other pennants were raised. The warriors went off, went north.

Uther Pendragon got his body of warriors on the other side of a river, traveled toward where the Vikings were reported to be, under the ancient castle at Ouralion, that is where Viking warriors were seen to be. Uther, within sight of them, set up his camp. He set up his dragon pennant and from it, spread a feeling of security and rightness. Uther Pendragon was the Father of All Tribes, the Mighty Enchanter. His look could freeze an army. He was the song which bards sang. So sang the bards.

Early morning, Uther's warriors were up. Uther called them to advance. He had stout knights of Caer Went as his special guard. Sir Aliduc was on one side: Sir Cador, on the other.

There were in front of Uther and his warriors a huge body of Viking warriors. The two sides met in a fury of slashing weapons. As the day wore on the Vikings were driven back to the castle. Many of them lay dead on the field and among these, Octa, Ebissa and Ossa, who was related to Octa. Many of Uther's warriors lay dead and many others, wounded and the wounded included Cyon, and Aldolf, and Lanyel, and Blaes, and Segurant the Brown, and Uther himself. Uther got a serious wound in the chest. And many got wounds which they patched up and did not mention to others. Uther had the wounded carried and, pennants flying, the warriors rode the ten miles southeast to London. In London, the wounded were taken to where women had skill in herbs. Uther kept, from that time, mostly to his quarters. He was cared for by Igerne, who was a healer. The winter came, Yule was celebrated. The news of the Vikings was spoken of. They wee building their forces. Colgrim was then their king and had taken charge of organizing the Vikings into a fighting unit.

Uther Pendragon organized his warriors. Lot and Cador did much of the organizing. Then King Budic was there with a good body from Amorica. Early in the spring Uther decided he needed to attack the Vikings. To get to Ouralion, he fixed a horse drawn carriage. When he and his army set themselves for battle, he dismounted stood holding a wooden frame. When the Vikings saw that, they all went into the castle. They sent out a messenger.

"Take King Uther home. Then come back with young men ready to fight. We do not fight the old and sick. He wants to die a warrior so he can go sit with the champions. Tell him to go home."

However, Uther stood firm. He was resolute.

Uther Pendragon gave orders to surround the castle. When King Colgrim saw this, he ordered his Vikings out, and they stormed out of the castle and attacked. There were many wonderful feats of arms. The Vikings fought long; then, after many were slain, they were driven off. Uther was helped into his carriage.

"It will be long before they again attack us," said Lord Geraint.

Uther Pendragon had his men start on the way to London, which was about ten miles down the road to the southeast. On the way, as Uther sat in his carriage, his face got blacker and blacker.

"One ninth part of my prowess goes to Arthur," said Uther.

Before he reached the Gate of London, he was dead.

Lord Lud held a dignified celebration of Uther and Uther was given a burial place on the top of Mount Snowdon.

King Budic was found to be among the slain, after the battle at

Ouralion, and he was taken to Margam, and there he was buried.

Knights and lords drifted off to their homes, as there was no leader to say why they should not. Then, in the spaces between the jurisdictions of the lords, there was lawlessness. Robbers and other criminals made their own laws. There were squabbles between numbers of rulers. A number of Kings tried to promote themselves as the replacement for Uther.

In the north and west in those lands a solitary wanderer might have sometimes been seen. Often, he was seen in the areas around the Teifi River. One day as he was seated by a spring, which was near the Teifi River, seated brewing herb tea; he looked up and saw a man in a ragged cloak seated near him.

"Have some tea?"

"That would be welcome."

Vortigern, for that is who the wanderer was, poured a cup and handed it to the second man. The second man took the cup, took a sip.

"I see you have learned a bit about herbs," he said.

"Ah, it is you, dear father," said Vortigern. "I am a learner. They seem quite a gift."

The two sat and sipped tea.

"Uther Pendragon is dead," said Merlin.

"King Uther."

"A king he was. But he was more. And is more. I see him, Chief of the Vessel of the Iron Door, which toiled to the hill."

Merlin picked up a flat stone, skipped it across a still pool, which was fed by the spring. A couple of wagtails flew up, out of the bushes.

"Come back down to the pool. You were in no danger," said Merlin.

One came back, sat on the bush: The other stayed up on a nearby tree.

"I will want more respect than that," said Merlin.

He waved his hand and the wagtails feet turned black.

"I'm not glad about the news," said Vortigern. "I am in a different world than all the lords and knights. I suppose the land will survive?"

"Arthur will be king. Another Dragon. Conceived May Day. A

good day for dragons. May Day, early morn, cut a square of turf with the dew still on it, put it face down on another turf which is covered with dew and they will produce a dragon. In this type, an eel," said Merlin.

The two had a second cup of tea. Merlin walked off.

Many were the roads which Vortigern walked as the days went on and on. Yule was, as always, good to the wanderer, provided he could keep warm. Beside a campfire, on a cold winter day, there again was Merlin. Vortigern looked up and there Merlin was. Vortigern poured Merlin a cup of tea.

"Last I looked, those wagtails feet are still black," said Vortigern.

"And they will be. And so, their Children's.

They sat and enjoyed the fire. The smoke rose up grey against the dark trunks of trees.

Said Merlin, "I have placed what one might say is a bit of a treasure in a cave. A few things the land might find mysterious and interesting. It will be found by an heir to it. And he will be a blond, blue eyed man.

"That is good to know," said Vortigern.

They sipped tea.

"I hesitate to ask about my family," he said.

"Your wife misses you. As do your daughters. Gotta is beautiful: favours her mother. Madrun would not, of course, remember you. She too will be beautiful. – About the treasure. I see a bell having a thing to do with its recovery.

They sat and watched the fire.

"And of course Hrothwena and Lady miss you."

"I do think about them."

"That will lighten their hearts. – And Uther has a second daughter. But she is out of this land."

After some time watching the fire, Merlin left.

The days moved on. Vortigern enjoyed the new spring. He walked up and down Watling Road, walked the roads which led off from it. He walked to the sea, walked up and down the coast. So the year passed, the leaves turned bright, then fell. Then he thought, he might be mistaken for Father Yule, he in his tattered cloak.

Then it was spring; May, and he was near the sea, sitting on a bank

66

of the River Conwy, and Merlin came and sat on the bank.

"This is an interesting place," said Merlin. "On the western bank is a spring which rises and falls like the sea."

The two sat and watched the sea.

"So many strange things in nature," said Vortigern. I could look at these things forever. The enemy is Time, Janus."

"There you are mistaken. Janus rolls with time as much a victim as we. Janus will become a god with no priests: will be hidden away in Arianrhod's cold tower."

The two sat and watched the river.

"I was just thinking on what you said about May, and Arthur, and the snakes," said Vortigern.

"Women will become snake like," said Merlin, "Cupid's arrows continue to wound."

They watched the river. Merlin continued, "Kings shall fight each other at the Ford of the Staff. For the sake of the Lioness. A tree shall spring up on the White Tower of London. An owl will nest on the walls of Gloucester. And from its egg will be hatched an ass. It is time for you to go home."

"I am a wanderer now. Even for them, I feel I am better wandering."

"Yes. But stop in for tea. Stay a day now and again. You can make tea for them. You and I will walk through the fields and we will talk about the flowers, and talk of teas. And some other marvelous things which flowers might do."

The two set off, walked through hills and meadows. When Merlin left, Vortigern thought about home. The next day, his footsteps headed in that direction.

Then, before too much time had passed, Vortigern was having tea in his own home. Then, before break of day, he was gone. Then, before he realized the summer was gone, there were fall colours. Then another Yule.

In the winter, Vortigern was again out on the road. He now wore warm clothes. It was cold, but there were beautiful things to see. It was good to be out.

Merlin had spent Yule with his half sister, a daughter of his mother five years younger than he was and she was staying in the castle of

King Rhydderch. His sister, Ganieda, had a friend there, Cerddglud Cynllaith, whom Merlin was interested in.

But here now, back in his home woods, he was comfortable with his black dog. When Vortigern came down the path, he had just then collected the top most twigs of an oak. He considered oaks to be special friends. They gave him stories. The sun was rising into view.

"You'd be surprised how many tales these oaks will tell you," said Merlin. "Oaks are special friends."

They climbed the rock, shrub covered side of a hillock.

"Then you have come here for tales," said Vortigern.

"The fact is, I have come for a snake egg," said Merlin.

They continued walking through shrubs and small trees. They reached the top of the rise. Where there were rocks and clumps of shrubs. Below them lay a shrub filled valley through which wound a brook. And to their right, they looked up at tall, blue hills etched against the pale sky.

"Time for tea," said Merlin.

The two of them walked down the hill, toward the brook. Merlin slowed to gather herbs: Trefoil, Cress, hedge hyssop, selago.

"You should keep iron away from this," said Merlin, pointing to the selago.

Down by the brook, over a small fire, they made tea.

"I saw, far out at sea, a white ship," said Merlin, "sailing the waves. The second time I looked, I saw but the calm sea."

The two sat over tea.

"I must be off," said Merlin, as he got to his feet.

He walked over the brook, up the hill, into the trees.

Vortigern walked up along the brook. He walked through the Valley of Gwrtheyn. He walked until in front of him was the four sided tower, a tower the sides of which sloped to a point. He walked around tall cliffs, walked over the flat, grassy field and up to Brecknock Castle.

The morning came, Vortigern was back on the road as the woods in the spring he found lovely and there were the spring flowers.

Merlin's path took him west, toward the sea, and he came to Caer Arianrhod, which was in a dark forest near the sea. There stood the castle, dark as night, and round windows stood each next to each in a complete circle around the castle. Like the windows; tall, thin doors, each next to each, went around the entire building. And all the windows and doors stood open; yet, few would have found this castle inviting. Shadow, like a gloom, seemed to hover around it. The trees which stood around it caught onto its somber mood and seemed to drip melancholy. Merlin let his feet take him to the castle. Lord Gwenddoleu, son of Ceidiaw, would be at the castle and he had the dark birds, and the song of the birds caused madness. He was called the Bull King. And he had the Secret Apple Forest. And this was protected by Olwen, daughter of the Hawthorn Giant. And with Lord Gwenddoleu would have been Lady Cerddglud Cynllaith, and the mother of the lady was called the Spirit of Slaughter. The sister of Gwenddoleu, Gwendoloena, was also a friend of Merlin's, who was at the castle. And she contained the Spirit of the Moon.

For a time, Merlin moved among flickering lights, among dark shadows, among dangerous pits of darkness. All the while, the windows, the circles of darkness, looked out on the outside world and little they told of what was on the inside.

Vortigern wandered through the hot summer, sharing tea with one other wanderer, with another wanderer. The leaves fell from the trees. Then it was winter. Then another Yule and then the trials of another cold season.

Through out the land, there were killings and retaliations, and on the roads were many robbers and rascals. And many young knights and warriors who wished for tests of strength and courage could find them. Lords would often be looking for warriors; especially, for those with good reputations, who might add to the protection of valued property. And lords, at times, would discuss among themselves the need for a central authority; for a leader, like King Uther, who would supply a general orderliness.

Not far from Ludlow was a small castle, one of a good number which were in that area, which gave protection from raiding warriors. This castle was the dwelling of Lord Kyner, the lord who provided security for farms in his area. And Lord Kyner worked with the other lords of his area to provide a general protection for the whole area. But the basic occupation of these lords was farming. The castles were, in a way, fortified farm houses. The lord's fortified buildings protected the food and belongings of the farmers who farmed his land; while, at the same time, regulating what needed to be done in order to keep the farm producing.

Lord Kyner was a well liked lord. He was thought, efficient and just. It was also thought, he had two sons who would be good lords in the future: one, at least. The other, become a knight of renown. The boys were considered the star figures of that section of the country. Kay was tall and athletic. He had taught himself many amazing physical feats. The second boy, one year younger, was very strong. Kay had been born to Kyner and his wife; however, Arthur, the second son, had not. No one of that area, except Lord Kyner and his wife, knew that. Merlin had given Arthur to the Lord and said it was important that all should think Arthur was the lord's own son.

Kay would often be cross, but he was fair. Arthur could be bad tempered. But he and Kay got on well together. And among the other boys of that area, they were considered leaders. All the same, the stern, glum Kyner Fairbeard made certain their heads did not get too big. Among the dozen of the boys who were their friends, most of them spent a good part of most days in doing farm work. An exception was the lad named Griflet. He lived in a neighboring castle and, like Kay and Arthur, spent much time in weapons training. Griflet was full of foolishness and a great tease, but he was so good humoured that Arthur and Kay put up with him. His father, Lord Do, claimed to be a descendant of the great lord, Lord Gilfaethwy. But in that part of the world, Kay told Griflet, that he was certain that a great many others could make that same claim. "Likely, hundreds," Kay had said.

Now and again Lords would come to call on Kyner, and now and again, their wives or other members of their family would travel with them. Kay wished to be introduced to those who came. Arthur paid little attention to them. And Lord Kyner seemed disinclined to make introductions. The visitors, he said, came to see him.

The year turned. There were the end of season celebrations, the preparations for Yule; then, the Yule celebration. The celebration observed ancient traditions, and these permitted much foolishness. Lord Kyner tolerated this without himself being foolish. But in keeping with the spirit of Yule, he was the generous host. There was joy in the central hall of the castle.

The main part of the castle was the central hall: thick stone walls around a frame of great timbers. And the walls rose up to form a squat tower. As one entered the hall, on the right side, rising from a flagstone floor, was a stair to a wooden floor on heavy rafters. And the stair went up to the roof. At the end of the hall was the great fireplace, the fireplace tools and utensils. On either side of the fireplace was a door to a back room. Kay and Arthur had the upstairs, over the hall. In the center of the hall was the long table which could be dismantled if the space was needed. Along each side wall were benches where men could sit, or at night, make beds.

In the fireplace a roaring fire burned, casting its flickering light off the walls where hung arms and battle gear and these, draped with ivy and bright cloths. And among these were branches of holly, pine and other evergreen. A laughing girl ran into the hall carrying a bowl of wassail, set it on the table so all could fill their horns. At the table there was laughing and talking. The Yule Log burned. At the foot of the stairs, boys and girls were laughing and talking. There were seven boys and eight girls there. A boy with curly brown hair was saying something funny causing the tall, slender boy, Kay, to rise up and start pulling the ears of the boy who had spoken. There was laughter.

"Make him stop, make him stop," said, between chuckles, the boy who's ears were being pulled.

"Griflet, I'm going to bust - - -," the tall boy was saying.

A stern faced man entered the room. There was silence. Lord Kyner had entered.

"Son, get your wraps. It is time we made our calls," said the lord.

Kay went to get his cloak. Outside, a horse neighed. It stomped its foot. Kay and the lord went out. Arthur looked out and saw the two horses gallop away.

"Well, at least he stopped pulling my ear," said Griflet.

A girl laughed. She was Elyned, daughter of Brychan.

"Pull his ear," said Griflet's sister, Lorete.

At the end of February, a couple of lords, a half dozen warriors with them, rode up toward Lord Kyner's castle.

"Slim," said Lord Kyner, when he learned that the visitors were on their way, "take Arthur with you and show him what you are working on down past the meadow. I want him to understand some of the needs of the place."

Arthur, from on his walk through the meadow, did not get a good look at the arriving lords.

"Likely, we don't know half, how many come and go," said Arthur.

"Can't never tell," said the slim man.

The two of them walked past the meadow. Arthur helped slim with work on a pen.

A couple of days later, Arthur was not at a scheduled weapons practice, but he was with men and oxen who were plowing. He insisted on taking a turn holding the plow.

"No. The horse is for other things. He is a noble beast. One does not bind him to a plow, – or any other thing," said a workman.

"Oh, there are noble ox. But he is separated out when he is born. And he does not work. No, not even as the noble horse works," said a worker.

Kay was at the castle with his teachers. In these days, Arthur's teachers were, more often, the workmen. From them, there was often a babble of voices speaking of this and that which, it was said, everybody knew, and of things which had happened in the long past.

"Down in those hills," said a workman, "Ludlow Castle has been there for countless ages. And for a good part of an age, one could talk about that."

Time passed and the days warmed. Arthur and Kay worked with teachers. At the sessions, there were comments as to the state of the land. Someone mentioned lords who wanted to take shipping away from King Erbin, as he had gotten old.

"That worries me not," said Lord Kyner." Anything we need, we can make it."

He left the conversation, became interested in other things. The teachers talked of the disorder in other places: in the area about the Severn. The people in their area had changed little through many centuries. Many said that Vortigern had let them down; though, in their area, little thought was given to him. Outside their area he would have been nearly forgotten. It was sometimes said, as in the castle of Lord Kyner:

"In the days of Vortigern – "

Vortigern was little more than a representation of times past. That he was wandering some place, some back roads, hardly anyone would have dreamed that could have been the case. However, Vortigern's family were everyday working gentry; mostly, just neighbors and part of their community. There were rare times when Vortigern's failings got thrown up to them; but these were mixed in with other complaints which life gives reasons for. Life there was hard and full of reasons for complaints. At that time, a Briton warrior was visiting at Brecknock. The Briton warrior had been complaining about Vortigern. Hrothwena spoke:

"Not meetly was the sword pierced upon the side of the horse. Not meetly did the man of the grey stone pillars mount the lofty steed. Dark was his spear."

The Briton warrior said, "Darker still is thy husband in his cell gnawing the jaw of a buck."

Hrothwena: "I hope he enjoys it. May he be supplied with a few."

Briton warrior: "Let the Lady of the Sea, let Branwen, only come hither. Then, o Hengist, thou mayest do, thou mayest kill, thou mayest burn. So said Vortigern, thou, o Venedotian with the haughty countenance regarded not counsel, did not attend the great swelling of knights who would give no accommodation to the Saxons. – I blame him much. None could have been less wise."

One, then another of hot summer days passed.

The Venedotian wanderer, Vortigern, walked in at Brecknock. He was, by his wife, then his family, made comfortable and given food.

"And here you are well and free," said Hrothwena.

"I've never been otherwise," said Vortigern.

"And I have lately been called, the Lady of the Sea, herself," said Hrothwena.

"Then your beauty was understated. You are even more lovely," said Vortigern.

He told of his days, through that summer, on this byway, on that. He told of his dreams. The next morning, he was out along the road.

At Lord Kyner's, the days rolled into late summer. Among other things, Arthur got experience with haying. A long day he was spending helping men get in bales of hay. Birds flew out of the herbage as the men who were haying moved forward. In the evening, there was plenty of food and drink. At evening meals, there was talk about conflicts to the north.

73

"One thing," said a worker, "having the Vikings for neighbors, we are not so much worried by the groups of quarreling rascals."

"That is, as long as we do not fight with Vikings," said another.

Nights and days passed. Then it was Harvest Festival. Kay and Arthur enjoyed the crowd of young people who gathered at the castle for the celebration. The celebration was boisterous, but rites, correctly done, as Lord Kyner oversaw what went on, and what went on needed to meet his approval.

Kay and Arthur then needed to get again with their teachers. The weather got colder, and time came when there was need to prepare for Yule. Then Yule was celebrated, and neighbors gathered at Lord Kyner's castle. Of food and drink there was a plenty. Cold and snow followed the Yule, and it seemed no time before it was spring: Easter.

There was trouble on the areas near the coast. Picts and numbers of lawless men were raiding Briton homesteads and Hrothwena knew she needed a tie with one or more other lords. She planned a Mayday for kings. King Urien and his sons and daughters were invited. Mayday, numbers of young people, including Morgan the Fay, with Urien and his son's and daughters were at the celebration. Morgan had been a long time friend of Urien's sons and daughters and was about their age. Urien's eldest son, Pasgen, had selected Madrun to be his partner, and Hrothwena could hardly find enough good things to say about Pasgen. It was thought best that Madrun should, at the end of the celebration, go with the family of King Urien when they returned to Rheged. Morgan the Fay approved of, and endorsed Madrun and hers was a powerful endorsement. Morgan the Fay had become recognized as a person of much wisdom and great ability in creating. Her mother, Igerne, had seen her promise and had sent her to Avalon so that gifted teachers could guide her development. Hrothwena said that the influence of Morgan the Fay on Madrun would be beneficial. And an alliance with King Urien would be most welcome. "Urien, King of Rheged, rules the West. Gold and silver quickly pass away. Better than both is union and harmony," said Hrothwena. "That is what we will have with King Urien, the Gold King of the North, the Lord of the Land of Evening and of Shadow, as his mother was out of the Land of Gore. King Urien, called the Dark Faced Lord of the Bright West, Lord of the Sunset, was listed as a most resolute of kings; savage, his spear

74

thrusts. Like death, his blue tinted spear. Relentless in battle is King Urien. And he is King of the cultivated plain. He is the gleaming spirit of the land. What bard does not praise King Urien," said Hrothwena.

King Urien, the dark faced lord, with his family, and with Madron, rode off toward the land of sunset. It was at this time, to the castle on the ridge, warriors of Lord Caradoc were seen returning from a raid on valley farms. The warriors rode up to their castle, which was on a ridge high over Watling Street. It was a castle protected by the rough stone outcrops which covered the hillsides below it. The warriors had taken the narrow way up the east side of the hill, to the east gate.

At a castle near Ludlow, Arthur was at work. The Mayday celebration was but a pleasurable memory. But nature seemed still in celebration: blue sky, white clouds and flowers. And news had gone around; a ship had sailed in, docked at Geraint's harbour. And at another harbour to the south, a harbour belonging to King Meirchiaun, it was said, a ship had unloaded.

"They should help in the celebration of nature," said Kay to Arthur, who was mending a fence.

Days passed. A crowd gathered at the castle for Midsummer Eve celebration. The day was hot and bright and the celebrating was joyful, but Lord Kyner made certain that those there were respectful, and that rituals were correctly done.

"And Lord Geraint and I stood and watched the ship being unloaded," said a lord to Lord Kyner.

Night came; there was a bright fire on a sacred hill. Arthur watched as fiery wheels were rolled down hill.

Midsummer Day held, for those of the castle, household and land rituals. In the afternoon, Kay and Arthur sat on grey logs of a pen. Below them, pigs oinked.

"Lord Caw has a large family," said Arthur.

"Yes," said Kay. "His sons: Hueil, my age; then Mabsant; then Dirmyg; then, Anghawd; then his young daughter, Gwenabwy was there. And his older sons, Etmic and Coth, were there with their families. And Lord Clydno's daughter, Eurneid, was there, and a person to notice."

"But not for us to notice," said Arthur.

"No, she was not," said Kay.

75

"Hueil seems full of himself," said Arthur.

"I do not much like him," said Kay.

They were joined by Griflet and a couple of other boys whom Arthur didn't know. And who didn't introduce themselves. They sat in a row on the logs of the pig pen.

"You have a crowd at the castle," said one of the boys. "Lord Caw and his lady, and Lord Clydno with lady, and his son, Sir Cynon. And Sir Coth and his wife. And Sir Etmic. Among others."

The boys entertained themselves until the sun sank low and they were called to their dinner.

From Midsummer, the days were hot and filled with work, with learning about that and about the land; and with training in weapons and in life as a gentleman. Harvest time came with the work; then, the harvest festival. There were harvest rituals which needed to be done. Then rains came and Arthur and his friends needed to entertain themselves with story and song. Then the cold weather came, the leaves fell; then it was the time to prepare for the Yule. At Yule, many people made visits to the castle of Lord Kyner and were there treated to food and wassail.

Cold weather came, and snow, and the work for caring for animals in the difficult weather. Some needed to be butchered.

At Brecknock, Vortigern went in from the weather.

Then it was spring. Apple trees of Glastonbury filled with bloom. And fruit trees throughout the land were filled with bloom. Lord Kyner prepared his men for Pict raids, as they had troubled a number of near by areas.

From Brecknock castle, family and men of the castle took Vortigern, in a flower covered wagon, to a grave site in Gwythern valley, on the side of a small knoll. Then it was May, the Mayday celebrations; then, the long hot days to Midsummer. For his celebration, Midsummer Eve, Lord Kyner invited a harper for the Midsummer fire.

The hot days of summer passed, the harvest was taken in; then, it was time for another Yule. Harpers and a bard entertained in the decorated hall. There was much clowning and foolishness, but the rituals were properly done. Then there was Imbolc. Then the long, cold winter.

Early spring, some warriors rode up. They were greeted by Lord

Kyner. Lord Kyner and a dozen warriors of the castle got horses and Lord Kyner and his men rode off with the other horsemen.

Work went on at the castle. Arthur and Kay helped with the planting. Then Mayday came, smaller than last year, but a fun family celebration. And sleeping became more pleasurable now that it no longer needed the covering of animal skins. But there was cool air, as the stones were cold that went from the floor to high above where Arthur slept. Before being called to the day's first meal, Arthur lay on the worn skins and gazed at the huge wooden beams high overhead, beams on which generations of spiders had woven networks of webs. Then there was the smoky smell of frying pork.

"Hog's ass and grits," said Kay. "Time to rise."

Arthur got up and began the day.

Arthur and Kay worked on weapons skills.

"Father would be pleased at our progress," said Kay.

Midsummer came, young people gathered at the castle. Arthur and Kay insisted that rituals be correctly done. Burning wheels were rolled down the long finger of the hill on which the fire burned.

The hot summer came, and time, under the old oaks, enjoying life in their cool shade. Then, harvest came on; Harvest Festival. Then the frost. Lord Kyner and the castle warriors came home. Then, it was celebrating the Yule. Then, the cold evening with the snow outside.

There was the melting snow and a warming sun. It was time to clean tools, get ready for plowing.

In the fields, then in the woodlands, flowers were seen blooming; then, a great many flowers. Easter was honoured with flower filled rituals. In the evening, a harper sang songs in her honour. Then all were busy tending the fields. Then it was Mayday Eve. The sacred fire was lit. Many young people came to it for rituals, some of which involved unclothed activities with one, then another, of the girls. Then, during the day, there were flower filled rituals. Evening came. Then morning. Lord Kyner and warriors of the castle were present.

"My father said, 'Best defense is attack'," said Kay.

Arthur helped with work in the fields. With Kay and a workman, Arthur went to a smiths to get tools repaired. Kay told Arthur about the smithy of Weland Smith, and about Weland, and Wade, and about Watling Street.

Midsummer Eve, the Midsummer fire was built. Young people gathered with older members of their families; then, when older people retired for the evening, had unclothed rituals. Arthur was sought out by one then another, of the young girls, for physical contact. On Midsummer Day there were rituals, then games.

Through the summer and into the fall, Kay and Arthur kept up with their training with weapons. Then there was the job of getting the harvest in. Kay and Arthur were taking more responsibility in seeing that all went well. They helped plan the Harvest Festival. Then the young people came and the celebration was held.

There was frost, the leaves fell. Lord Kyner and the warriors of the castle returned. The weather turned colder. The castle was decorated for Yule. Holly and Ivy were hung on the bright shields. Brightly coloured cloths were hung, and harpers played for the Yule Eve and Yule feasts.

"Our boys deserve to have a good Yule," said Lord Kyner.

The castle was visited by a group of girls and boys and these, sang and acted out bawdy takes on old tales, and for these, the visitors were given drinks and cakes.

The Yule music drifted away across the snow. Yule decorations disappeared. Soon, there were many candles. Girls, for Bridget, put alehoof on their dresses. The herbs were decorative and gave off a pleasing, minty smell. The candles were also to honour Kalliste. Also, a harper came to the castle to help in the celebration of Candle Fest; or, Imbolc.

Said Lord Kyner to Kay and Arthur, "It is important to do things that have always been done."

The weather turned cold. Arthur and Kay went out in the woods to gather firewood.

"Kay, I enjoy this time of year: the snow and the dark woods. And the feeling of being in great space," said Arthur.

"I like it hot," said Kay.

The boys trudged back through the woods and on the path up the hill to the castle, waited for lunch to be served. Soon they were called in to sit at the long table. Above them at the table, the warriors joked and laughed. They were served steaming food.

The season turned. In spite of the frost, little flowers peaked out from the leafy floor of the woods. Time for plowing: Arthur now enjoyed plowing and he was good at it.

Up to the castle, Arthur said, "Those oxen are friends of mine. The ox is surely as noble as any other animal."

"Make sense when you speak," said Lord Kyner.

The men ate. Full platters of food were on the table. The food eaten, Arthur rushed down to the fields.

The sun warmed the land. Easter was honoured with flowers.

"We can not say about Easter, but we appreciate the flowers," said Arthur.

A couple of days passed. Warriors rode up, filled the lunch time table. Lunch finished, Lord Kyner and his warriors rode off with them.

"Battles never end," said a workman as he watched the warriors ride off.

Said Kay to Arthur, "We need to get better with weapons."

Arthur nodded. Still, he went down to the fields, paid attention to getting the crops in. A couple of hours went by, Kay went down to the fields, watched what was being done.

May Eve came and young people gathered to aid in the ritual, and Kay put himself in charge of the activities. There were many flowers collected by the girls, and the girls danced around the fire. Arthur chose a dancer and the two of them enjoyed physical activity. Other boys also got together with one or another of the dancing girls.

Mayday, the girls gathered May dew, put it on themselves and the boys of their choice. The day was spent in May games and in these, Arthur was an enthusiastic participant.

There was warm weather. Arthur and Kay worked with concentration on weapons practice.

"You know," said Kay, "if we do not watch ourselves, we will get left behind in the finer points of horsemanship by those in the bigger, richer castles."

"I'm not worried," said Arthur.

Arthur was getting to be quite strong. He and Kay got their horses and rode off around the countryside.

Warm weather brought a spell of rain.

Midsummer Eve brought thunder and rain, but the fire was lit, danced around. The girls put their clothes in a lean to when rains began again and danced unclothed.

Midsummer Day, there was rain, so the celebration was in the castle, that which could be inside.

The year turned. Arthur and Kay worked on skill with weapons. Harvest time came. Arthur and Kay made certain that the workmen kept up with it. Arthur and Kay's mother was pleased with the job the boys were doing with the farm work.

The harvest festival was much fun for Arthur and Kay and the young people who gathered there in mid September. Kay supervised the rites done for Mother Earth.

The evenings got dark early. Then Lord Kyner and the warriors were there. Dinner was dark and silent. The fire crackled. The wind sighed through the turret and was silent.

"Kay, tomorrow early, you and I are going to inspect the farms. Be ready," said Kyner.

"Yes sir."

Bedtime came early. In the cool darkness of early morning, Kay was up. He dressed and was gone. Arthur, after his breakfast, went for a walk in the dark woods. The wind sighed in the tops of the trees.

Then, the weather got cold. The castle was decorated for Yule.

Yule came. There was a bard, and there were musicians with strings and pipes. Young people came and there was joy in the castle.

The castle was quiet after Yule. Then there was the Candle Fest. Then, the cold winter. Cold air puffed through the castle. The boys continued with weapons practice. Lord Kyner watched, nodded approval. He made suggestions.

"Kay, you will be going with me this spring," said the lord. "Arthur, I am pleased with what I hear of your duty with the farm. I need that to continue."

The day passed. The warriors were at the table. They ate and left and Kay went with them. No farewell. He just left.

The weather warmed. Flowering trees came into bloom. Flowering trees circled the green hemisphere that was the mountain of Glastonbury. A man in a cape, a hood, a man with a staff, walked up the path on the green mountain. With his staff he tapped on the gate. The gate swung open. A good number of armed knights stood in the hall. None of them challenged the man in the cape. He passed on.

"Who was that?" said one of the knights.

"Who knows," said another. "But likely someone a wise man stays clear of."

"Yes, this is a strange hill," said the first knight.

King Avalach was standing in his garden among the blooming plants and trees. The garden was still. Except for the sound of trickling water. The king looked back and there was the hooded man.

"Father Merlin!" said the king.

Two girls rushed out into the garden.

"You know my daughters."

"I do. Rieingulid and Rieinmeth, The Lightning Princess."

Another girl rushed out.

"And Dwyanedd," said Merlin.

"There is a special reason for the visit?" asked the king.

"One must be where one is," Merlin smiled.

"That is reason enough," said the king.

A knight came out bowed to Merlin.

"You know my husband Sir Oswy?" said Rieinmeth.

"I do. How do you do Sir Oswy?" said Merlin.

"Quite nicely, Father Merlin, thank you. It is good to see you."

"Let us sit and reconstruct the land," said the king.

"Rieingulid, do see what the service is doing."

Merlin sat on a bench by the water. He said:

"It seemed it was time to locate myself in this place."

"Meaning," said King Avalach, "a thing might be happening here that you might want to be part of."

"Or might need to be part of," Merlin suggested.

Young women brought out tables. Set them up. Food was brought out, put on the tables. Merlin, the king, his daughters and Sir Oswy took seats around the table. They sampled the food in between long spells of gazing at the reflections of the flowers on the water.

"Soon, there will be hosts of foreign people in this area," said Merlin.

"I see," said King Avalach.

He sat and thought about it.

Merlin sat and thought. He thought of Arthur who was plowing.

Arthur then was telling workmen what duty to be doing. He was standing in a plowed field. Tall dead weeds bordered the field, and weeds, left for Old Nick, were left in the unplowed corners. The field was surrounded by little hillocks on the left, the hillocks sat in front of brush covered hills.

Arthur left the plow and walked over the field to see what some other workmen were doing.

Said Merlin, "The castle should be over that way. And beyond the castle, Lyonesse."

The day passed. Then King Avalach was working on the castle. Merlin and Sir Oswy stood looking at the sun shine on the bright blocks of stone on the rising structure.

"It seems Lord Geraint needs constantly to defend himself, his holdings, against the raids of envious lords," said Lord Oswy.

"A problem with being rich," said Merlin.

They stood looking at the new building.

"This building seems not to proclaim great muscle," said Lord Oswy.

"It will have another strength," said Merlin.

Then it was Mayday. At Glastonbury, very special rituals were held for Lady May. And very beautiful. Then, the palace was rising on the bright hill. Bright in the sunlight. Many Glastonbury knights, in their bright clothes, rode through the hilly green meadows where the palace was going up.

At evening, there was laughing and drinking in the mead hall at Glastonbury. It was speculated that King Avalach might be living in a larger house. Then the talk turned to King Lot and the battles he was having with the Vikings, and how Igerne must be worried for her daughter, his wife.

"And such a pretty young girl," said a knight. "And always full of laughter and smiles."

"If there is a quite area," said a knight, "it is in the middle of things. Lord Brychan has his hands full with his own family. That is two young daughters: Elyned; then, Gwladys: both soon to be needing husbands."

There was a mumble of conversation around the table. All the while, cups were filled with fine mead.

The day passed. The weather got hotter. There was talk around the table of battles in the north, squabbles between contentious lords.

Then it was Midsummer. On various high hills Midsummer fires could be seen. In Glastonbury, a feast was held in honour of the day. The day passed, then there were thunderstorms. The bright lightning lit up the green hills. Dark clouds sailed over.

Harvest time came, harvest festivals, then it was Yule. Cold frosts covered the land. Imbolc came; then the days began to warm. It was difficult for people to travel from place to place because of the gangs of lawless men.

Arthur was in charge of the plowing.

"When you get that field done, I want you to work on the weapons practice," said Lord Kyner.

Arthur finished the field. He walked up to the castle. He got weapons, and the practice tools he needed out of the cold castle store room with its dusky darkness and its uneven, rounded stone floor. He took them into the back courtyard where Kay was busy with practice. After Arthur and Kay had been a while at practice, Lord Kyner walked back to see how practice was going. The lord was a hard looking man. He looked, then walked away to look at other things.

"When Father shows up, workmen make certain they look busy," said Kay.

He and Arthur continued practice until they were called to their evening meal. They went in to their long table. The stern faced Lord Kyner sat at the head of the table. Arthur was passed steaming food.

Days passed, then it was Easter. Arthur went in to the first meal. There was the stern face of Lord Kyner at the table. There were flowers up and down the table. Even more than last year.

"Times might be hard," said Lord Kyner, "but that is no reason why we should not be proper. And show respect."

The warriors of the castle sat and ate. They got up and left for the armory.

"Good day for one to do his best," said the lord. "And Arthur: Be with the workmen today. So they can be certain we are doing our duty."

Arthur got up to go out.

"And, of course, we will be doing our what all tonight," said the

83

lord.

Arthur walked toward the fields. Along the sides of the path and in the hedge vegetation was sending out new growth and flowers were blooming.

On the road past Somerset, in which Glastonbury tower stood tall, on a green hill in Lyonesse, a palace was rising toward the sky. King Avalach walked into the castle, started looking. Everything needed to be right.

Days passed. At Lord Kyner's castle, twilight had settled in. Arthur went in, sat at the long table. Lord Kyner was at his place.

The lord said, "We decided to watch our own areas this summer. – Too many bands of rascals on the prowl. – The bother is, there is no one ruling this land. – We need someone with a crown on his head sitting behind those lions."

"That is the talk I hear from all over," said one of the warriors.

The men sat, ate in silence.

"And," said Lord Kyner, "we, I mean all of us, joined with Lord Brochwael, had a good victory to settle the center, as you well know. And as Lord Bassa is now dead and gone, thanks to Lord Brochwael, it gives some room in that center."

Above them, through the tower stonework, the wind huffed and sighed.

The men sat and drank ale. Arthur went up to his bed.

The morning birds were singing. The sun came up and brightly shown on corn green with new growth.

May Eve came and a crowd gathered at Lord Kyner's castle. There was joy as the animals were gathered for their part in the rituals, and Lord Kyner, on the hill where the fire was to be lit, stood and observed that rituals were correctly done. The May Eve fire was lit and rituals associated with the fire were done. Girls crowned Kay and Arthur with flowers and insisted on taking them around the fire. Arthur went to sleep before the fire burned low, went to sleep with the sound of the pipes in his ear.

Before the sun was up, the girls were among the flowers gathering the magical dew. Then the girls drew up games which they insisted that the boys and young men needed to join in playing.

The day passed. Lord Kyner insisted May second have an early start, then Kay and Arthur get busy with weapons practice. Then it was time for the Eve of Midsummer. Again, there was a crowd ready to celebrate and many were the young friends of Arthur and Kay.

With the sinking sun, the fire was lit. Leaves and sticks from plants and trees were gathered to give to the fire, which burned brightly on its sacred hill. The stars, with night's darkness, came out and filled the sky. Many miles away, on its sacred hill, the light from another fire could be seen.

Kay set wheels on fire and there was a boisterous chasing of the wheels down the hill. The girls tried to keep up with the young men, and many of the girls were quite fast, but none could keep up with Kay. Tired from running, Arthur and a couple of the girls got naked wrestling on a patch of cool moss which was under a tree.

Morning came and all needed to be alert for morning rituals. Lord Kyner was strict that the rituals be done honourably, and correctly. The day passed. And the next.

Merlin went from Glastonbury, took himself along a lane to where the new castle, a palace, was taking form. He was pleased. He went down a lane to the road to Caer Went, took himself along that road until the Golden Dragons of Caer Went were in front of him. Inside, he found Arch Druid Dubric, and he with druids Bithen and Colfryd.

"Merlin. Delighted to see you," said the druid.

"It is indeed my pleasure," said Merlin. "I have a job for you. I want it announced far and wide, Yule will be celebrated here and all are to be present. The lords of the land will decide who is to govern until the true king shall claim his throne. A great tourney shall be held, great honours going to the winner."

Merlin left the palace, took the road to Glastonbury.

The news went through out the lands. The feast and the tourney were much talked about, as there had not been a big tourney held for a long time. Lord Kyner and his warriors got the news. They sat at the long table.

"Kay," said Lord Kyner. "This is what your practice was all about. And from now until Yule you will work extra hard. You will be ready for the tourney. I will say nor more."

The lord left.

Said Arthur, "So you now take your place beside knights and other

85

warriors."

"A day I have long awaited."

"Would you like me to be your squire?"

"Of course you shall serve as my squire. You hardly needed to ask," said Kay.

Kay and Arthur left the table, walked down the hall, through the doorway past the fireplace where smoke curled from the burnt ends of logs, down flagstones in a gradual drop to a stone floor, walled in by ragged stone walls. From racks on the walls they got what was needed for their practice.

Days passed. Kay and Arthur, excused from help with the harvest, spent that time in their physical training. Two old warriors were assisting in the training. The boys, on the old floor, listened as a warrior made a suggestion.

"And this is as hard work as is harvesting," said a warrior.

"Harder," said Kay.

At Caer Went, on a high porch, stood Merlin. He was speaking with Druid Dubric.

"I have a feeling about this coming Yule," said Merlin. "Spirit forces coming together. This celebration must be hosted by Prince Anladd. You will need to inform him. He is that rare leader whom few could accuse of being ambitious."

"And the young can see what true nobility looks like. A thing so lacking in today's world," said the arch druid.

"Exactly," said Merlin. "And at the harvest festivals, some of the old golden light will glitter around his name. And the day will come, they will see him standing here, not a tired elder, but as fine a prince as you would want. And his lady will be beside him, a beautiful queen, and any accumulated failings shall be whisked away by the Yule air."

"I shall make certain each harvest festival within reach has a loud voice speak of our Yule Fest," said Dubric.

The two stood and watched the light and shadow on the green fields on which the bright hot sun beat down.

Days passed. One after another, fruits and grains were harvested from the lands. Prince Anladd was to host the Yule Festival.

Harvest festivals passed. Days got shorter and colder. The Yule drew near. Arthur, Kay and Lord Kyner and Lady were on their way through London, where many had taken rooms so as to be with in a short ride to Caer Went, where the Yule Festival was to be held. The warriors of Lord Kyner's castle had gone on to pitch tents in a field near Caer Went. Lord Kyner led the way down a narrow street which had buildings rising from close to each side of the street. The horses clomped over the uneven, worn stones, turned onto a road which went out into fields, went back and forth between rolling hills. The lord rode up to a small castle which was on a low mound.

"Here, make certain to take in all you will need," said the lord.

Arthur and Kay loaded themselves down, followed the lord and lady, as grooms took charge of the horses. In the castle, Arthur and Kay were shown to a small room, and were told, they could dine as soon as they were ready. They washed in a large crockery bowl, went to the hall below where food was served on a long table. Lady and Lord Kyner joined them and, with a number of other men and women, they had the evening meal.

That eaten, Lady and Lord Kyner, with others of the more senior men and women, retired to their rooms, which left young people, and they had congregated around an old hearth where fire off the logs threw off heat and light, which was welcome, as the hall had darkened. Three young men and four young women all were talking and their voices were getting louder. There was merry laughter. A stern faced man walked into the hall. There was silence. The corners of his mouth, under a graying, blondish mustache, dropped down in a slight frown. This was Lord Kyner. He spoke sternly.

"Kay, you and Arthur retire for the evening. You will be up early. Kay, see that the horses are ready at sun up."

Arthur and Kay got up. Kay went to see the horses. Arthur went up to his room, washed and took care of his toilet. There were skins on the grey boards. Arthur pulled a skin over himself and slept. – A bell was ringing. It was morning. Kay was already gone out. Arthur, up, washed and dressed, went down to the long hall. Lady and Lord Kyner and another couple were seated. "Lady, Lord Baldwin, this is my son, Arthur," said Lord Kyner. "Arthur, Lady and Lord Baldwin."

Kay entered the hall and was introduced. Arthur sat and ate. He listened to the low conversation between Lord Kyner and the young lord as his thoughts were on the good food and not the mumble of words.

Lord Kyner stood up. All the others with him, Lady and Lord Baldwin, and all went up to their quarters. Arthur changed into good clothes. Kay pulled over a toilet. While pissing, looked around and said:

"So Lord Baldwin believes a study with druids will help him manage his lands."

"Something to think about," said Arthur.

"You think so? Perhaps you're right."

Their good clothes on, Arthur and Kay went out to their horses. Lady and Lord Kyner waited, already mounted. All mounted, they rode leisurely toward Caer Went. A short ride, on the left, in a field, were pitched a good number of tents and pavilions. A short way on, they were riding beside the castle park and in the park, a number of people, and groups of people, were wandering around. Lord Kyner and his family rode between the two golden dragons, rode through the gate at the front of Caer Went.

The great doors to the front hall were in front of Lord Kyner and his family. Four grooms appeared to take their horses. Lord Kyner went forward, introduced himself and his family to the porter and was announced to Prince Anladd, who, with Queen Marcel, looked grand at the end of the hall. Lord Kyner and his family were shown to places at the center table. Lord Kyner greeted Lady and Lord Baldwin, who were seated down to his right. Good food was put before Lord Kyner and his family. Between lady and Lord Baldwin and Lord Kyner's family was a young knight and his lady.

"Lady, Sir Askil, these are my friends, Lady and Lord Kyner and their sons, Kay and Arthur. This is Lady and Sir Askil," said Lord Baldwin.

Greetings were exchanged. The company ate. Others came into the hall, filled up spaces at the tables.

"It seems it just rose out of the ground," said someone.

"Strange," said another.

"The Lords were to have met after the dinner," said a lord up the table from Lord Kyner, "to plan that too."

"And are we not?" said Lord Kyner.

"Certain it is, it would serve but little now," said the lord.

88

A lord, who introduced himself as Lord Neithon, spoke:

"It was this. People had been walking about, getting ready to celebrate; for some time, meandering cheerfully about; then, someone said, 'What is this?' and a crowd of us went to look. A cube, about four foot all around. One minute, it was not there: the next minute, it was. The stone so heavy that all of us together could not have lifted it. So how did it get there? We could talk our heads off, but until the druids study the problem, little would come of it."

While the company dined, Druid Dubric announced that a ten knight guard would be put on the stone and the guard, be of worthy knights who would not seem to be overly concerned with the message on the stone. The stone would be guarded until its riddle be solved. Nothing done to it until the day of the tournament, New Year's Day, when any man who felt worthy might, while observed, give the sword a try.

There was a murmur of voices. The crowd in the brightly decorated hall continued eating. A druid came down the hall, went to Lord Baldwin.

"Lord Baldwin," said the white robed druid. "I am Druid Nertat. You are asked to be part of the honour guard for the stone."

"I am honoured to serve," said the lord.

The druid went down the hall.

"That means, the druids believe I will not be personally involved in the message of the stone. It is said, the stone is to say who is to be king."

"I know many who could do worse," said Lord Kyner.

The men laughed.

"But I'll let that pass," said Lord Kyner.

A bard then entered the hall. He played the harp and he sang as he moved down the hall. The many guests stopped eating and listened to the notes of the harp as they rose and fell. The harp fell silent. Kay looked down around the room.

"I see a number of faces here which I recognize," said he.

Arthur looked. He did see Griflet. And Lorete. And Lord Caw, and he, with members of his family. The harp began again. The harper was singing about Uther Pendragon. In turn, people filled their mugs with wassail. The song came to an end. Loud voices gave cheers for the Yule. Then, voices called back and forth about the words on the stone.

Said Lord Kyner, "We have a good ride ahead. Lady, Lord Askil, it is good to know you. Lady, Lord Baldwin. Take care that rock does not get away from us."

"I'll give it my best. Have a good ride Lord Kyner, Lady. And best of Yules."

"By all means, good Yule to you. And Lady and Lord Askil," said Lord Kyner.

He led the way out of the hall, told the porter he was ready for horses. Lord Kyner and his family mounted, rode between the golden dragons. Rode out on the road.

"We will not be adding to the picture here tomorrow, or at any time until the New Year, at which time we will be present for the tournament. And good and rested so that we can look as we should," said the lord.

The lord and his family rode on to the small, low castle. Inside the gate, they dismounted and gave the horses to grooms. Arthur and Kay went up to their room, used the toilet and changed clothes. They went down to the fire in the center hall.

"What did you make of this stone thing? Kay asked.

"Not much. I was taken with the building itself, the fine designs in the stonework."

"All the same," said Kay.

Three young men, the ones at the fire the day before, came down to the fire.

"Hi. May we introduce ourselves. I am Ner, and this is Aidan; and this, Ufelwy."

"Hi, I am Kay."

"And I, Arthur."

Ale and food were brought in, put on the long table. The young men filled mugs. Arthur broke a piece from the loaf of bread, listened while the others talked of this and that.

"Yes," Ner said, "it would be well to look good in front of the many young girls; some, pretty enough."

"Yes," said Aidan, "This would be a bigger thing than I have ever seen: so many big people might well be there."

Arthur watched the fire. He drank ale while the talk mixed with the crackling of the fire. Then Lord Kyner was there.

"Let us close the evening," said Lord Kyner.

Arthur and Kay bid good night to the three young men, followed the lord out, up to their rooms.

Next morning, Arthur and Kay were awakened early. They washed, went to breakfast. Lady and Lord Kyner were at the table.

"Half an hour, we'll be on our horses," said the lord.

Arthur ate, went to his room, took care of his toilet, went to the front entrance. Three horses were there. Nearby stood a groom. One horse stomped, switched its tail. Arthur mounted up, followed Kay and Lord Kyner down the road.

"Keep us from getting stiff," said Kay.

Although the air was cool, the sun was warm. The thin layer that had fallen in the night had already melted in areas warmed by the sun, but lingered in shaded areas under trees. The horses clomped along the muddy road. The road led through patches of woodland, dipped in and out among hilly fields; then, took a turn back to the old castle.

"I'm ready to eat," said Kay.

A groom took their horses, as Arthur, Kay and the lord dismounted. Arthur went up to his room to wash for lunch. When Arthur went down to the center hall, a number of men and women were at the center table. He took a seat, with his family, next to Kay.

After eating, Arthur walked out the huge front entrance and out into the cold air. He walked to his right, away from the road, to where a finger of the forest crept up a gully that was between two hills, walked in among the trees, walked out and up the shrub covered hill to his left, walked back to the castle, washed, and soon it was, supper was announced. He joined his family in the center hall. Lord Kyner was speaking to a gentleman.

"And Sir Catlon, this is my son, Arthur," said the lord.

Behind Sir Catlon was the crackling fire. Arthur sat and ate. The room filled with many warriors and their families, and as many entered, the hum of conversation increased. The increase made audible many words about the sword and stone, words of many speculations. The increase of the noise of excitement might have reflected the expanding news of the astonishing appearance of the marvelous, enigmatic sword and stone. The stone which ten senior knights, in shifts, guarded. It would be guarded until the day of the tournament, at what time any man who felt himself qualified to be the king might step up and attempt to draw the sword.

Time passed. After breakfast, the day of the tournament, Kay and Arthur went up from the main hall to their quarters to ready themselves for the day. Kay was slow in dressing.

"I want everything to look exactly right," said Kay.

Lord Kyner entered their quarters, looked them over.

"Now, get together and get out front," said the lord.

Kay fiddled with this and that, admired his shield, dusted it off; then he and Arthur rushed down to where the frowning, impatient lord and his lady sat horsed and waiting.

"Time's wasting," said the lord.

Kay and Arthur mounted and followed the lord and lady out onto the road. The road dropped down to the bottom of the rise, turned left and away from the castle, which sat behind its scattered trees. To the right, a thin woods crept down the gradual grade of a low hill.

The woods became scattered groups of trees. The Lord and his family rode forward. Left, the flat wet fields glistened in the sunlight. Beyond the fields rose hills covered with the bare trees of a wood. The road rose up, turned right. Arthur could see a number, a good number, of riders along the road in front of him.

Beyond where Lord Kyner and his family rode, in the courtyard in front of Caer Went, a crowd had gathered around the strange stone which held the sword. Druid Dubric was near the stone to observe and determine the correctness of each attempt to draw the sword. First to try were strong knights, Balamorgineas, and Bedivere.

Said Druid Dubric, "Sir Bedivere, you are considered honourable and known to be strong. Do you believe yourself to be the one destined to rule the kingdom?"

"Sir, I do not."

"Then be the first to attempt to draw the sword."

Sir Bedivere stepped up, tried, but could not budge the sword. Sir Balamorgineas was quick to step up.

Said Druid Dubric, "Sir Balamorgineas, you are known to be a bruiser and skull buster, and of a good size as any might see. If strength is what is needed, that sword might be yours."

Sir Balamorgineas grabbed the sword but could not draw it. Mador of the Porte attempted to draw the sword. Kings and lords, one by one, stepped up to have a try at it. First, the powerful King Lot tugged at the sword but failed to draw it. He was followed by King Carados, and he, by King Urien, and after King Urien, King Ryence attempted to draw the sword. He was followed by King Fion, and he, by King Nentres. King Nentres was followed by Lord Clarence, and he, by King Ban. King Ban was followed by King Leodegrance of Cameliard. King Leodegrance was followed by Lord Caradoc. Then King Pelinore attempted to draw the sword, but the sword held fast. No others who were there stepped up: no others, at that time, presented themselves as being more qualified than those whom they had seen try to draw the sword and fail; as those who had tried had included powerful kings.

Said Druid Dubric, "It seems we must wait for another day, for one who is pure in heart, who is noble enough to meet the needs of the sword and stone. So let us attend to our tournament, as the spirit of the tournament was put forth as the way to hold us together."

A mass of persons hied to the field, down past the castle, which had been prepared for the festival. There was a blaring of horns. The crowd hurried along.

Lord Kyner and his family heard the horns. They passed the courtyard with its tramped on mud; followed, behind other riders, the tramped on track to the field below the castle. In front of them, over the stands, were bright flags and waving pennants. Lord Kyner's lady rode off to be a part of a group of ladies. Lord Kyner, Kay and Arthur rode forward.

"Oh my," said Kay.

"How's that?" said the lord.

"I've forgotten my sword."

The lord stopped.

"Thunder," he said. "That's not a thing you can do."

The lord sat there. He gave Kay a blistering look.

"Arthur, go to the castle and get Kay's sword," said the lord.

Arthur took the road back to the castle. The castle was closed up. It seemed, all were gone from it. Arthur remembered seeing a sword by the side of the road. He returned along the road. The sword was where he remembered seeing it. He stopped his horse, dismounted, went into the courtyard. The sword was through an anvil and into a stone. Arthur pulled it out. He went back to his horse, mounted up, rode down to the flat field, rode to where warriors were gathered and located Kay.

"Arthur, did you get my sword?"

"No, the castle was closed up. But I found a sword by the side of the road."

"Blast. That roadside sword. I'll bet it's rusted."

"One more word of complaint and back to the castle we go. If covered with rust, it's more than you deserved."

Arthur gave Kay the sword and Kay put it in his scabbard.

"Say, it really looks rather good," said Kay.

"It had better look good," said the lord. "Good to hear words of appreciation."

Kay and Arthur went with the lord to get lances for the lord and Kay. For a while the field seemed a whirlwind of contending warriors. Trumpets blared and names were called out. The names included Kay of Bonmaison. Bonmaison was the name of Lord Kyner's castle.

The stands were filled with women in bright clothes and with the many men who were not in the lists. There was a decorated section for King Anladd, Queen Marcel and their family.

Kay, it seemed, was doing well. Arthur saw that Kay was matched against a huge knight who was announced as Sir Balamorgineas. The contenders met. Kay unhorsed the larger knight, rode back to the other horsemen. Curious about what sword Arthur had found for him, Kay drew it to look it over. Sir Ulfin, nearby, looked and saw it.

"That looks strangely like the sword I have been guarding. May I get a look at it?" said Sir Ulfin.

"Why, this is the sword of the stone!" said Sir Ulfin.

"Then I am king," said Kay.

"That, you are not," said Lord Kyner who had ridden up.

"How came you by this sword?" Sir Ulfin asked.

"Honestly enough," Sir Kay answered peevishly.

"Kay. Apologize to Sir Ulfin. And you tell him all you know of the sword, as it is his duty to ask," said Lord Kyner.

"I apologize, Sir Ulfin, it is the one Arthur gave me."

"Arthur?" said Sir Ulfin, much surprised.

"There is some mystery. Arthur, step this way if you would, son," said Lord Kyner.

Arthur walked on over to where the three stood.

"Arthur, this is Sir Ulfin, who is honour guard of the marvelous stone. We must ask, how came you by this sword which you gave to Kay?"

"I saw it from the road. When I rode back to it, I saw it was stuck through an anvil and into the stone. I went to it, pulled on it to see if it was tightly stuck. It was not."

"Let us visit the stone," said Sir Ulfin. "There, the stone itself might aid in answering our inquiries."

Arthur returned to his horse, mounted, rode to where the others waited. Together, the four of them rode from the field, up to the courtyard, through the courtyard, to the stone from which the sword was now missing.

"In my duty as a guard, I will return the sword," said Sir Ulfin.

He said, "Now, Lord Kyner, would you test it to be certain it is well secured."

Lord Kyner walked to the stone, gave the sword a mighty pull. The sword held fast.

"Kay, see if you can draw the sword," said Sir Ulfin.

Kay walked up, struggled to get the sword from the stone. He had no success. He shook his head, returned to his place.

"Arthur, may we request that you draw the sword," said Sir Ulfin.

Arthur went to the sword, pulled it clear of the stone and anvil.

Lord Kyner went down on his knee.

"You are the king of this realm. You are my king."

"Father, I beg you to rise."

"You do not beg, you command me to rise. Command me to rise, I rise."

"Rise Father."

"I hold a truth which the time has come for me to share. I am but your foster father and the name of your true father I know not, but it is certain he is one more noble than I. Newly born, Merlin brought you to me, charged me with the care of a person whom he valued: yourself. You are king of the realm. You are my king."

"You are the only father I have ever known. Therefore, I am always your obedient son."

"No, that must not be. You must obey but yourself, only your own conscience. I ask but one favour of you. You will have the position of seneschal to fill. Make Kay your seneschal. He will give you good service."

"As long as we two shall live, he shall be my only seneschal."

"My king, I suggest you return the sword to the stone. Then a time should be set when a great mass of interested parties might observe you draw out the sword. If the sword should hold fast: know, that should not be a time for grief; for, as you are young, there will be another day. I, if you like, will get the advice of Druid Dubric," said Sir Ulfin. "And also Merlin," he said.

"If you would, that would be my wish," said Arthur.

Arthur gave the sword to Sir Ulfin. Sir Ulfin returned it to the stone.

Sir Ulfin, Lord Kyner, Kay and Arthur returned to the tournament. Kay continued to do well. Among a number of other young warriors, Kay, by King Anladd, was made a knight of Caer Went.

Darkness came, Lord Kyner and his lady, Kay and Arthur rode up to Caer Went. Horns announced them as they entered the castle. They entered the hall, sat at a table filled with food. While they were eating; in the hall, horns blew. A lord held his hand up for silence.

"I am Sir Lucan. I am here to announce that on Imbolc the sword will again be presented to those who wish to attempt to draw it."

There was a mutter of conversation. Kay, in his new state and title as Sir Kay, was silent and seemed thoughtful. Lord Kyner and his family, dined.

"Time to be on the road," said Lord Kyner.

The lord and his family left the hall. At the front entrance, in the torchlight, Lord Kyner had his horses brought to the front, where he waited. He and his family mounted, rode up the muddy road to their quarters.

"We will be on the road early," said Lord Kyner.

At Caer Went, Merlin sat with Druid Dubric and Ulfin.

"It was good fortune," said Merlin, "That no one saw it when Arthur first drew the sword, and that it was Ulfin who saw that it was out of its stone."

"Strange, that stone should have come," said Ulfin.

"Yes," said Merlin, "If you mean unusual. Like rocks hidden under ground, slowly building force unseen; then, after a long build up, the force shifts so that many must see. Or, in less time, air becoming hotter; so that, after a wait, it must rise to meet cold air, give birth to thunder. When forces build to a point, it is time for a rare event."

"One feels the forces," said the druid.

Said Merlin, "At Imbolc, have a good force here. Geraint, with Cador, should be alerted. I will get word to a number of those who will help."

Candles were extinguished. Caer Went became dark and quiet. The hooting of owls, now and again disturbed the silence.

The Castle Bonmaison sat quietly in the darkness of the winter morning. Candles, at first meal, flickered and smoked.

"Men," said Lord Kyner, "we have two new men with us. I reintroduced my son, Sir Kay. And Arthur, of whom I am most proud, joins those numbered as men."

Arthur finished his meal; then, following Lord Kyner's suggestion, he took himself to the armory, took swords in his hands and began an exercise. Kay went to the armory, walked to the swords, selected two for his workout.

"This makes me feel, back in the world I know," said King Arthur.

"Yeah," said Sir Kay. "Nothing more like a grimy, smelly exercise room to do that."

Arthur changed swords for axes. He worked on and on. He went to the shed, relieved himself, washed at a basin. He waited outside, under some old maples, for the call to the noon meal. The day passed. The night found King Arthur in his old familiar sleeping space.

Time seemed hardly to have passed when King Arthur, hearing roosters crowing, hearing animal noises, realized it was getting up time. Up he got, went out to the shed. The smell of burning cakes made him happy to be back home. He sat at the hall table, sampled cakes, hot cider.

"Today, I'll pay my respects to Lord Do," said King Arthur.

"I would have suggested it," said Lord Kyner.

"Would you tolerate company?" Sir Kay asked.

"I would."

Down in the old stone walls, with the horses, Arthur said, "Hard to find better horses than these of Fathers."

"We live in Horse Country," said Kay. "And good thing. Little better than to be on a horse."

He and King Arthur got their horses ready for the ride. Arthur went to the shed, relieved himself. He went to the kitchen. Kay was fixing meat and bread.

"Few places I like better than the kitchen," said Sir Kay.

King Arthur said, "You should love Lord Do's kitchen. In his great oven, one can put a whole ox."

"There are bigger kitchens than that," said Sir Kay. "I'm certain the Caer Went kitchen would be great to be in."

"However," said King Arthur, "I can not think the food from any kitchen would be better than that out of ours."

The two of them packed the food, went out to the horses. They set out down the road, which curved its way down the hill. They took the way over flat fields, onto wooded hills. They stopped, dismounted. It was high noon. They got out their food. Here and there on the fields below were small groups of buildings. Some had their walls protected by high banks of mud.

Finished eating, King Arthur and Sir Kay each pissed on a bush, then mounted up. Over wooded hills they rode, rode down to a flat area, crossed over a bridge, rode up a tree covered hill toward the mossy stone walls of a small castle. The road curved up to a square tower in which was a gate. To the left, the rocky land dropped off steeply to the Tene River. Old round towers were to the left and right of the square tower. Beyond the square tower was an open space sparsely covered with low plants, which the two could see from where they were admitted. An old round tower rose from the right rear of the open space, and beyond that, the stone wall of the great tower. Griflet rushed up to meet his visitors.

"Arthur, Kay, great to see you, I was just thinking of you."

"Good to see you. But first," said King Arthur, "I would like to step into that old round turret."

"Be my guest," said Griflet.

King Arthur walked into the gate house, up a winding stair to a passage which led to an old round turret where, built into the wall, there were holes into which one could relieve himself. King Arthur used one of the holes in the stone, returned along the passage and down the stair to where Sir Kay and Griflet stood waiting.

Kay excused himself; went, as King Arthur had done, into the gate house tower.

King Arthur nodded at the old round tower to the right front. "That is a spooky looking tower."

"It was old when the castle was built. It was a sacred space for Lud and has never been anything else. We can – ."

Kay returned, interrupted Griflet.

"I appreciate the use of it, but I must say, I prefer our more primitive whatsit."

"Ours is as old as the castle. That is centuries. Hard to get more primitive than that," said Griflet.

"Let us pay our respects to your father," said King Arthur.

Griflet led the way across the weedy patch of ground. The three of them entered a square tower building, climbed the stairs, went into a room where an elderly gentleman sat at a tall, thin window.

"King Arthur, Kay, good of you to come."

Lord Do stood up, greeted King Arthur and Kay.

"Please, will you not sit." said Lord Do. "There is much I would be pleased to hear."

King Arthur told Lord Do and Griflet of how he found the adventure at Caer Went. Kay added some of his experiences to the story. He told of how he found the tournament. The conversation went to the conduct of tournaments. While on this subject, there was a clang.

"We are being called to evening meal," said Lord Do. "So let us be prompt to be at it."

The four of them went to the dining hall. There, over their ale, they lingered until time to retire.

In the morning, after they had eaten, Lord Do made certain they had food for on the way back to Bonmaison. Griflet walked with them back to their horses.

Said he, "It is great, you were the one. Between us, I thought perhaps the sword was meant for me. My family, you know. But all the time, you were a Pendragon."

"Griflet, I will want you at Caer Went. Sooner or later, I am sure to be there. So be ready," said King Arthur.

King Arthur and Sir Kay made their way out the gate and down the muddy road. They rode down the hill and on toward their castle, Bonmaison.

The winter set in. The snow fell and cold weather came to the land. Two days before Imbolc, which was a day honouring the Bear and Sheep, Lord Kyner, Kay and King Arthur set out for Caer Went. The road took them to London and there, they dined and spent the night. The next morning, after their meal, they took themselves to Caer Went. As the three entered between the golden dragons, there was a blare of horns. A groom rushed out to take charge of their horses.

"This castle gives a proper welcome," said Lord Kyner.

He, King Arthur and Sir Kay were met at the entrance by Sir Lucan and two other Knights, and were shown to fine rooms.

Said Sir Lucan, "The trial of the sword will follow directly after our day's first meal. If I might advise, I would suggest to the king that he, by the many, be first seen tomorrow."

"That seems wise," said King Arthur.

"We will dine in these rooms. By your leave, Merlin will join us," said Sir Lucan, who was the butler of the castle.

"It will be our pleasure," said King Arthur.

Sir Lucan left. King Arthur, Sir Kay and Lord Kyner washed, changed clothes. Dinner was brought in. Lucan entered with Merlin. The group sat and ate together.

"As the son of Uther Pendragon, the crown is rightfully yours," said Merlin.

"And have I brothers and sisters?" Arthur asked.

Merlin said, "Your mother has four daughters, two by her late husband, Lord Gorlois. But you wished to know of your father. By him, you have two sisters; Anna and Affrela, and they, born to different mothers. Anna, the elder, has a son whom you should know. He is Prince Howel."

"And I will want to have loyal associates," said King Arthur.

"That is a thing to plan on," said Merlin.

King Arthur became involved in his own thoughts. The company ate. Merlin and Sir Lucan went out. Squires entered, cleared up after the lunch.

"I will walk around a bit," said King Arthur.

He went to a stair, climbed to a turret, looked out over the wide landscape, looked out at bare trees and snow. Looking away from London, and to left and right, the hills were covered with dark, bare trees. All was still. Except for the circling of a few dark birds. Arthur walked down the steps, walked through the dark passage ways of the castle, climbed a tower which had a toilet on the wall. He used that. He walked down, through a passage, up stairs to another tower. Below him was the road and beyond it, tree covered hills. He looked up the road, saw horsemen coming toward the castle and beyond them, more horsemen. Arthur walked down, found another passageway.

Arthur returned to his rooms. Supper was brought in and he, Lord Kyner and Kay sat at the table. While they ate, Sir Kay told of going to the great hall, of meeting knights there. "Sir Dyvyr I met; and, said he had met father. Sir Bedivere was there. And Sir Ulfin. And Lord Do and Griflet, but there, I avoided more than a polite how do you do, good to see you. Others? Sir Naram, Lord Baldwin, Lord Geraint, Sir Cador, Sir Brastias. Sir Lucan said it was not a really big lot."

"Weather is against it," said Lord Kyner.

"Imbolc. What can one expect?" said Sir Kay.

The three finished eating, retired to prepared bedding.

King Arthur woke to the blare of horns. He walked up the steps to the turret where a toilet was; walked back to his rooms and washed. He, Sir Kay and Lord Kyner walked to the great hall.

Lords, Knights and ladies were seated at the long tables. King Arthur, Sir Kay, Lord Kyner, sat and enjoyed the good food. They sat and sipped cider.

Horns in the courtyard gave a call. Those in the great hall filed out to the marvelous stone, stood attentive to what would come next. Druid Dubric walked to the stone.

"For any man who believes himself qualified, we invite you to attempt to draw the sword," said the druid.

Arthur waited. All seemed to be watching him. He walked up to the stone, pulled the sword from the stone, returned it.

"Now, where are the kings who should have witnessed," said a knight.

"My King, I would suggest more witnesses," said Druid Dubric."
On Easter's day, the weather should be better. We could meet here and
at that time there would be many to see you draw the sword."

"That seems wise," said King Arthur.

"Lord Kyner," said the druid, "Would you entertain an honour
guard of a dozen knights to be with the king until that time?"

"I would."

"I ask Sir Ulfin, Sir Cador, Lord Baldwin, Sir Britael, Sir Aliduc, Sir
Nasciens, Sir Brastias, Sir Jurdan, Sir Aron, Sir Cyon, Sir Morien and
Lord Gornement to serve as guard."

"That is an honour," said Lord Kyner.

"And I am above you," said Lord Caradoc.

"And I, close by," said Lord Do.

"Thankyou for the support," said King Arthur.

"For those who wish my company, I intend to depart for London
shortly past noon," said Lord Kyner.

Lord Kyner, Sir Kay and King Arthur went up to their quarters,
dressed for the road, went down to the noon meal. Next to King Arthur
sat a handsome knight.

"Good day, King Arthur. I am Sir Elis and I am certainly at your
service," said the knight."

"Good to see you, Sir Elis. I will be wanting knights for my castle
here, and I would be pleased if you would be one of them."

"I would be much honoured."

Arthur ate, got from the table with Lord Kyner and Sir Kay. With
them, he bid farewell to Druid Dubric, thanked Sir Lucan for his
service. Outside, the horses were ready, and waiting also were twelve
knights. Together, they took the road to London.

Lord Kyner led the party to a good sized inn. He, Sir Kay and King
Arthur were, by the innkeeper, shown to their rooms. They washed,
took care of their toilet, then went to the dining room. There, they
joined the men of the honour guard. Together they drank ale, ate
supper, sat and talked. Arthur sat and listened to what the men had
to say, as much talk was about the condition of the land. But as often,
many conversations were going on at the same time, much was lost in
the rumble of noise. Early in the evening Arthur retired to his room.

Morning came. King Arthur got from his bed in candle light, got himself ready for breakfast. He took himself to the dining room, hurried through breakfast; then, the horses were ready. The company was off to Bonmaison Castle. Sir Cynon and Lord Clydno caught up to them as they were nearing Banbury.

"We now call you King Arthur and offer our service," said Lord Clydno. "Which would never have been in question."

"Thankyou. I was certain of it."

King Arthur and his companions took a way which went more to the right and so, parted from Lord Clydno and Sir Cynon. King Arthur rode toward low, wooded hills.

King Arthur dismounted, gave his horse to a lad who worked with the animals, went to the washroom, which got crowded with the host of riders. All insisted he be the first to wash. He washed, went to the candle lit hall where food was being brought in, set on the table. Men entered and the table filled with diners.

"Be good to get in my own bed," King Arthur said to Sir Kay.

Morning came. Darkness slowly gave way to light. This found King Arthur up, washed and ready for what would be brought from the kitchen. He sat and ate as others were joining him at the table. Arthur ate, went to the armory, began working with swords. Kay was also spending time with weapons practice.

"No one has spoken of celebrating your drawing the sword," said Sir Kay.

Said King Arthur, "From what I gather, these knights have a duty here. And that is not to party. There are a number who did not draw a sword. These knights are to watch out for some of those."

Days went by until mid March. Mid March was the time for honouring horses. The day, Equirria, was to be celebrated at Ludlow Castle. There, not only horses, but Sir Kay and King Arthur would be given special recognition. With King Arthur and Sir Kay, Lord Baldwin, Sir Cador, Sir Cyon and Lord Gornemant would be attending.

March thirteenth: King Arthur, soon after breakfast, and with his company of knights, set out for Ludlow. The company rode down and through fields, which were showing clumps of early green; then, up to the wooded hills, and here they stopped for a bite to eat. Then, on the road, they made their way to and up the hill on which stood Ludlow.

At the gate, there was a blare of horns and Griflet and his friends welcomed the company and led them to the inner courtyard where Lord Do was there to greet them, to escort them to the table on which was a fine feast of food. And while the meal was partaken of, two harpers, each in turn, supplied music.

Arthur ate. He went to the courtyard where Griflet stood with three other young men.

"Hi, King Arthur," said Griflet.

The other young men said, "Hi."

King Arthur stood and listened to the conversation.

"Griflet," said King Arthur, "show me the place where you all sleep, and we will have my bedding there."

Griflet excused himself, walked with King Arthur to a stone stair. King Arthur followed Griflet up the stair, up to a stone floor where bedding was spread out.

"Here is a place near me. I will go get bedding for here."

"That will be fine."

Griflet went off. Soon he was back. King Arthur spread out bedding to his liking. He was soon asleep.

Then ist was morning. King Arthur took himself to a wall where a toilet was. He washed, went back to his bedding and dressed, went to the hall where many were eating. He took a place at the table, enjoyed a quantity of food.

Lord Do entered, went to King Arthur.

"Good morning, King Arthur. After you have eaten, at your pleasure, we will go to the lower fields."

"Very good, sir," said the king.

He ate, walked to where the lords waited: With Lord Do, he recognized Lord Gornemant, Lord Baldwin, Lord Clydno, Lord Caradoc, and Sir Kay with them. And there were a number of other lords, and among these, Lord Caw. He went with them to the castle gate, out and down the mud road to the lower fields. There were decorated stands set up and many flags and pennants which the winds were disturbing. He was welcomed by a blare of horns. He and the lords took seats. And his, in the center, next to that of, on his right, Lord Do.

Horses: a horse was brought to the field in front of the stands. It was brushed and fine looking. The groom who was with it shouted out the name of the horse and the estate to which it belonged. Brought forth at a walk, it then had to trot: then, to run. It then jumped hurdles. Brought out by a groom, a second brushed horse was brought forth; its name called out. Horse after horse was brought forth. A horse of Ludlow came onto the field. Last: a horse of Bonmaison. The groom shouted:

"The horse of Arthur, our King."

There was a great cheer, then a general movement toward Ludlow Castle. King Arthur, beside Sir Kay, walked up the path.

King Arthur said, "It seemed as if the cheers were for some ghostly spirit king of all things, not one of us."

"I know what you mean," said Sir Kay.

In the great hall of the castle, tables were set for the feast and, with joy and hilarity, the company sat and dined.

"You know many more of these people than I," said King Arthur to Sir Kay. "If there any you think I should know, give me knowledge of it."

"Likely, it would be best not to meet people at this time. It seemed, father had you off some place when there was a great number of people you might have met," said Sir Kay.

Sir Kay went off to visit with some of his friends. Arthur left the table, walked here and there, an observer, not joining in on the conversations he encountered. At sundown, food was brought out to the tables. Arthur sat, sampled food, listened to conversation, ate more of the food, sat and listened to conversation, took more scraps of meat to have as bits to go with his ale. He got up, made his way up old worn stairs, around to a turret where there was an ancient toilet, a hole in the stone. He used that, walked down and to a hall. He stopped at a narrow window, looked out at the dark, star filled sky. He took his way down the worn stone stair, around to the center hall. The center tables had been cleared away. A harper was playing and many ladies and gentlemen were standing in the cleared space listening to the harper and conversing with each other. And among them, there were a good many young people, many whom had not before come to his notice. There were a number of good looking young women. Arthur went on the cleared floor. He looked over the group of women, walked over to one who was attractive, invited her to dance. They danced. The harper switched to another tune. King Arthur thanked the young woman, selected a woman who was near the entrance to the hall. He asked for the dance. With the young woman, Arthur began to move further in.

Hueil had been standing nearby against the back wall. He walked up.

"Hey, this was my dance. Why did you not say no?"

"You do not own this woman," King Arthur said.

"You keep your mouth out of my business," said Hueil.

"You get back where you were. And keep a mannerly mouth," said King Arthur.

"You come with me," said Hueil.

He grabbed the woman's arm.

King Arthur struck him. They began fighting. Hueil pulled a knife from under his clothes, struck at the king, had the strike deflected, but managed to stab King Arthur in the thigh. King Arthur threw him back against the wall near the entrance. Hueil left the hall.

King Arthur grabbed a bright cloth decoration, walked up a dark stone stairway, went to a turret where a washbowl sat on a stone. King Arthur, with the cloth, washed the wound, then bound it up. He returned to the hall, stood near the stairs and listened to the harper. He saw no more of Hueil that night.

The harper paused for time to have a drink of ale. King Arthur went to the harper, said:

"I enjoy your music. How are you called?"

"I am Eliot, and at your service, sire."

King Arthur raised his horn, "Lords and Ladies."

There was silence.

"Here we shall drink to our harper, thank him for the fine music.

There were cheers. The people drank.

The harper returned to his harp, sangd of Uther, the magical king who gave magical protection over wide areas of land. He sangd of Uther and his rainbow belt which gave protection from men and demons, as it held the spirit of Uther. "His belt had been a rainbow enveloping the foe. Uther, the defeater of Diluvian Giants, the inspirer of courage: Uther, the plougher of fields, the Protector of Darkness. Uther, the Demon of Bards, was a mighty enchanter: His was the great Round

Table at which sat a mighty Spirit Host. 'King Uther, in those days of old with milk of goat was fed, and, like his sire before him, wore a helm of burnished bronze, and for the crest, it had a leek, with dreadful nod, the head.'": ."

The song switched to, "Arthur, the Bear King who came with corn and honey, and other good things to bring."

The song went on, but King Arthur's mind wandered. In his own thoughts, he slipped up the stairs to the turret with the toilet which he had before visited. He went down to the narrow corridor of old irregular stones, which led to the area where his bedding was. He changed out of his festive clothes, went to bed.

Next morning early, King Arthur was up. He went through the corridor, up the steps of the turret, made his toilet, washed, returned to where his bedding was and dressed for the ride home. Down he went to the center hall where many were seated at the food covered table. He entered the hall, all stood to give him welcome. The king took his seat.

"Please be seated," said the king.

King Arthur enjoyed his breakfast. He got up to leave the table and all present stood. He and Sir Kay walked to where Lord Do stood.

"Lord Do, thankyou for the fine and worthy festival. I do have one thing you should know of. I had a quarrel with Hueil, son of Lord Caw. I intend to solve that problem and that, with as little disruption as I can manage. Again, thankyou for the hospitality and the most enjoyable festival."

"King Arthur, it is shocking to hear that one of my guests misbehaved, and I beg your pardon for that."

"It was not in any way a fault of yours, nor does it reflect on your hospitality. I bid you good day," said King Arthur.

Horses were at the gate and the lords and knights who had come with Arthur and Sir Kay were mounted and ready to ride. King Arthur and Sir Kay mounted up, and the body of horsemen were on their way toward Bonmaison. Midway, the horsemen dismounted, took a lunch break. Late in the day, they dismounted. Sir Kay and King Arthur were back home.

King Arthur's leg had become stiff and sore. He walked stiffly in to the hall where, on the table, a welcome supper was set. With some effort, King Arthur sat; then, took his time eating. While the fire sparked and burned, he sipped his ale. He made his way to his own comfortable bed. Rain came up in the night.

Next day came with a dark, rainy morning. King Arthur took himself, through a drizzle, to the shack and there, he made his toilet, washed. He walked stiffly to the hall, which was filled with the smells of cooking.

After his breakfast, King Arthur took himself to the armory, tried to get the stiffness out of his leg. He kept at his exercises through the morning. Time to take a lunch break, he went to shed, used the toilet, washed, walked up to the center hall, sat across from Lord Kyner.

"Father, as many good things to be said about the celebration of Equirria, one thing to be said which is other. I got in a fight with Hueil. He pulled a knife and stabbed me in the leg."

"As all there know you are king, his act was treason. First, we must send for a healer."

King Arthur finished lunch, returned to the armory.

Two days passed. The third day, before evening meal, a tall woman rode up, introduced herself as Indeg. She unloaded two packs from the horses. She was tall and thin and dressed, as a warrior, in a helm and with a sword.

"You are the healer?" asked Lord Kyner.

"I am."

"I hardly thought you would be here so soon."

"When my father, Lord Garwy, got word of Lord Do's need he sent me right along. I wasted no time, grabbed my things and jumped on a horse, set out."

"Yes, it would not have been possible for you to have been the one I sent for. So: Garwy the Tall. If he sent you, I am certain you are gifted. So: Come join us at the table. Then certainly the king will want his leg healed. That over there is the wash room and I hope it meets your needs."

"It will be a splendid fit."

She turned her horse over to a groom, went to the shed.

Food was put on the table. Men and women went in. King Arthur came up to the door.

"I want to put a visitor in a place next to you, if I may," said Lord

Kyner.

"It would be a pleasure I am sure."

Arthur joined the group entering the hall, kept the place next to him open. Lord Kyner entered the hall with Indeg, had her take the seat next to the king.

"You looked fine on that horse. Your horse handles well," said King Arthur.

"It is a favorite of mine," said Indeg.

The company ate. King Arthur and Indeg finished eating.

"May we now go to a place where you are comfortable: And where I may look, from your limp, at what must be your leg?"

They went to where King Arthur had his bed. Indeg helped him out of his pants. Indeg looked, touched the wound.

"You stay put, I'll need to ask the cook for hot water."

Indeg got up went out. She was back with an iron kettle full of hot water. She washed the leg with water and an ointment, rubbed another ointment into the wound. She closed her eyes.

"May I help you out of these clothes?" asked the king.

"Yes, you may," said Indeg.

The two had a night of copulation. Morning came.

"I have never slept so well," said Indeg. "Stay here."

She took the kettle to the kitchen. She was back with hot water in the kettle. Again she treated the king's leg, washed all of his lower body. They dressed, went to the shed, washed, they took themselves to the center hall, sat and ate.

"Lord Kyner, I am confident I can cure the king's leg," said the healer.

Arthur and Indeg finished eating and left the hall.

"What now?" said Indeg.

"I usually have weapons work," said the king.

"That sounds good, if I may?"

The two went to the armory.

"We can make suggestions to each other," said Indeg.

The two exercised with the weapons. The sun rose to its mid day position. Indeg and the king went to the shed and washed. There was a clang outside the kitchen.

"Go hold my place," said Indeg. "I need to go to my supplies."

109

King Arthur went into the center hall, took his seat. A bit later, Indeg came in, asked for a cup of water, boiling hot. When it was brought to her, she mixed in ingredients from her pouch, stirred it well, waited, took a sip.

"Drink this," she said.

King Arthur drank it.

"That becomes one of our things to do." said Indeg.

King Arthur and Indeg ate. They left the hall.

"Likely a walk would be a good thing," said Indeg.

They took a path past an animal shelter and down the hill. They walked toward a wooded slope.

"I enjoy the woodlands. As now, plants are beginning to take life," said King Arthur.

The two walked slowly up the grade, into the sparse woods.

"We will take our time," said Indeg.

They walked away through the woods, took their time with their walk. They got back to the castle as men were going into the hall for dinner. Arthur and Indeg followed them into the hall, took their seats.

King Arthur and Indeg finished with dinner, went to the shed and washed. Other men were in and out. Indeg and King Arthur got hot water from the kitchen, took it to Arthur's bedding and there, Arthur undressed. Indeg washed and treated his wound. She then slipped off her clothes, lay close to the king. The two moved into copulation. After a bit, together, they went to the shed and washed. Then it was morning.

"What a wonderful night," said Indeg.

"Yes." said Arthur. "Yes, it was beautiful."

The two got up, went to the shed, washed. They went toward the center hall, as they smelled pork and cakes cooking. They went to the table and sat. Breakfast was brought out.

King Arthur and Indeg stopped off at the shed. From there, they went to the armory. They took pleasure in working with their muscles. Time came to eat.

King Arthur and Indeg walked to the center hall.

"I should visit my horse," said Indeg.

Arthur said, "It is a grand looking horse. Be sure, it is being well treated."

They went into the hall. Indeg called for a cup of hot water, mixed Arthur his drink, waited until it cooled.

Having finished their food, Indeg and King Arthur walked to the enclosure where Indeg's horse was. Indeg fed it some of the grain. From there, they walked over rolling farm fields.

"These will soon be covered with grain," said the king.

The two chatted happily as they walked over the fields, then back. Coming up the road were three bright figures: two men and a woman. They rode up: three finely dressed riders on fine horses. The woman rode up to them. The three dismounted.

"You must be Arthur," said the woman in her clear, bright voice.

"I am."

"I am your Aunt Rieinmeth. And let me introduce Sir Oswy and Sir Illtyd. My nephew, King Arthur. And may I ask, whom are you with?"

"Aunt Rieinmeth, this is Indeg. Sir Oswy, Sir Illtyd, Indeg."

"You are Lady Lightning?" said Indeg.

"So I'm told," said Rieinmeth. "I am flattered you know of me. Arthur, first, I am concerned about your injury."

"With much appreciation to Indeg. It is healing well."

"Wait here. We will pay our respects to Lord Kyner. Then the three of us will have a hard look at the injury."

Grooms had come up. They led away the three horses.

Lady Rieinmeth and the two knights walked toward the castle.

"She is very beautiful," said Indeg.

"She is," said the king.

"And fresh looking. As if she had just now fallen from the sky," said Indeg.

"That is a good picture," said Arthur.

Lady Rieinmeth was back out.

"Indeg, take us to where you do your magic," she said.

The three went to where Arthur's bedding was. Indeg helped him out of his clothes. Arthur lay down so that his aunt could inspect his injury. She felt it, felt all over his thigh.

"It was quite deep," she said. "But your leg is healing nicely. Indeg, tell me what all you are doing."

111

Indeg gave an exact account of what she had done.

"That seems a good system. I might suggest a drink which I brought. It is stronger than the one you are using. Also, I have one for you. A spoonful a cup. Start with it next October. And what I leave for Arthur, same amount for a cup as you use with yours. And Indeg, you are always welcome at Glastonbury. Tell them there you have come to see your Aunt Rieinmeth."

"Thankyou. What a marvelous aunt to have. Arthur, I believe we learned something."

"Now let us go see what they'll feed us," said Rieinmeth.

Arthur dressed and the three went to the center hall.

While King Arthur dined, he listened to lively conversations. They were still talking when Indeg pulled him up, led him through a hall, up the stairs to the room where they slept. Indeg went back to the kitchen to get hot water. Back with Arthur, she treated the injury.

While rubbing in ointment, she said:

"I might give three things which I learned: one, the thing which I did not know about which I should know about which I should take in October. Two: I do not belong in a palace. Three: I'm to have your child."

"Why do you not belong in a palace?" Arthur asked.

"I belong with the woods and wilds."

She undressed, lay beside the king.

The two got up, went down the steps, out to the shed. Back in bed, Indeg and the king again copulated. Then they slept. Then it was morning. The king and Indeg got up, walked down, went to the shed, washed.

The king and Indeg went in, to the table. Rieinmeth and Sir Illtyd and Sir Oswy were at the table, as were all the other lords and knights. There was much lively conversation. Indeg was beside Arthur and was happy.

Breakfast over, King Arthur and Indeg went outside. Three horses stood waiting. Sir Illtyd and Lord Oswy bid farewell to Lord Kyner, to each of the other lords and knights, to Arthur and Indeg. Rieinmeth gave Arthur and Indeg each a hug. Rieinmeth and the two knights mounted and were down the road. Indeg took Arthur's hand and together they watched the riders go into the distance.

"Back to work," said Indeg.

"Yes, always," said the king.

They headed for the armory.

Days went by. And nights. Arthur, his hand around Indeg's waist, walked up the grey steps, onto the old grey boards of the sleeping quarter.

"I feel like I'm home where I will be forever," said Indeg.

Arthur looked at the slender, handsome girl at his side. He would be going away.

"Part of me will always be here – with you," he said.

"You are my first, first real –," Indeg said.

"And Time itself can't take that away, – from you and me," The two slipped out of their clothes. "and now we have tonight which will give us joy," said the king.

The two of them lay together in the warm blankets, put out the candle.

April came in. A week went by. The lords and knights of the guard got their packs ready for the road. Indeg got her things ready for her trip home. She and Arthur went in to the table.

"Now is Arthur patched up as good as new?" asked Kay.

"Almost," said Indeg.

"If I were promised such a good healer, I would go out, get my leg stabbed," said Sir Kay.

"I am certain, I would do my best," said Indeg.

The dinner finished, Indeg took Arthur to the dark stairs, made their way to Arthur's bed. Indeg tested, cleaned and worked with the injury.

"After rides on your horse, use this ointment," she said; then, "Now let us make this night a bright light to remember always."

"Do not forget to keep contact with my aunt – and with me," said the king.

Morning came. King Arthur and Indeg got up, went to the shed and washed. They followed the others into the hall. Indeg ate, then sat deep in thought. The diners left the table. Indeg and Arthur followed them out. There was Indeg's horse, her pack on it. Indeg gave Arthur a warm embrace, jumped on her horse and was gone.

Sir Kay went up, stood by the king.

"She had nearly ten years on you," he said.

"We knew that," said the king.

King Arthur went to the armory, worked with weapons, then it was time for lunch. There was a clanging of the bell. The king went to the shed, used the toilet, washed, walked up to center hall, took his place at the table. Lord Gornemant was across from him, and next to Lord Gornemant, Lord Baldwin. And next to Sir Kay, Sir Cyon, then Sir Cador. The seat between the king and Sir Kay sat empty.

"Today, the armory – seemed a lonely place," said the king.

"She was indeed a lovely companion," said Lord Gornemant.

"Nothing is forever," said Lord Kyner.

King Arthur ate his dinner. He sat and listened to the conversation of the men as they drank their ale.

King Arthur left the table, walked down to where the horses stood in their enclosure. A couple of horses stuck their heads over the boards, waited to be petted.

The hours slipped by. It was supper time. King Arthur went to the shed, washed, walked up to the hall, went in, took his seat. There were lively conversations around the table.

"Time we were going to Caer Went," said Lord Kyner.

"It is," said King Arthur. "We'll have horses packed and ready to leave first thing tomorrow."

"I will see to that," said Sir Kay.

"That sounds good to me," said Lord Kyner.

King Arthur ate what was on his plate, left the table, went out, walked over the dark fields, observed how bright the many stars were. He went in, up to his bed, got his belongings packed, ready for travel. He clomped down the board stairs, out to the shed, got ready for bed.

King Arthur walked up the old familiar wooden stairs, got in bed, moved over close to the lumpy stones in the old wall. Next he knew, birds were singing: one of them, a dove.

King Arthur got up, took his pack down the wide steps, fixed it to his horse. He went to the shed, made his toilet, washed. He joined with the other men who were going into the hall. Breakfast was brought out. Quickly, he ate. With a number of others, Sir Cyon and Lord Baldwin, he went to the shed, made his toilet. Then he was out by his horse. Lord and Lady Gornemant, Lord Baldwin and his Lady, Sir

Cyon and Sir Cador. His stepmother came out, mounted.

"Are we all ready?" said Lord Kyner. "Then we are off."

The ride was leisurely: the break for lunch, pleasurable. The men and women of the castle were handy at setting it up. Then, the tent for night. And there were sufficient blankets. Then breakfast: the castle's people got that together nicely. And back on the road, the ford was easily crossed. So it seemed like no time, the group from Bonmaison was riding up to the Dragon Gate of Caer Went. There was a blare of horns. Sir Lucan and a number of knights and men came out of the castle and up to King Arthur. They bowed, took charge of his horse and belongings. Said Sir Lucan:

"Sire, if you will, Merlin would speak with you."

"Yes, of course."

Lucan led the way in at the white arched doorway, which was encircled by many carvings into its stone. Lucan and King Arthur walked up curving, wide marble stairway, passed curving marble arched ways, into a handsome space: a large room, handsomely furnished.

Merlin, who had been looking out of the window, turned to greet the king.

"Good to see you, King Arthur. I was your father's chief advisor and I hope you will find me of service."

"Thankyou Merlin. Your advice will be most welcome."

"I will leave you two to talk. And I am, of course, delighted to be of service," said Sir Lucan.

Said the king, "Thank you, Sir Lucan."

"This was your father's area," said Merlin. "He enjoyed this palace; though, for major festivals, he found larger castles more convenient. Have you given much thought to what in the near future your course of action is to be?"

"Some. A lady friend of mine inspired me to give it some thought. And before that, I had considered some of the things with which I would be faced."

"Very good. I will leave you to prepare for dinner. When you wish, ring that bell and attendants will be at your service."

Merlin made his exit. Arthur looked through a narrow window. The sun was close to setting. King Arthur cleaned up, saw a wardrobe where there were many fine clothes which were ready for him to wear.

He dressed in what he thought would be fitting. He rang the bell. In a short time, Lucan and six other gentlemen were at his service. Sir Lucan introduced Sir Glyddiew, Lord Dweyl, Lord Brochwael, Lord Brychan, Prince Kyngen and Lord Goreu.

"So let us present you to the amazed multitude," said Lord Brychan.

Together the five gentlemen walked with King Arthur down the curving marble stairs. They walked across the floor, into the great hall. The table shown with crystal and silver.

"Ladies and gentlemen, Arthur the King," said Sir Lucan.

There was a great roar, "Hail the King."

King Arthur walked in and was seated at the head of the table. The food brought out was a feast worthy of a king. King Arthur took pleasure in it.

"You have many members of your family here," said Lord Brychan, who was on his right.

"And Lord Brychan has done his part to make it large," said Lord Brochwael.

King Arthur looked at the fine looking company which sat at the table.

"Surely one could not but be pleased by looking at such a fine company," said the king.

He took his time eating, took pleasure in sitting with his ale. He enjoyed seeing the many people there drinking their ale, but most of all, chatting and enjoying being part of the company. It got late.

"I am retiring for the evening," he said to Lord Brychan.

Lord Brychan stood, "People, we are glad King Arthur has come. Hail to the King."

The king rose, he and Sir Lucan walked up the marble stairs, around on the marble floor to the king's area. He and Sir Lucan entered that area.

"Do you think of anything you might request for this evening, your majesty?"

"I would like to see Sir Kay and Griflet son of Lord Do, if I might. Sir Kay is my seneschal, so here to forward, any help you can give him will be most welcome."

"I will have them here shortly. And that cord will ring a bell and so, fetch a body to tend to your request."

Sir Lucan departed. Sir Kay and Griflet were soon in the room.

"Ah, here you are," said King Arthur. "The day after tomorrow I expect to draw the sword; so, will not be returning any time soon to Bonmaison. Or I should say, we will not, as I want both of you to get to know the palace of ours. Sir Lucan will give you help. Anything you need from Bonmaison or Ludlow, we can send for it. So, how are your days going?"

"Right well," said Griflet. "I thought I might be staying, so, brought things I thought I might need. One thing might interest you. Father sent to Lord Caw to have Hueil return to Ludlow for explanations. Lord Caw said Hueil never returned home and he had not heard from him."

"You will need to practice 'Your Majesty'," said Sir Kay.

"I suppose I will," said Griflet.

King Arthur smiled.

Sir Kay said that he liked the place and would make it his duty to learn everything about it.

The three chatted about this and that.

"One thing I miss," said Sir Kay. "In the great hall, there was no smoky smell of burnt bacon, no fragrance of egg and onion."

"Indeed, I caught the fragrance. But not the smoke," said King Arthur.

"I like smoke," said Sir Kay.

"I am certain you'd find plenty of that in the kitchen," said the king.

"If I may, I will track down Sir Lucan, take Griflet, and have him show us what room the palace has to offer us,' said Sir Kay.

King Arthur pulled the cord. Sir Lucan came right in.

"Your Majesty?"

"Sir Lucan, you have met Sir Kay, the seneschal, and the warrior, Griflet. As part of the castle staff, they should be shown where they are to locate."

"Of course. Gentlemen, if you are ready, this way."

The three went out. King Arthur looked to where his bedding was. And beyond that, the washing and toilet area. It was all very grand: a different world. The king prepared himself for bed.

King Arthur was up early. It was a warm spring day. He made his toilet, washed, selected for wear what he thought, neat and comfortable. Somewhere a bell was rung. Into the long hall he went. Many others, Lord Kyner and his lady among them, all stood around the table. The king took his seat.

"Please be seated," he said.

Others came and took places. Sir Kay entered with three other knights, one of whom was Cador. They took seats.

"I enjoy a good breakfast," said Lord Gornemant, who was seated on the king's right.

"And this, I find quite good," said the king. "I wonder if it is smoky enough for my seneschal?"

"Ah, your seneschal likes smoke," said the lord.

"He enjoys country living," said the king.

"My guess is, Fortune will throw more than enough of that in our path," said Lord Gornemant.

King Arthur finished eating, took his time with his drink. He got up. All at the table rose.

"Please be seated," said the king.

He left the hall, went to his area.

A few minutes later Merlin was there.

"May I come in?" he said.

"Yes, come in. Good to see you."

"Well, how do you like what you see?" said Merlin.

"I feel right at home: but like I was dropped into a dream world."

"This is, however, your world. And you are a member of a family who will want to get to know you. And they will see much of your father in you. Have you given thought to your crowning?"

"You mentioned that important festivals were usually held in larger palaces. To me the crowning is my important festival and I will not look kindly at anyone who, for no good reason, avoids it."

"Your father would have spoken in much that way. Your father would have likely selected the City of Lions, Caer Leon. Many would find it easy to travel to. And it is a symbol of power, a symbol of majesty and influence. And now, you will want to know from a wizard, what would be the best day for the coronation. I am a wizard and will now tell you. Much of your strength is in trees, so one inquires of the trees.

Your father and I favour our friend, The Oak. Your mother's people are lords of the Land of Apples. Here, we are in good fortune. There is a day sacred to Oak and Apple. It is known as Ambarvalia, and Oak Apple Day. And this day, May twentyninth, will be here shortly.

"So Easter, we will make that knowledge known," said the king.

"Between Easter and Ambarvalia there will be time for us to chat about the situation here, how the situation has developed from past history. But now I am certain you will want to spend time with your family."

Merlin slipped off into the shadows and was gone.

"Hello, King Arthur. Can I be of help with anything?" Sir Kay was at the entrance.

"Yes. Spend the day listening to people and learning about the palace, how it is managed."

The king used his toilet; from the ceramic bowl, poured water down the drain. This was a different world. King Arthur sat on a handsome stool and rested. Sir Lucan was at the entrance.

"Sire, will you see Lord Brychan and his family?"

"Yes, I will."

"Glad to see you, King Arthur."

Lord Brychan entered. With him were a number of handsome young women, a young man and an elderly gentleman.

"King Arthur, this is my uncle, Lord Erb."

"How do you do, Lord Erb?"

"Nicely thankyou. How are you, sir?"

"And this, my son Sir Nevyn."

"How do you do?"

"How do you do?"

"And this is my son in law, Sir Tugdual."

"How do you do?"

"And my son in law, King Kyngen."

"How are you sir?" said the king.

"Fine, thankyou, how are you."

"And my daughters, Neffydd, Gutuyl, Tudful, Pyslyl, Drynwin, Bethon, Elyned and Gwladys, and she is my youngest."

"And whom, I must say, I have had the pleasure of previously meeting," said the king."

119

Together they stood on the marble floor. The ladies told the king about this and that. Sir Lucan came to the entrance.

"Sire, more of your family to see you."

"Yes yes. Invite them in."

Lord Geraint and his lady and his sons Sir Kyngar, Sir Iestin and Sir Selyn and their ladies. And his brothers, Prince Ermid and Prince Dweyl and their ladies.

The group talked to each other and to King Arthur. The young ladies kidded among themselves and engaged in banter with the king.

"Listen not to them, your majesty. These women have not a brain in their head," said Lord Brychan.

Pystyl said, "Just think, all the time, you were our cousin."

The king talked with his family. The time passed. There was the sound of a horn. Sir Lucan came to the entrance.

"Sire, your dinner is ready," he said.

"Very good. Thankyou Sir Lucan," said the king.

The king and his family walked out of the entrance, down the marble hall, down the curving marble stairs. He entered the great hall.

"Ladies and gentlemen, His Majesty, the King."

King Arthur took his seat.

"Please be seated," he said.

King Arthur took his time with his meat and drink. He listened to the babble of many conversations. After a spell he stood. The company all stood.

"Carry on," said the king.

He left the hall and went up the stairs, he returned to his quarters, sat and gazed out of his window.

Shortly, Sir Lucan was at the entrance.

"Will you see members of your family, Sire?"

"Have them come in."

Lord Brochwael and his lady, and his son, Sir Glyddiew, and his lady entered.

"So good to see you, your majesty," said Lord Brochwael.

"Good of you to come," said the king. "Won't you be seated?"

The king sat on one of the benches, one to the right of the window, and the four guests sat on benches across from him. Lord Brochwael gave account of where they lived and what they did. And Lord Brochwael said:

"And as the information of us being members of your family has come newly to you, you may have questions about who we all are. I will, if I may, give a picture of the family, of its various groupings."

"As our cousin's women folk would have had scores of other things to talk about - and many of them all at the same time, - we doubt if you have gotten much information about the family from them. That is, presented in such a way that it made sense," said Sir Glyddiew.

"Indeed. Although Lady Erduduyl did say somewhat of who their family was."

"So we will fit that in," said Lord Brochwael.

Lord Brochwael began by telling of the early days, of Cymbeline, of Ynyr, of Ergyng, of the brother kings, Nynniaw and Pebiew, and of their sins.

"And if you have questions, stop us," said Sir Glyddiew.

"Yes, there are so many details," said Lord Brochwael. "As the connection of your father, as Chief Dragon, with dragons, his Father Theoderic's Uncle Casnar was called the Dragon of Went; so, King Uther was not the first Dragon King of this castle. Before King Casnar, King Moruawr would have been the Dragon King. So: You are part of a line of Dragon Kings. So: If Theoderic, who was called The Great, had styled himself as The King, he too, would have been a Dragon King. And the Dragon seems to have its dark, Underworld relationships: your father with Igerne; his father, Helen of the hosts: then, our Grandmother Elaine. With her is an association with Arawn, King of the Underworld. And with Cob, the Goblin King. Yourself, although I have lived for many a year, it seems you have always been here: the Dragon King on his throne."

"Then we are called to be here by the Spirit of the Dragon," said the king. "The Spirit is ever here: we're here because we're here because we're here."

"Quite. So, here we are and here we are and here we are," said Lord Brochwael. "And we'll talk more on this. But, with your leave, we will make our departure at this time."

"It has been a good conversation," said the king.

The guests bowed to the king and departed. The king sat and

rested. Sir Lucan appeared.

"Have you a minute, Sire?"

"I have."

Lucan entered.

"Sire, am I to understand, you will have crowning at Ambarvalia, and are you to go from here to that castle?"

"You are. I am. We will go from this castle the nineteenth: The second day after Easter. I plan a leisurely trip: up above Gloucester, then to Caer Leon. Keep our way to yourself. You and the major part of your staff will take charge of Caer Leon, and the staff there will work with you. Sir Kay is seneschal, but I want older knights on the staff to give help."

"That gives me what I need."

Sir Lucan bowed and made his exit.

The king sat and watched out of the window. The white clouds sail and change.

The horns sounded. The king got up, took himself down to the great hall. Announced, he took his seat. He enjoyed the well prepared meal. The number of people at the castle had been increasing. Many wanted to see the new king. Around the tables there was much talk and laughter. King Arthur sat, enjoyed the many conversations.

King Arthur stood up. Everyone in the hall stood.

"Carry on," said the king.

The king departed the hall, went up the curving, marble stairs. Shortly thereafter, he retired to his bed.

The king was up early. It was Easter. Then Sir Lucan was there.

"Sire, shall breakfast be announced?"

"By all means."

Sir Lucan went down the stairs. There was a blare of horns. The king walked down to his breakfast. Women were wearing Easter decorations.

"Hail, King Arthur." "Hail Arthur, our King," shouted the standing subjects.

The king took his seat, said:

"Be seated."

King Arthur enjoyed his breakfast; stood, and all stood with him.

Said the king, "The time has come for me to reclaim my sword from the stone."

King Arthur walked out of the great hall. Merlin and Druid Dubric were beside him; the druid, on the right. Horns sounded. The heralds walked in front of the king, toward the palace doors. Knights carrying flags took places behind the heralds with horns. Lords walked behind King Arthur. These were followed by women wearing wreaths of flowers, and some of these carried baskets of flowers. Flowers had been put on the path from the palace.

The heralds led the way, and along the way were wreaths of flowers on each side. The king was being guided toward a shrine.

"Of course," said the king.

In a flowered covered wooden frame was a statue of a female: Easter. In front of Easter were three life sized statues of rabbits. The king was given a wreath and this, he placed at Easter's feet. At Easter's feet was a scabbard.

"The scabbard is for you," said Merlin. "Scabbards are protected by Mother Earth."

King Arthur took the scabbard and put it on.

The heralds led the way around and to the stone. The procession stopped. King Arthur walked to the stone, pulled the sword from it, held the sword up, put it in his scabbard.

"Now hear this," said the king. "My crowning will be held at Caer Leon, held on Ambarvalia, the Day of the Oak and the Apple. For that day, I declare a King's Peace, and expect all my subjects, those who are not ill or ailing, to be there."

The king, Dubric and Merlin took their steps back along the path to the palace.

"Let us go up to my section," said the king. "Where we can chat."

The three went down the path, in through the doors of the palace, up and around on the stairs and to the king's area.

"Won't you be seated," said the king. He said:

"Druid Dubric, I would like you, as guide to things of the Spirit, to place the crown on my head."

"That will be a great honour."

"Now for the look at how your vast country will be ordered," said Merlin. "What plans have you?"

"As I am a continuation of the force of my father, Uther, I should study how his laws functioned and from where he got his aid."

"Some of those who served under him, and performed well in their duties, are at hand and would be willing to serve you. Some are not. I see you will need to have a war force which can win victories. Your first strength is in your relations. You will need your own force, and it must have new, young leaders, as many of your father's commanders, though loyal, are old. You will need to take the lead. Your fathers leaders: Sir Ulfin, Sir Aliduc, Lord Clydno, Lord Eidiol, Lord Aldolf, Sir Morien, Sir Brastias, Lord Cenon, Lord Cinric, Sir Cyon, Sir Britael, Sir Jurdan, Sir Naram, and there were many others who supported these: word should be sent out to these warriors. And to King Uther's friends and relations over the waters. Your nephew, King Howel, should be sent for. And at your crowning should be King Ban and King Bors. They will give aid now, as they will need your help later. And you will give it," said Merlin.

"So, you will contact King Howel, King Ban and King Bors. Sir Lucan and Sir Ulfin can inform those others that their service is needed, as they will be here. Some will see you before the day is out. On Ban, Bors and Howel, see Sir Cador."

"That is a long list," said King Arthur.

"It is one you will know," said Merlin. "And some whom I did not mention have, by yourself, already been included."

Said Druid Dubric, "I had in mind to put Druid Arwystyl at Caer Leon. I believe you will find him a help, and I find Lord Caradoc a man of wisdom."

The three chatted about this and that. Merlin and the druid went out and down the stairs. The king sat awhile in thought. The horns were blowing: King Arthur walked from his area, down the stairs and to the great hall.

"His Majesty, King Arthur," he was announced.

All stood until the king was seated.

King Arthur ate leisurely his well prepared dinner, stood, and the company stood with him. He walked up the curving marble stairs, went to his rooms. He used his toilet, sat to rest, when Sir Lucan was at the entrance.

"Sire, Lord Caradoc, if you are available."

"I am, Sir Lucan. And I wish also to see Sir Cador."

124

"He will be here shortly."

"Good to see you, Lord Caradoc," said the king.

"It is I who am glad to see you. I can think of no one whom I would rather have seen draw that sword from the stone. As you certainly know, my strength is at your service."

"I was certain of it. In the past, I have felt thankful that your strength was with us."

"As I am certain this is a busy time for you, I ask your leave to depart."

"I thank you for your being considerate," said the king.

King Arthur walked to his window. Sir Lucan was at the entrance.

"Sire, Sir Cador to see you."

"Your Majesty, you wished to see me?"

"I do. Thankyou for being prompt. At my crowning, I would have it attended by King Ban of Benwick, King Bors of Gannes and my nephew, King Howel of Armorica. I am told you can have them notified."

"I can, Sire. My father, Lord Geraint owns one of the three major fleets of ships, so can send ships for the companies of those three kings."

"Very fine. And who owns the other two fleets you mentioned?"

"King Mark of Cornwall owns one and the other is owned by King Gwenwynwyn, son of Naf. King Mark: he would be the son of King Merchiaun."

"Ah, I see."

"And let me not be the last to express joy in having you as our king."

"It pleases me much that I have you as my subject."

"If it is your wish, I will get going on my duty."

It is indeed, and I appreciate your promptness."

Sir Cador made an exit.

Sir Lucan was at the entrance.

"Sire, will you see Sir Emeraw?"

"I will see him."

A knight entered.

"Your Majesty."

"Yes?"

"I am Sir Emeraw. I have come to offer you my service."

"I will be glad to have it."

"Thankyou, Your Majesty."

"Take my good will with you."

Sir Emeraw made his exit. Sir Lucan stepped in.

"Sire, a knight to speak with you. Will you see him?"

"I will."

"Good day to you, Your Majesty, I am Sir Ozana."

"Good day Sir Ozana."

"Sire, I have come to offer service to you."

"I will be glad to have it. You may ask Sir Lucan what your duty is to be."

Sir Ozana bowed, made his exit.

King Arthur sat by his window and rested. Sir Lucan was again at the entrance.

"Your Majesty. Lady and Lord Kyner and Sir Kay."

"Delighted."

The lord, the lady and Sir Kay came in. The king took their hands and led them to comfortable seats.

"Tell me how your days have been doing?" said the king.

The king's stepmother told of enjoying the courtyard, the lands of that area. She spoke of admiring the halls under the great swing of the arches, the echo of her footsteps as she walked the long halls.

Sir Kay said he was impressed with the marvels of the kitchen, as at the greatness of the ovens and the neatness of the work tables, and the richness of the steams and smokes.

"But how about your study in the duties of being seneschal?" asked the king.

"Oh," said Sir Kay, "Sir Ulfin and Sir Segurant the Brown have been walking with me, telling me about things."

"Kay will hold things together," said Lord Kyner.

Said his lady, "I recall, when Kay was born, my lord said, 'Damsel, if thy son be mine, his heart will be always cold and there will be no warmth in his hands, and he will have another peculiarity, if he is my son he will always be stubborn, and he will have another peculiarity, when he carries a burden, whether it be large or small, no one will be able to see it, either before him or at his back; and he will have another

126

peculiarity, no one will be able to resist fire and water as well as he. There will never be a servant or an officer equal to him'."

"You do draw a man of value," said the king.

"Humph," said Sir Kay.

"You will surprise yourself," said Lord Kyner to Sir Kay.

"And Druid Dubric will get together a crowning ceremony, and Merlin assures me it will be pleasing," said King Arthur.

King Arthur and Lord Kyner discussed the trip to Caer Leon. Lord Kyner had some knowledge of the roads. Then Lord Kyner spoke of what work might be waiting at Bonmaison.

"Sounds like you have things at home in good order," said King Arthur.

The horns: the four of them heard. They walked down to the great hall.

King Arthur ate his dinner, retired to his rooms, to his bed and was soon asleep.

King Arthur woke in the early light of dawn, took care of his toilet washed and dressed for the road. Sir Lucan was at his entrance.

"Ah, Sir Lucan, I have these to pack on my horse."

It was early. The horns were blowing.

"Good to hear the horns, Sir Lucan."

"Early start anticipated, Your Majesty."

King Arthur walked down the curving, marble stairs, entered the great hall.

"His Majesty, the King."

All in the room stood.

"Be seated," said the king.

The king took his time with his breakfast. He stood. The company stood with him, followed him, followed him out to the waiting horses. The king mounted. Here was a blare of horns. Pennants were raised and the leading pennant, the red dragon. The king shook the reins and the company moved forward.

The morning was clear and bright. The road led around hilly meadows. It turned, led into the dark forest: A long ride on the narrow road through the trees: Out into fields, on past Gloucester, across the river. West they turned, rode over sunny fields. They rode between a couple of high, round topped hills, and high up, beyond the round topped hills, to the right were tall forms of mountains; one, in the distance against the sky, a dark blue, pointy peak. The company rode forward. On the left was the river and beyond it, rock cliffs.

Lord Gornemant rode beside the king. He looked down at the river.

"Ships from over sea can come up the river there," he said.

To the front were green meadows on which were groups of trees, then on a tree covered hill, rising above the trees was Caer Leon, a splendid sight, its many roofs glittering golden. King Arthur rode toward it. In front of him, along the Usk, left and down from the road, was a handsome town. It was a marvel to behold: buildings artfully built and shining in their whiteness; the rooves, bright golden.

Along the road, green, grassy fields formed parks in which were artfully spaced groves of trees. There was a blare of horns. There was a shout, "His Majesty the King." The gate sailed up. King Arthur rode into the courtyard of Caer Leon.

King Arthur dismounted. There was a knight at his service.

"Your Majesty, I am Sir Brys. May I show you the king's rooms?"

"Certainly. I presume you are the butler."

"I am."

The two walked in at a wide door, walked up stone stairs, into a room which looked out on the courtyard.

"Where are you from, Sir Brys?"

"I am from the black fernbrakes in Pictland."

"Very good," said the king.

Sir Brys left the area.

"May I enter, Your Majesty?" said Sir Lucan.

"Certainly."

"Here we are. All of us. All seems in good order. I suggested to Sir Kay, he work with those here in working with our line of supply. Our Caer Went staff will aid the Caer Leon staff where they can, all under Sir Kay's authority, or course."

"And you are Chief Butler, Sir Lucan."

"Yes Sir, thankyou Sir. And Sir Brys will be a good man to work with."

"He tells me he is from Pictland."

"Yes, Brys, the son of Brysethach. Some mysterious places in

128

Pictland. It is said, he was the first to call for Mother Earth to give a sign as to who the rightful king should be."

"I suspect many had that question in their thoughts," said the king.

There was a blare of horns.

"So, I will now wash up for supper," said the king.

"By your leave," said Lucan, and he departed.

Washed and having taken care of his toilet, King Arthur took himself to the stairs down.

"Hail King Arthur," sounded a chorus of voices.

King Arthur took his place at the table.

Harpers, filled the great hall with song. Wine replaced food, and the harpers were replaced by Eliot, the Bard of Ludlow. The king sat long listening to the skillful Eliot. However, after hearing a number of long songs, the king got sleepy and made his exit.

The day passed. King Arthur walked through a long castle hall: through another. The castle gave the impression of great wealth. And many workmen were then involved in, for the coronation, enhancing that impression.

There was a blare of horns. The king walked into the great hall. There was a shout:

"His Majesty the King."

The king sat, ate. A harper began playing.

The king sat over his wine, listened to the music. He got to his feet, retired to his rooms.

"May I enter, Your Majesty?"

"Certainly."

Sir Brys came in.

"Is there a thing which we might supply you with, Your Majesty?"

"I think of nothing."

"Fortunately we keep a well stocked larder. And it helps to have your seneschal have an interest in material needs. And it is good to get to know your staff of Caer Went. So, if there is any help we can be."

"Not this night. So, I will bid you a good evening."

"Thankyou Your Majesty."

Sir Brys bowed, went out.

The king was up early. He dressed, waited by the window which seemed to give the best view of the Usk. A ship was sailing up and past the castle. There was a blare of horns.

The king was quite ready. He walked down, into the great hall.

"His Majesty, the King."

King Arthur took his seat. He enjoyed his breakfast. Breakfast over, the king walked out of the castle.

"King Arthur, would you tolerate company?"

It was Sir Kay.

"I think I could."

"This is Sir Bedivere. He was one of the boys, us boys, who rode up north of here to chase the rascals," said Kay.

"Good to see you, Sir Bedivere,"

"And he was one of the strongest."

"And a welcome attribute that will be," said the king.

The three walked out of the gate, around the wall to where a wide, circular grassy mound enclosed a plate of grass. The inside of the grass mound was a circular stone wall. In the wall; north, east, south and west; there was a gateway of stone.

"A fine area for meetings," said the king.

The three walked down a grassy slope to a green meadow, to a road which was at the side of an impressive building.

"This is the school of druidic teachings," said Sir Kay.

"Very good," said the king.

On streets which led to Usk River there were warehouses and shipping counting houses. People nodded politely to the young, handsome knights who were walking through the town. The three returned to the castle. Then the horns were blowing for the midday meal. The three walked toward the center hall.

"What has Griflet been busy at?" said the king.

"Doing what squires do," said Sir Kay. "He has good instructors here. I do not but in."

"Quite true," said the king."

"His Majesty, the King."

King Arthur waved all to their seats: sat down. He enjoyed the lunch, returned to his rooms. He watched the cloud shadows pass over the river Usk, the clouds sailed over the handsome landscape. There was a blare of horns. A good number of warriors were entering the castle.

Sir Brys was at the entrance.

Your Majesty, will you entertain a visit with Lord Geraint and his sons?"

"I will."

"King Arthur great to have you with us. You have met my son, Sir Cador. And this is Berth, son of Cador."

"Your Majesty."

"Nice to see you, Berth."

Geraint continued: "And this is Prince Cyndrwyn, son of King Ermid."

"And I believe you have met my sons, Kyngar, Selyn and Iestin?"

"Glad to see you," said the king. "And to see you, as you seem, in good health."

"We'd do well to be," said Geraint. "It can get tricky around all this shipping."

"All the same, good to see ships coming in," said the king.

"And, Your Majesty, to have someone to do battle with," said Sir Cador.

The conversation went on to supply and to trade relationships and to diplomacy.

"And, as we said, all of us are delighted to have you as our king." said Lord Geraint.

"It was good to see you," said the king.

Lord Geraint and his family made slight bows, departed.

There was a cheer for Lord Geraint when he entered the hall.

As King Arthur rested in his room he heard the noise and commotion in the halls below. Then the horns wee blowing. King Arthur went down the stairs to his dinner. "His Majesty the King," was announced. Lord Geraint, at the table, sat on his right. A harper played a lively tune which was heard through a cacophony of conversations.

The days passed. When King Arthur was in the castle courtyard, Sir Kay walked up,

"King Arthur, tomorrow is Beltane."

"That I know quite well."

"Father would be annoyed if it were not observed."

"I am certain Lord Geraint will do sufficient observation, - and since I am here, I will be requested to be part of it."

Said Sir Kay, "You and I, like old times, could scout around and see what the countryside is doing."

"Not a bad idea to see what is doing in the country. See that the kitchen has lunch for us to take with us. Our horses should be ready for us to depart after our quick breakfast," said King Arthur.

King Arthur retired for the evening.

In the early light, King Arthur was up and quite ready when the blare of horns gave the call for breakfast. He took himself down the stairs to the great hall.

"Arthur the King."

He quickly ate breakfast, walked out of the castle to where horses were waiting. Then Sir Kay was there. King Arthur mounted his horse.

We're off," said the king.

The two rode down the road, through the valley of the Usk, rode on the slopes, make their ways though the trees. On they rode through the morning, winding their way through the hilly land. They stopped on a low hill where there was an out cropping of rock and on the rocks set the packs which they took from the horses. Out of the packs they took food for their lunch. This they ate, then were off again down and up hills.

Near the top of a wooded hill the king stopped:

"We will stop here while I feed some bushes."

He dismounted. Sir Kay dismounted also. When the king returned, he and Kay walked up the hill to where among bushes and low trees was a circle of tall trees. In the center of the circle was a dark, moss covered mound which was entered between two tall stones and these, covered by a stone slab. Between the stones was what seemed a huge, white robed oger. And in his hand, he held a large double bladed axe.

King Arthur walked up to him:

"What man is that, guards the gate?"

"The severe, hoary one with the wide dominion."

"Is there a porter?" asked the king.

"Truly there is. It is Glewlwyd Mighty Grasp. Who is he that asks?"

"It is Arthur and fair Kay. How goes it with thee?"

"Truly the best way in the world. What good attends thee? Into this house thou shalt not enter unless thou wilt preserve."

"I shall preserve," said the king.

"What following hast thou?" asked Glewlwyd.

"Truly, the best men are mine."

"To my house thou shalt not come unless thou plead for them."

"I will plead for them and they will preserve," said the king.

Sir Kay, "I will preserve it and thou shalt behold. Though the Birds of Wrath should go forth and the three attendant lords should fall asleep: Mabon, son of Modron; Gwynn, King of the Unkown – ."

Said Glewlwyd, "Severe have my servants been in preserving their rule. Manannan, son of Lear was grave in his counsel. Mabon, son of Lightning, stained the straw with gore. Lugh Windyhand was a firm guardian of the encircled mount. I rendered them complete. Kay, I solemnly announce, though all three should be slain, when the privilege of the grove is violated, dangerous enforcers shall be found. The Earth Ark of Lady Rhoia shall be respected."

King Arthur and Sir Kay walked past Glewlwyd, down old stone steps to a stone floor enclosed by circular stone walls. In the center of the room was a circular, stone walled room below the first, and it was reached by a winding stone stairway; and on this stairway King Arthur and Sir Kay walked down.

The shadows of the trees got longer. King Arthur and Sir Kay walked into the sunlight, nodded to Glewlwyd, walked down the hill where their horses waited.

"That was an unexpected find," said King Arthur.

"Father would have been pleased," said Sir Kay.

King Arthur and Sir Kay rode back through wooded valleys toward Caer Leon. The shadows got longer. The sun sank behind the hills. Then on some of the tall hills fires could be seen.

Said King Arthur, looking up at the tall hills, "I see the Sun is being honoured with plenty of light."

"Yes, Beltane; Great feast for the Sun," said Sir Kay.

Through the valleys along the two horsemen rode. They came to the green meadows and tree covered hills near Caer Leon. They rode up to the gate.

"King Arthur with Sir Kay."

"Enter, Your Majesty and Sir Kay."

King Arthur, Sir Kay, dismounted, gave their horses to grooms, went in the courtyard, the castle hall. The king went up to his rooms. He cleaned up, made his toilet, went down to the hall.

"His Majesty, King Arthur."

King Arthur took his seat. Food was brought out for him. There was a harper playing for the lords and knights who were there. Lord Geraint was in his seat beside the king.

"Many of the Lords and knights are at this or that festival. Perhaps you made a visit to one or another of them," said Lord Geraint.

"I was part of a celebration. It seemed to fall in my way," said the king.

The king sat and drank. He listened to the harper.

Said Lord Geraint, "The town will continue the celebration of life tomorrow. It is hoped you will bless the celebration."

"I will be glad to," said the king.

He stood and walked up the stairs to his rooms.

King Arthur woke in the early light, washed and dressed in what he felt would be fitting for the day. There was a blare from the horns. The king went down to breakfast.

"His Majesty, King Arthur."

All stood to welcome the king. Many were dressed in bright clothes. The breakfast was quickly eaten.

"Shall we see what the town is doing?" said Lord Geraint.

Lord Geraint and the king left the table, walked down the hall of the castle, through the courtyard, out the gate and around the castle to the huge, circular bowl. They were followed by a procession of lords, knights and ladies. There was a blare of horns. There was a shout:

"Hail King Arthur."

Lord Geraint, with King Arthur, went to the East Gate, entered the bowl. The sun was behind them. Lord Geraint and the king walked to the elevated seats at the east of the bowl and were seated. All the town people who were in the bowl, as a body, came forward and bowed to Lord Geraint and the king.

"King Arthur, many people are off celebrating at more backwoods locations: sacred hills or sacred waters: We here would be thought too city like," said Lord Geraint. "A favourite location," he said, "is Caradoc's Well. It is a favourite place for fairs."

Town people wearing flowers and carrying baskets of flowers were doing dances around a girl dressed in flowers. The musicians played while dancers threw flowers at the May Queen.

King Arthur noticed there were eight gates at the bowl: north, south, east, west and a gate between each of those gates.

A May King crowned the May Queen with a crown of flowers. Buckets of water were thrown on the May Royalty.

Lord Geraint and the king made their exit.

Lord Geraint and the king, followed by knights, lords and ladies, walked around to the castle gate.

The king entered the castle, walked up to his rooms. He rang the bell. Sir Lucan appeared at his entrance.

"Yes, Your Majesty?"

"Sir Lucan, I wish to speak with my seneschal."

"I will inform the seneschal, Your Majesty."

King Arthur changed into riding clothes. Sir Kay was at the entrance.

"Come in, Sir Kay. Sir Kay, after lunch I would like to ride out into the woods and fields. And in this, have your company."

"May I bring a friend of mine along, Sir Bedivere? He and I had already planned an outing."

"That would be fine."

The blare of horns announced lunch.

"I want horses at the gate by the time we finish eating," said the king as he and Sir Kay walked toward the stairs.

King Arthur finished his lunch, went out to where the horses were waiting. Sir Kay and Sir Bedivere appeared. The three mounted and rode forth down the road.

King Arthur and the knights rode up the valley of the Usk. In the distance, on the other side of the river, there were tents and pavilions. The three rode through farmlands: the hills and green meadows with, here and there, clumps of trees. The horsemen rode onto a grassy, round topped hill. King Arthur pulled up his horse, dismounted.

"We can see a good way from here," he said.

"A rest is welcome," said Sir Kay.

Bedivere got out some dice.

"Yes," said Sir Kay, "we could have a game."

King Arthur and the two knights sat on the grass on the hilltop, began rolling the dice. They became engaged in the game.

The three saw, riding through the valley toward them, a knight carrying off a woman. She struggled against the knight as they came forward. King Arthur looked up:

"I have a great penis urge. Why are you not stopping that knight, getting me that maiden? I could lay with her behind that thorn tree before those following knights get here."

"The reason we are not, sire, is because it is the duty of a king to aid the weak, to protect the honour of women," Sir Kay said.

"Yes, chase unworthy thoughts from your mind, sire," said Sir Bedivere.

"Well, since you will not get her for me, if you must be noble, take her from that knight and ask him on whose land he thinks to be lawless on."

"That's what we became knights for," said Sir Kay.

"Then we're off," said the king.

The three mounted, headed to cut off the fleeing knight. And he, seeing them getting close, put the woman down, raced away.

King Arthur stopped.

"Ho, ho" he shouted." The girl is safe. That is sufficient."

"Oh, thankyou, King Arthur."

It was Gwladys, youngest daughter of King Brychan.

"That was Lord Gwynlliw Vilwyr. He and his warriors had just lost a battle and that had upset him. He might have thought, because he is a loser, Father would not have accepted him," said Gwladys.

"That should have been your choice," said the king.

"Yes. But Father would be accepting any knight who is not wicked. He's had a job finding knights. We are so many."

"Then, give me a hug, and Sir Bedivere will take you to your father whom I see coming this way."

The king and Sir Kay rode up the hill on the way back to Caer Leon.

King Arthur and Sir Kay rode over a hill, through a valley. Sir Bedivere caught up with them.

"Sire, Lord Brychan sends his most sincere thankyou. 'There is, as men should learn,' he said, 'a right way of doing things.'"

King Arthur and his knights rode up the river valley. Darkness came. It was dark when they came to the gate of Caer Leon. King Arthur, with pleasure, walked into the great hall. The company stood, shouted:

"Hail, King Arthur."

Food was brought out for the king and Sir Kay and Sir Bedivere. There was a harper, and there were a couple of musicians playing flutes.

The day passed, and another, and a whole week had fled by. King Arthur looked out of his window at the green woodlands which lay in front of the castle walls which he could see from his window.

Sir Lucan appeared.

"Sire, King Howel has arrived."

"Splendid, have him come up."

King Howel entered, and he was a splendid looking young man who seemed to be near to King Arthur's age.

"King Howel, so good to see you. Being my cousin, you should get to know all this well. How was your trip across?"

"I, and I think, all the others, had a most enjoyable trip. I brought a good crew."

"I appreciate that. The more to join the celebration, the better I like it."

There was a blare of horns.

"Are you ready for your dinner?" asked King Arthur.

"Oh yes. Indeed yes."

The two kings walked to the stairs and down. Lord Geraint had King Howel placed on King Arthur's right; and himself on King Arthur's left.

Said Lord Geraint," I like to see my nephew, Howel, looking so good. His land is fortunate to have his energetic, young arm as a guide for its future. In his land, all can center on him."

"Thankyou Uncle Geraint. That is what I intend for my land."

"Lord Geraint," said King Arthur, "I would wish King Howel to meet any of our leaders whom he might not know."

"Sire, I will see that he does," said Lord Geraint.

Then the harper was playing and words of a number of conversations became mixed with the musical notes from the harp, and the hours of evening passed. King Arthur stood, raised his cup:

"Prosperity to our land."

"Prosperity to our land and health to our mighty king," said all present, as they stood and raised their cups.

King Arthur climbed the stairs to his rooms.

King Arthur woke with first light. He washed, attended to his toilet, dressed in light clothes. He took the stairs down, walked through the courtyard, had the porter open a gate. The king walked out. To the right, below the wooded slope, was the town, its most handsome buildings with their bright rooves. Already smoke could be seen rising from the town, from its forges. Beyond the town was the water, and it was bright in the morning sunlight.

This morning, King Arthur took the way to his left. Below the wooded slopes below the castle were bright green meadows, groves of green trees and parks bright with flowers. Groups of young men and women were out in the parks.

Beyond the meadows and parks were the woodlands, and beyond them, the blue peaks of mountains; one, a lonely point. The king took the path along the stone wall to where the land dropped away. From there, he could see, across the water, bright cliffs, golden in the early rays of the sun. There was a blare of the call from the horns. King Arthur, along with others, took himself toward the castle gate. The king took himself into the great hall, in for breakfast.

Breakfast over, King Arthur made an inspection of the castle. He checked for areas which might be difficult to defend. Sir Kay came and walked with him.

"I remember our young years, our old instructors explaining how Bonmaison should be defended. Even with this palace like building, much would be the same," said Sir Kay.

"I picked up on much of that. That is what old instructors are for," said the king.

"This castle is a marvel," said Sir Kay. "The kitchen, everything falls into place. And the washrooms. I mean water that falls from the ceiling. And all rendered with an eye to grace."

"Yes," said the king. "I suspect we will be spending, off and on, a

138

fair amount of time in this castle."

Sir Kay and the king continued their walk, inspected the battlements at the top of the castle.

There was a blast from the horns. Sir Kay and King Arthur went down to the great hall.

"His Majesty, King Arthur."

"Be seated," said the king.

The king, seated between King Howel and Lord Geraint, ate a hearty lunch. And he listened to the conversations which were going on around him.

King Arthur stood, went up the stairs to his rooms. He sat and looked out of his window at his tree covered slope, at the bright rooves below the slope. Lord Lucan was at the entrance.

"Sire, will you see Lady Gwladys?"

"I will."

Lady Gwladys went in.

"Oh, King Arthur, thankyou for keeping me from being carried off."

"Sit down. And tell me about it."

"Well, to start, you are still a part of past summers?"

"Yes, I did all those things."

"Then it was like that. Only, one must know where one can not go. It might have been fun."

"Living has its rules."

"Yes, of course. But with a proper wedding. Father said he was still on the guest list. If I wished, I could refuse to see him."

"Life goes past quickly. Keep that in mind."

"Do you still give hugs like times past?"

"With you, I do."

Gwladys gave King Arthur a warm hug as the king stood to embrace her. Gwladys made her exit.

Lord Lucan was at the entrance.

"Sire, King Stater has arrived."

"Very good. I will see him."

King Arthur sat in an official looking chair. King Stater entered bowed.

"Your Majesty," he said.

"Good to see you, King Stater. Is all well with your kingdom?"

"It is Sire. In a general way. King Vortigern left a bit of a mess. However, we have obtained order to a good degree. I hope all is going well here?"

"I believe it is," said King Arthur. "Now tell me what has been happening in your kingdom. And do be seated."

King Stater gave King Arthur an account of who was who in the Kingdom of Demetria, and of what each was doing, as far as he could tell.

"Thankyou, King Stater. I appreciate being informed."

King Stater stood, bowed, made his exit.

Sir Lucan was at the entrance.

"Your Majesty, Lord Brychan, Lord Brochwael and Sir Glyddiew to visit, if it is convenient?"

"It is. Have them enter."

"Your Majesty," said Lord Brochwael, "we wanted to drop in to be reassured that the days are doing well, and that should there be aught which you would like us to do, we are at your service."

"And I would like to add my thankyou to that of my daughter for bringing an end to some silliness," said Lord Brychan.

King Arthur chatted with the three men. They talked about this and that. There, the horns were blaring. The four men walked down the stairs to the great hall.

The day passed.

The next day came in with wind swept rain. King Arthur watched it whipping past the windows. He washed, made his toilet, watched the grey rain sweep past the windows. There was a blare from the horns, and it was mixed with the sound of the falling rain. King Arthur walked down the stairs to his breakfast.

He was announced, "His Majesty, King Arthur."

"Be seated," said the king.

Breakfast finished, King Arthur walked up the stairs to his rooms.

A little time passed. There were the sounds from the clearing up of the great hall. There was the sound of the rain.

"Sire, will you see Lord Neithon?"

Sir Lucan was there.

"I will."

A thin cadaverous looking gentleman entered, bowed to the king: "Your Majesty."

"Good day, Lord Neithon."

Lord Neithon expressed his pleasure at having Arthur King of the land. He made his exit.

Sir Lucan was again at the entrance."

"Sire, King Iddon to see you."

"Have him come in."

King Iddon entered.

"Your Majesty, we come to wish you a great future."

"Thankyou, King Iddon, and we hope this will bring good to all in the land who are of good will."

King Iddon told King Arthur about how his, Iddon's, land was doing. He made his exit.

The rain swished past the window, shushed on the leaves of trees below. King Arthur stood by the window and watched it. The rain slowed. The steady fall of rain increased, blocked out the sight of all but the nearest trees. The horns were blowing. King Arthur walked down stairs.

The rain continued through the day. And the next.

The weather cleared. Then numbers of people did wend their way to the castle. There came to be a sound of turmoil in the downstairs halls. Then Merlin was there.

"Ah, Merlin" said King Arthur. "What I wish is a crowning which would be grand. But I would have it one which my father, King Uther, and his grandfather before him, and on into the past, would recognize as a correct way for a king to receive a crown."

"It will be a proper crowning and done so that kings who follow will use your crowning as the example of how theirs should be," said Merlin.

There was the blare of horns. King Arthur and Merlin went down the stairs.

"Hail His Majesty, King Arthur," went the spirited shout."

King Arthur took his seat.

King Arthur, as he ate, gave thought to the future. Finished eating, he walked up the stairs to his rooms. Merlin entered.

141

"You wanted me, Sire?"

Sir Kay was at the entrance.

"I do. Come in Sir Kay. As I am to announce my staff, including yourself, see that tailors have ten grand, matching robes.

Said Merlin, "I suggest sky blue trimmed in ermine. The tailors of the town have them ready."

"Very good," said the king.

"Many details have been neatly tied," said Merlin.

"Very good," said the king.

"And I suggest there be hunts for a stag, as there was an old custom, the procession for the crowning led by the head of a stag. Theoderic had such a procession."

"Then I must have one," said the king. "And we will need a great chorus of pipes and horns. Sir Kay, see that we have one."

The king and Merlin talked about the order of march. "The march," said Merlin, "should be led by three arch druids: Druid Dubric, Druid Bedwini and Druid Arwystyl, the Druid of Caer Leon, and he would walk to the left of Druid Dubric."

The discussion went to the hunt. Merlin explained how the hunt would be organized.

There was a blare from the horns. The king, with Sir Kay and Merlin, went to the stairs and down.

There was a jubilant cry:

"Hail, His Majesty, King Arthur."

"Be seated," said the king.

He stood at the head of the table:

"There are things I have to relate. First: duties are assigned. The seneschal is Sir Kay. The butler is Sir Lucan. The constable is Sir Bedivere. The chamberlain, Lord Baldwin. The chancellor, Sir Ulfin. The wardens, Sir Brastias and Sir Naram. The advisors, Lord Caradoc, Lord Gornemant and Lord Clydno. First thing tomorrow, there will be a stag hunt. The head of the stag will be presented to Druid Dubric on the point of a spear. Let us eat."

The crowd at the tables, while eating, enjoyed music of harps. The feast continued, the music swelled as the harpers gave way to pipers. King Arthur went up the stairs to his rooms.

There was a blare, in the dark before sun up, a blare of horns. King

Arthur was up and dressed, down the stairs, and on his waiting horse, a bow and arrows packed conveniently with it. He rode out the gate and was joined by a multitude of riders. Merlin, on a large black horse, rode by his side.

Down through green meadows they rode, up into wooded hills. There was a large stag. King Arthur and Merlin dismounted, crept quietly up. The king shot it. He blew a blast on his horn. Horsemen rode up.

"Have the Lord Stag removed to the castle," said the king.

He and Merlin took their way to the castle gate, dismounted. There was a blare of horns. King Arthur went to the great hall, to breakfast. More and more riders entered the great hall for their most welcome breakfast. More food was brought in.

The king went up to his rooms.

"Sire, will you see Druid Dubric?"

Sir Lucan was at the entrance.

"I will," said King Arthur.

"Sire, it will be an honour to carry your Lord Stag."

"Delighted you consider it so."

"To march in support of me," said Druid Dubric," if they be welcome. And these: Druid Nertat, Druid Berthgwyn, Druid Bithen and Druid Colfryd."

"They shall march four abreast behind thee."

"Thankyou, Sire."

The arch druid departed. Merlin was there.

"King Arthur, I believe the procession has fallen into order, subject to any change you might care to make.

"Now, what do we have?" King Arthur asked.

"The arch druids, Druid Dubric with, of course, Lord Stag; the Dragon Pennant, and I suggest it be carried by Lord Eidiol; the Crow Pennant and the Bear Pennant following, two abreast: Aldolf, the Bear, Sir Segurant, the Crow; Following these, your chosen staff in robes of duty. Following these, kings and lords. Following these, knights; then, warriors. Following these, druids, bards, then musicians. Following these, your family: The family of Lord Brychan, the family of Lord Brochwael, the family of Lord Geraint, the family of King Ermid, the family of Prince Dweyl, King Glywys, Lord Kyner, Lord Do, and behind the last, yourself. I plan to be with the druids; as so, I have been numbered. You alone will be horsed; I advised Druid Dubric, not that he needed advice."

"Then it is together," said King Arthur.

"It is together," said Merlin.

He stepped out and was gone.

King Arthur watched, through his window, the clouds over the water, over blue hills, and thought about the coming ceremony. The horns rang out. King Arthur went out and down the stairs.

"Hail His Majesty, King Arthur."

The enthusiastic cheer. The king took his seat. The hall filled with excited conversation, scraps of which reached the ears of the king. Men up and down the table were dressed in fine bright clothes.

"Your Majesty, I wonder what the women are up to," said Lord Geraint.

"We can but wonder."

"I suspect much of their concern has to do with clothing," said King Howel.

"This ceremony, though, will give them other things to worry about," said Lord Geraint. "A new king will cause great movements in many things. Especially, as King Arthur is young and not set in his ways."

"And he is unmarried," said King Howel.

"That need not worry them," said King Arthur.

"But certainly, it will. I could wager on that," said Sir Geraint.

King Arthur nodded. He was served another helping of the good food. Conversations down the table turned Lord Geraint's, and King Howel's, attention to other things. King Arthur's attention settled on the fine flavour of the ale.

King Arthur stood. Those in the hall stood.

"Hail to King Arthur."

The king nodded to Prince Anladd, to King Howel, to Lord Geraint, to King Ermid, to Prince Dweyl. He walked to the stairs, walked up the marble stairs to his rooms.

There was a sound of many voices coming from the great hall. King Arthur sat in his chair and rested. A cacophony of noises came from the downstairs, clashes and clatterings as new arrivals and new arrivals, one followed another. Sir Lucan was at the entrance.

"Sire, will you see Lord Bridlaw?"

"Have the lord enter."

"Your Majesty, I am Lord Bridlaw."

King Arthur was seated in a large, handsome chair.

"Good of you to come," said the king.

"Your Majesty, we are delighted to have you as our king. I have heard whisperings that some foolish Vikings were not happy, so planned to disrupt the coronation; therefore, I brought a unit of warriors in the case that they might be helpful."

"That is considerate."

"And we wish you a good day tomorrow."

"Thankyou, Lord Bridlaw."

Lord Bridlaw bowed and was gone.

King Arthur pulled a cord that rang a bell. Sir Lucan entered.

"Your Majesty?"

"Sir Lucan, is Merlin available?"

"Where, Sire, Merlin comes from and where Merlin goes is a mystery. I would never know that, Sire."

"That being the way it is, I would speak with Lord Geraint, with Sir Kay and yourself."

"We will be with you directly, Sire."

Sir Lucan went quickly out.

King Arthur sat in his large chair, waited.

Sir Kay, Lord Geraint and Sir Lucan entered.

"Your Majesty?" said Lord Geraint.

"I wish to know of how we will dispose of any disturbance which there might be to our functions."

Said Geraint, "Sire, we will have scouts and these, join the march in their place, as warriors, in our ceremonial march, when their scouting is complete. Every man in the march would be armed, so no small, hidden body of men could stop the ritual."

"And, Sire," said Sir Lucan, "no where in the land would one find a group of swordsmen who would be so stout."

King Arthur said, "We'll be watchful. And Lord Bridlaw is here with a unit of warriors. Lord Geraint, know where he is in case you want to use him. You are familiar with this area, as you defend shipping.

Sir Kay will help you organize. That is all I have."

"Thankyou, Your Majesty," said Lord Geraint.

The three knights bowed to King Arthur, departed.

King Arthur got up, got his new sword, took it from its sheath. He went to the center of the room, swung the sword several times, looked it over, top to bottom. He felt its weight, put it back into its sheath. He sat in his chair and contemplated.

The horns blared. King Arthur walked down the marble stairs, which were bright from hanging, bright silver candle holders. And on his left were clusters of tall pillars of bright stone. Then, beneath his feet were tiles; their colours in graceful designs. He walked into the great hall. All rose, shouted:

"Hail King Arthur."

King Arthur motioned the crowd to be seated. He took his seat. There was a huge crowd of knights, lords, other warriors. The sound from the harps mixed with the roar of laughter and conversation.

"It looks like we have a good bit of support," Lord Geraint was saying.

"Seems a truth," said King Dweyl.

King Arthur took his time with his drink. Men came and went from the table. The king slipped away, up the stairs to his rooms.

There was a blare of horns. It was just then getting light. King Arthur took care of his toilet, washed, quickly dressed, went to the great hall.

"Hail King Arthur," shouted the standing crowd.

"Be seated," the king, in a loud voice, said.

King Arthur ate. Druid Dubric walked up and stood stiff and scowling behind the king.

"Your Majesty, may I inform the company what is expected of them?"

"Certainly."

"Company, we will form a line along the road beyond the gate. A general way, the marchers will take places in this order: the arch druids, the four castle druids. After these, the pennants and these; the Dragon Pennant, carried by Sir Segurant the Brown and with Sir Segurant, Prince Anladd and Prince Erb, son of Conan. Then the Bear Pennant, carried by Lord Aldolf, and the Crow Pennant, carried by

146

Lord Eidiol son of Ceidiaw. These will be followed by King Arthur's staff; and these, by kings, lords and knights and these, as far as I have received their names, and not including the family of the king; King Stater, Lord Cadwallon, Prince Riagath, Lord Cenon, Lord Cinric, Sir Cynon son of Lord Clydno, King Iddon, Sir Caurdaf son of Lord Caradoc, Sir Morien, Lord Bridlaw, Lord Gwynlliw Vilwyr, Sir Blaes son of Llychlyn, Lord Cursal, Lord Jonatal, Lord Doldam, Sir Ligger, Sir Gwider, Sir Bredbeddle, Sir Gwider of Peyto, Sir Lanyel, Lord Bose, Lord Ingemer, King Ethelfrid, Sir Cleremond, Lord Gorthmol, Sir Britael, Lord Warewik, Lord Urgent, Sir Blois of Case, Sir Cardol, Sir Glinneu son of Taran, Sir Gurguint, Sir Florence, Sir Ladin, Sir Guy of Bloy, Sir Grasy, Sir Hervy of Revel, Sir Phariance, Sir Placidas, Sir Flanned, Sir Morwith, Sir Anneck, Sir Borel, Sir Ozana, Sir Brys Brysethach, Sir Mador of the Port, Lord Askil, Lord Catlon, Sir Balamorgineas, Lord Neithon, Sir Nasciens, Sir Dyvyr, Sir Elis of Climon, Sir Emeraw, Sir Eiddilig, Sir Aliduc, Sir Jurgans, King Bagdemagus, Sir Aron, Sir Dinas, Lord Llwydeu, Sir Beof, Sir Cyweddiau, Sir Gorwal of Ergyng, Lord Guitolin, King Cadwyddan, Lord Idnerth, Lord Ruduedel, Sir Cyon, Sir Cadog, Sir Petroc, King Mark, Lord Dewrath, Sir Cadwathlan, Lord Gwenwynwyn, Sir Traher, Lord Ionatas, Sir Arnold, Lord Balien, Lord Wigen, Sir Argal, Sir Kegein the son of Eluath, Sir Grimarc the son of Kinmarc, Sir Guitard, Sir Margoitt, Lord Dunwale the son of Apri, Sir Aedlein of Cledauk, Sir Aikan, Sir Clofard, Sir Madoc, Sir Gerin, Sir Elidur Pen Llarcan, Lord Gonwais, King Doldanim, Sir Howeldin, Sir Layer, Lord Peredur, Sir Kincar. After the knights, other warriors. Following them, druids; then, bards; then, musicians, and these, with their instruments. The King's section, next, will be forward of the king. First, King Ermid, Lord Geraint, Prince Dweyl and family. Next, Lord Brochwael and family, and then, Lord Brychan and family. The next, King Glywys, Lord Oswy, Sir Illtyd, King Kyngen, King Tewrig, Lord Do, Lord Kyner, King Howel. And, on his horse, will come King Arthur. So. Let us celebrate. Let us honour our king. Hail King Arthur."

There was a thundering reply. "Hail King Arthur."

There was a rush to get out on the road. King Arthur took his time. He walked sedately with King Howel, Lord Geraint, King Ermid and Prince Dweyl. They were followed by the princes: Iestin, Kyngar, Selyn and Cador; by Sir Berth and Sir Cyndrwyn and Sir Custans son of Dweyl. King Arthur found his horse, finely fixed for the ceremony, outside the gate. Mounted, he had a view of hillsides. Overnight, they had become filled with cities of tents. And with the tents were the horses and wains. Near the gate, a great number of ladies in their bright clothes, and many more ladies who had their lines stretching on down along the road.

Word came back, "We are ready for the horns to announce the march."

There was a blare from the horns.

Slowly the march moved: The sun shown on the motion of bright colours. The march moved on the road that ran through fields filled with crowds of people who had come to see the king who would take the land's throne.

The march moved forward, the pennants blew in the May breeze. The sun shown on golden crowns.

At the entrance to the great hall King Arthur dismounted. He walked up the isle between rows of kings, lords and knights, each dressed in certainly that which was his best. The king walked down the great hall to the marvelously made area where the throne was. Behind the throne, dressed in a gown covered with sacred symbols and holding, which was fixed on the head of a spear, the head of the stag which King Arthur himself had slain. And, five to the left, five to the right, King Arthur's staff, standing stiff and stour in their ermine trimmed robes of sky blue.

King Arthur, by the four castle druids, was fitted into the royal robe of the Pendragons. He took his seat on the throne. There was a blare from the horns. Druid Dubric handed the head of the stag to Druid Bedwini, picked up the crown. To the right of Druid Dubric was Prince Anladd, and on his right, Prince Erb. To the left were King Kyngen, Sir Tugdual and Sir Nevyn. Right and left of these were other members of King Arthur's family. King Glywys, at the far right of the line in the throne room.

Druid Dubric held the crown high in the air over the head of King Arthur. He spoke:

"Under the direction of Lord Oak, who was favoured by King Uther, the father of King Arthur, and who, in turn, gave support to King Uther. Under the direction of Lord Apple, who rules the mysterious realm where lives King Arthur's mother, the lovely Igerne. And this under the great Apollo, who is even now blessing the sacred burial ground with his presence, as is his custom, once every nineteen years. And, by the authority of Mother Earth, a stone hath risen, a stone that containeth within it a sword, and on that stone were letters of gold which declareth that whoso pulleth the sword out of the stone is of right the King of the land. King Arthur, son of King Uther, hath accomplished that requirement; and so, with the crown which is rightfully his, I crown him King."

"Hail Arthur our King," was the great shout.

There was a blare of horns. The company of men retired to tables in the great hall. The ladies retired to the ladies' hall. King Arthur went up to his rooms, dressed in light, handsome clothes, but with his crown on his head, went down to his place at the table, where, shortly, there was food set before him.

"How is castle security?" King Arthur asked Lord Geraint.

"I have sent the scouts back out."

"I was certain of it," said King Arthur. "We will soon have the whole land functioning as a single body."

King Arthur retired to his rooms, sat in his chair, watched, through the window, the white clouds, the silvery waters which wound their way up through the hills. Sir Lucan was at the entrance.

"Will you see Lady and Lord Kyner, Sire?"

"I will."

"Good to have you here. Please be seated," said King Arthur.

"King Arthur, you were impressive," said Lord Kyner.

Lady Kyner said, "It must have been tiring for you."

"Not at all," said King Arthur, "I was the one on the horse."

"You might find that being king is much like that: that there is not that much that really needs doing. Some, that really needs not doing," said Lord Kyner.

"Very likely," said King Arthur.

"Kay has been very busy," said Lord Kyner.

"Glad to hear it," said King Arthur.

The three of them spoke of the little events which were part of the process of living. There was a blare from the horns. The three walked to the marble stairs, walked down to the great hall, to where food was being brought in to the long table. All there seemed to get joy from having King Arthur at the head of the table. Up and down the table there was eating, drinking, laughing. King Arthur took time with his food and drink. People were up and down along the table. Harpers played throughout the eating and drinking.

King Arthur went up to his rooms. He was soon asleep.

King Arthur woke early, washed, dressed for the day. The day was starting warm and clear. Clouds to the east and southeast were bright rose. The sky filled with light. There were the blaring horns. King Arthur put on his crown, went to the marble stairs.

"Hail His Majesty, the King."

"Be seated. A good morning to all. Tomorrow I will hear petitions from those who wish to speak. Now let us enjoy breakfast."

King Arthur listened to the conversations at the tables. Scraps of some of these he could understand. Just that he was there seemed to be some cause of joy. The king, after he had dined, returned to his rooms, sat in his chair by the window. Sir Lucan was at the entrance.

"Your Majesty."

"Sir Lucan, do enter. – What reports do you get concerning the ceremony?"

"Your Majesty, many were overwhelmed with the grandeur of it. We of your staff, I must say, have had more praises than we have deserved, partly due to the magic of the tailors. And the arch druid with the head of the stag was startling to behold. And many have remarked on how magnificent was King Howel. Some said, except for yourself, he was the lord who was the most grand. And the masses held their breath to see the crown placed on your head."

"Good to have had it go so well." said the king.

"All seem quite content. And many ladies are now in the gardens, or on the meads, or by shaded, fish filled brooks, with the knights and other young men," said Sir Lucan.

"Another thing, Sir Lucan. Tomorrow, after the noon meal, in the time I have set for hearing petitions, I wish to have my advisors behind my throne: Lord Baldwin, Lord Caradoc, Sir Ulfin, Sir Brastias, Sir Bedivere, Lord Clydno, Lord Gornemant and Sir Naram. And, Sir Lucan, have Sir Kay come up."

"I will, Sire."

Sir Lucan left the room. King Arthur waited.

"King Arthur, you wish to see me?"

"Come in, Sir Kay. I do. Tomorrow, after the noon meal, I will be hearing petitions. I want to discuss how the event should be conducted."

Sir Kay and the king conversed about that, then discussed other things.

"Then, let me ready myself for the mid day meal," said the king.

Sir Kay made his exit. The king washed, made his toilet. The horns were blaring. King Arthur went down the marble stairway. Lord Geraint came up.

"Your Majesty, I have a scout report: A body of men headed toward Caer Leon and the flags displayed are those of five kings: King Lot, King Nentres, King Cradelment, King Clarence and King Urien."

"I am pleased that they have made this journey to honour my crowning. I will have Lord Clydno, Lord Gornemant and Lord Baldwin go welcome them, and I will send them gifts. Lord Geraint, you select a fine gift for each of the five."

King Arthur went to his lunch.

"Hail His Majesty, King Arthur," was the loud cheer.

"Be seated," said the king.

The king ate lunch, returned to his rooms. He rang for Sir Lucan. Sir Lucan was promptly present.

"Sir Lucan, I would see Lord Gornemant, Lord Baldwin, Lord Clydno, and Sir Brastias."

"Yes, Sire."

The king sat and waited. The four appeared.

"Your majesty," said Lord Gornemant.

"Yes, come forward. Lords, we have five kings on the way. To show my appreciation for their visit, I am having you welcome them and give them gifts, ones which Lord Geraint will select."

"It will be done, Sire," said Lord Gornemant.

The lords made their exit. King Arthur sat and waited for the return of the lords. The sunlight fell in bright patches across the stone floor.

Merlin entered the room.

"Sire, your welcoming lords have returned and the message they

151

bring is not good."

"I see."

The three lords were at the entrance.

"Your Majesty," said Lord Gornemant."

"Do come in."

"Sire, we have rude replies to report," said Lord Gornemant.

"How so?"

"We rode to where the five kings were riding forward. Said I, 'Greetings, King Arthur bids you welcome. And to show his appreciation, he has gifts for you.' Then King Nentres it was, said, 'We do not come here to receive gifts.' Said King Clarence, 'But to give gifts.' Said King Cradelment, 'Indeed, to give gifts. Of hard blows.' King Urien said, 'One, the gift of a sword between the head and the shoulders.' Said King Lot, 'I'll accept no gift from a beardless boy.' We turned our horses around, returned to the castle."

"There is a commitment to make those kings suffer for their brash statements," said King Arthur.

"I will have a word with those kings," said Merlin.

He and King Arthur went to the castle gate. Out front were the five kings demanding the surrender of the castle. More and more warriors of the five kings were coming up the hill and spreading around the castle.

Merlin, in his cloak and hood, rode out on his black horse, rode up to King Lot.

"King Lot, you five kings in a war with King Arthur can not come out a winner. King Arthur is the son of King Uther and Igerne, as I know because I was there. My advice, recognize Arthur as King, meet with him, work out any concerns."

"We do not need advice from a raggedy dream reader," said King Lot.

"From a prattling, stick throwing juggler," said King Nentres.

"If you are wise, as some declare you to be, you will be gone quickly," said King Lot.

Merlin sat and gave King Lot a hard look. A cloud of dust swirled off the ground and blew into King Lot's face. Merlin looked at King Nentres. King Nentres' horse bucked and King Nentres fell.

"Be gone," shouted King Lot.

Merlin turned his horse, returned to the castle and the castle gate shut.

There was confusion inside the castle as knights and lords had not organized into fighting units. At the table, King Arthur, his staff, and the lords and kings discussed battle plans. There was a blare of horns. The evening meal was served. Still men talked of the coming battle. One problem: the great number of warriors from the five kingdoms. After dark, a number of knights and warriors came into the castle to give heir service to King Arthur, which the confusion outside the castle had permitted. One of the knights who had been one of Lots sat at the long table not too far from King Arthur. The knight spoke.

"A number of us thought it foolish to go against the wise Merlin who has predicted so many things."

King Arthur went to his rooms. Then Merlin was there.

"We must attack them," said King Arthur, "or, 1 would ever after look like a king who could be trapped."

"Of course," said Merlin.

Merlin went out. The king went to his bed.

Day came. King Arthur, up, dressed for the ride on his horse. There was the blare of the horns. The king went down the stairs, went to his place at the table. The shout went up:

"Hail His majesty, King Arthur."

"Be seated. Today, after we eat, we will dress for battle."

King Arthur ate his breakfast, went to his rooms. Sir Lucan and Sir Brys entered with battle gear, helped the king into it. King Arthur went down the stairs. The horses were being brought into the courtyard. King Arthur's horse was brought up. He mounted. Merlin rode to where the king was. He said:

"King Arthur, use the sword to which you are accustomed until you feel you should show something different; should startle the enemy. It is then, draw you new sword."

In the confusion, Merlin rode over by the gate. He held the dragon pennant.

"Throw open the gate," said Merlin.

"They are not ready," said the porter.

Merlin grabbed the ropes from the porter, flung open the gate, rode furiously forward, the dragon flying above him, King Arthur and his warriors riding out to catch up with the flying pennant. In front of Merlin horses threw their riders and there was confusion. King Arthur set an example for his knights to follow. With the sword with which he had spent hours in practice, he slew knight after knight. The five kings were caught completely off guard. They fell back before the experienced warriors of King Arthur. Then did King Arthur change the old sword for the new. The raised sword picked up the early sunlight so that it seemed to shoot off fire. King Arthur swung it at the knights who were backing away. Then the knights in front of him were fleeing. The knights of the five kings were fleeing into the trees; then, down the road and away from Caer Leon. Merlin, on the road in front, blocked King Arthur's way.

"Enough," said Merlin.

Sir Kay came up.

"The wounded shall be taken into the castle," said King Arthur. "And have Lord Geraint take charge of those who are dead."

King Arthur rode his horse back to the castle gate, rode it into the courtyard, dismounted, and a groom took his horse. The king went into the great hall, up the stairs to his rooms. He washed, changed clothes.

There were the blaring horns. King Arthur walked down the stairs, went to his table.

"Hail King Arthur."

Up and down the table there were blood soaked bandages, but few missing places:

"They were not ready to fight. That is King Lot and those," said King Howel.

"The bad thing is," said King Ermid, "that they should have been with us protecting against the Vikings."

"And do not think words of their poor show will not get to Viking ears," said Lord Geraint.

"They will need to get with us," said King Arthur.

King Arthur ate, returned to his rooms, cleaned his arms. He put on his crown, went down the stairs, went back to where the throne was. He put himself on the throne. Most were thinking about the clean up after the battle. King Arthur was bowed to by people as they passed by him as if he was where he was expected to be.

The horns were blaring. King Arthur went in and took his place at the table.

"Be seated," said the king.

It was a quiet meal in respect for the dead. A harper was playing and he played, he or another, through the evening. But it was still early when King Arthur retired to his rooms.

King Arthur woke. The day had come in brightly. There were the blaring horns. The king washed, dressed, went down to breakfast.

"Hail His Majesty, King Arthur."

"Be seated. – Today, after the noon meal, I will be again in the throne room. Tomorrow, early, I plan to depart from Caer Leon with much appreciation to the staff at the castle and especially to Lord Geraint. Let us eat."

Breakfast over, the king went to his rooms. He sat and rested. Sir Lucan appeared at the entrance.

"Sire, Lady and Lord Kyner." "Have them come in."

The king rose and greeted the lord and lady.

Lord Kyner said, "My lady and I are, this hour, returning to Bonmaison. We were pleased with the way you and Kay received King Lot. I am certain King Uther could not have been more impressive. Have a happy trip back to Caer Went."

"Thankyou, and you enjoy your trip back to the castle. And I hope you will come often to where I am."

The lord and lady departed. Sir Lucan was at the entrance.

"Sire, King Howel."

"By all means, have him in."

"Uncle King Arthur, I have my crew on the ship. I have enjoyed the ceremony and thank you for the hospitality. If you have a need, we are right over the water."

"Thankyou, King Howel, it has been nice to have you."

King Howel made his exit.

King Arthur sat, watched, from his window, the bending tops of the trees which were part of the woodland which circled the castle. The wind sighed high overhead through the castle turrets. The many flags over the castle flapped in the wind. White and grey clouds covered the sky. They passed slowly over. There was the blare from the horns. King Arthur got his clothes together, went to the stairs, went down to

155

the great hall.

"Hail His Majesty, King Arthur."

"Be seated," said the king.

King Arthur ate his lunch. He left the table, went up to his rooms, saw to his toilet needs, put on his robe. He went to the throne room, sat on the throne. Druid Dubric came to the throne, said:

"Sire, would you favour the renewal of a grant made by King Brithgon? It is this."

King Arthur put his mark on it.

"Thankyou, Sire. And this, made by King Cynfyn, which is an agreement between King Cynfyn and King Gwylffer, son of King Gurgon."

King Arthur put his mark on it.

"Thankyou Sire."

Lord Brochwael and Druid Comereg entered the throne room.

"Sire," said Lord Brochwael, "I have made a grant to Druid Comereg. We would appreciate your mark on it, if you favour it."

King Arthur put his mark on it.

"And there is space for witness," said Lord Brochwael, "Druid Dubric?"

The druid signed.

"Lord Baldwin?"

The lord signed.

"Lord Caradoc?"

The lord signed. Lord Gornemant signed; then, Lord Clydno. Cyngen, who had part in the agreement, signed it also.

Many stopped at the area where the throne was, where King Arthur sat on the throne, but this was to bow, admire and move on. It was a hot day. Many were anxious to move on out to the parks, to be together among the flowers.

"I believe those who have desired to do so, have seen me here. I suggest we enjoy our parks," said King Arthur.

The lords and knights of his staff bowed and left the throne room. King Arthur went up the stairs to his rooms, changed into what seemed to him a handsome summer garment. He put his crown off, went down the stairs, went out the gate of the castle, turned onto the left path, then walked down into the blooming gardens. Many young were in the gardens laughing and talking. These, King Arthur avoided. He walked down into the clean green woods, walked down to a brook. He followed the brook until, with a gurgling, it fell into a pool.

King Arthur watched the fish swimming in and out of shadows from the branches of hanging shrubs. He walked down the brook, walked around boulders, walked up through the trees to a garden. He walked around the castle wall to the gate. There was the blare of the horns.

The king went to his rooms, changed clothes, fitted the crown on his head, went down to the great hall.

"Hail His Majesty, King Arthur."

"Be seated," said the king.

The harpers played while the company, while they ate, laughed and talked.

King Arthur returned to his rooms, got things ready for the morning ride. It had been a tiring day.

There was the blare of the horns. King Arthur dressed for the road. He took the marble stairs to the great hall.

"Hail His Majesty, King Arthur."

"Be seated," said the king.

He hurried with his breakfast, took the stairs back to his rooms. There were, at his entrance, two squires with Sir Lucan.

"Your Majesty, Sir Kay sent us."

"Very good. These here go to my horse."

Sir Brys was at the entrance.

"Your Majesty, it has been splendid having you. Have an enjoyable trip."

"Thankyou, Sir Brys, and I hope all will be doing well here."

The king went to the stairs, went down and to the gate where his horse was waiting. Three pennants flying, King Arthur called for the march to move forward. The king, near the front of the march, rode down the grade, up the river valley. He rode through the morning. At noon, the company dismounted to eat the packed lunch and do what their toilet needs were. King Arthur found a convenient clump of bushes; then, ate what had been provided for lunch.

The company saddled up and set out for a place on the river above Tewkesbury, where there was a crossing. The way took them then past Gloucester, then into a deep woods. Then, King Arthur observed that it was Merlin who was riding beside him. They rode past the cut off to Caer Went.

"We are not going to Caer Went," said Merlin.

They rode on.

"We are not in Somerset now," said Merlin. "Nor are we in Dorset, but are indeed in Lyonesse. You do not know of it? You will know much of Lyonesse, and of Camelot, and we are going thitherward."

The line of horsemen moved on. There was the clump and crackle of the hooves of horses. King Arthur rode through quiet darkness under the trees.

King Arthur rode out of the trees. The path came out under a late afternoon sky. Before King Arthur were rounded hills; some, woods covered; and wide, flower filled meadows. Here and there, groups of fine looking horses grazed. The road dipped into a little valley, crossed a small brook, rose onto a low hill and there, not too far in front of them was, on a rise, a marvelous palace. The setting sun made its many spires and towers glisten. The sun sank behind a wooded hill.

"That is Camelot. Your grandfather built it for you," said Merlin.

King Arthur gazed at the marvelous structure as he rode forward. Twisting turrets swept out of towers.

"It is very beautiful," said King Arthur as he rode forward.

"Is it not a bit arrogant to have a place like that?" the king suggested.

The road curved around a hill, – curved around another. King Arthur watched Camelot, which was ahead of him.

"And we will find Camelot staffed. There are cooks in the kitchen, grooms in the stable," said Merlin.

King Arthur said, "That is welcome news. Especially the part about cooks in the kitchen."

It was indeed dark when the castle war reached. King Arthur and the knights and ladies of his company dismounted in a grand court yard. They were told that dinner was ready to put on the tables.

King Arthur hurried up curving marble stairs behind the nicely dressed castleman.

"Your Majesty, these rooms have been reserved for you," said the castleman.

They walked on a balcony with rails, which looked as if they were made of giant snowflakes, to fine spacious rooms. The castleman bowed and left. King Arthur washed, dressed in fine clothes which he found in the room. He went to the stairs, down to the dining area where he found long tables set with food. All stood when he entered.

"Be seated," said the king.

The king, the other men at the table, with relish ate the food which was presented. And it was not late when King Arthur retired to his rooms. Then Merlin was there.

"Ban and Bors were not at the coronation," said Merlin.

"I thought nothing of it. They are under no obligation to me."

"However, their status should have caused them to wish to be at an event as important as your crowning. I suspect they are having problems which keep them at home. What I advise is that you send envoys who, in your name, will agree to aid them, with the understanding that they, in return, will support you now, when you are getting the land lined up and in order."

"I hope, when he has the need, I will have the power to be of help."

"You can be certain of that. The chief trouble for the Kings, Ban and Bors, has been King Claudas. And King Claudas has a great fear of wizards. Not long ago, he put one o f his knights, a Vocontian, to death for carrying, on his person, a serpent egg, an object which marked the knight as a wizard. As I will be with you, King Claudas will be so frightened he will be worthless as a battle leader."

Merlin made his exit.

King Arthur rang the bell. Sir Lucan was at the entrance.

"Sir Lucan, I request the presence of Sir Brastias and Sir Ulfin."

"Yes, Your Majesty."

In short order, Sir Brastias and Sir Ulfin were at the entrance.

"Your Majesty?" said Sir Ulfin.

"Enter in. Sir Ulfin, Sir Brastias, in the morning, I want you to go to King Ban in Benwick. Inform him that if he and King Bors will support me while I am putting an order to my lands, I will give him aid if at some future time he should have a wish for it."

"Yes, Your Majesty," said the knights.

"Then have a good rest tonight."

The two knights bowed and made their exit.

King Arthur retired for the night.

King Arthur woke. He got up, made his toilet necessities, washed and dressed. He went to his windows, looked out on green hills and patches of woodland. There were bells ringing. Sir Lucan was at the entrance.

"Your majesty, the bells are to announce breakfast."

"Very good. Thankyou, Sir Lucan."

King Arthur put on his crown, went down the stairway, took his place at the table.

"Hail King Arthur."

"Be seated." said the king.

King Arthur enjoyed his breakfast. When he returned to his rooms, Merlin was there.

"King Arthur, I have a tale to relate. At your birth you were visited by seven blue mist elves. And these each brought a gift. The first brought the dazzlingly white helm, which is called Goswhit. The second brought the shield, Prydwen. And this has the peculiarity that it can be made to become a ship, which can sail on oceans which you know of, and, also, oceans which you know not. And the third brought the spear. It was made in Arianrhod's castle by Griffin, who is also called Gofan. And it has the name, Rhongomyniad. However, it is usually called Ron. The fourth elf gave the burnie and this was made by Witeze, who is the son of Weland. And he made it in the smithy which is not far from where your father slew a dragon, and where the dragon's blood flowed out, there it is yet void of vegetation. The fifth elf gave the dagger, Whitehaft. The sixth elf gave a white mantle which had the name of Gwenn, and it had this peculiarity that it would hold no colour but its own. It was always pure white. And the seventh elf brought a square blue sheet, a gold sun in each corner, and this, from Avalon."

Merlin made his exit. King Arthur looked into the magical compartment. He spent time in making himself familiar with each marvelous item.

The bell was ringing: the noontime meal. King Arthur returned each item to its place.

King Arthur put on his crown, went down the stairway, took his place at the table.

The day passed. Days passed. King Arthur, on walking into the great hall, from his after lunch walk, was met by Sir Lucan.

"Sire, a couple of gentlemen from the court of King Ban are in the hall."

"Sir Lucan, have them, into the reception room."

King Arthur walked up to his room, dressed in formal clothes, went to the reception room, sat on his throne. Sir Lucan, two knights, walked up.

"Your Majesty, Sir Lionses and Sir Phariance."

"Nice to see you. What news have you?"

"Your Majesty, I am Sir Lionses. Sir Brastias and Sir Ulfin, after a short delay along the road, reached us with the welcome offer."

"Tell me about the short delay," said the king.

"As I said, the two knights came to some trouble: this, in the form of eight knights whom Sir Ulfin and Sir Brastias supposed were loyal to King Claudias. Three of these they quickly slew and the other five fled. But your knights got to Benwick in good order, and as fortune would have it, King Bors was at that time visiting Benwick. The two kings sent us to say they would fit out ships and bring a force here shortly."

"That is indeed good news," said King Arthur.

Life in Camelot fell into routines. Camelot was a fine palace to live in and it provided much pleasure. In the evenings, fine clothes were worn at the tables and there were meetings and entertainments with the brightly dressed ladies. The gardens and patches of woodland were much employed.

It came the middle of July, a great force of knights was seen on the road coming toward Camelot. It was seen that the force was that of Ban, and of Bors, coming from Benwick and from Gannes. King Arthur went to his quarters, dressed in fine garments, went to the reception room. The force of Ban and Bors' was soon at the palace; Ban and Bors, taken to the presence of the king.

King Arthur was delighted with having with him that great number of knights from Gaul and Benwick.

"By all means, let us see them," said the king.

He, with King Ban and King Bors, went through the palace hall, out to the courtyard, gazed upon the lines of stout knights and each knight, on a fine horse.

"At Camelot, we will have a grand tourney at the Lammas festival, then it will be seen how many fine horsemen we have to put on the field," said King Arthur.

King Arthur had King Ban and King Bors up to his quarters.

"I have never seen a more marvelous palace," said King Bors.

King Bors and King Ban discussed their situations with King Arthur. King Arthur rang for Sir Lucan, had Sir Lucan show King Ban and King Bors their quarters. King Arthur took the time to catch some rest.

The bells were ringing for the evening meal. King Arthur walked down to the great hall, took his place at the table. King Bors was on his right, King Ban, on his left.

"Be seated," said King Arthur. "In honour of the coming of King Ban and King Bors, and of the fine knights which they have with them, there will be a tourney on Lammas. The knights of Camelot can show our distinguished guests how good we can look on our horses. Let us eat."

Harpers played during the meal and into the evening. The day passed. On the next morning, constructions and decorations were worked on in the lower field where the tourney was to be held.

In short order, the field looked most festive. King Arthur looked at it and was satisfied.

It was two days before August first, many women were walking and talking in the gardens, and in the bordering woods, with handsome knights. King Arthur put on fine, but casual, comfortable clothes, went down and out into the garden. He kept away from the groups of knights and ladies so as not to be recognized. He slipped into the woods, walked down through the trees, down a grade to a brook. He followed the brook as it wound its way around pale boulders. Over some rocks the brook fell into a pool. There by the fall was a young woman. She turned and smiled at him.

"Hi," said King Arthur.

"Hi," said the young woman.

The two stood together for a bit.

"Did your lady friend run off?" the woman asked. Or is it that you prefer Mother Nature to human company?"

"He looked at her. She was blond with very blue eyes. A teasing smile flitted across her face.

"No. It is very complicated."

They stood together for a time.

"My time is also complicated. My time here. I was expecting my lord. But he had a change in plans. So.

The two stood together and watched the water.

Said the woman, "I was about to take a cooling dip in the water. Do you take a dare?"

"Seldom it is I do not."

The two took off their clothes, stepped into the cool water below the fall. They played together in the water. They lay back on the bank, took pleasure in the loving movements of their bodies. They copulated: lay together.

"I am hoping this can be ever our secret. For if my lord got wind of this; likely, I would need to learn how to die bravely. I will tell you who I am and you likely will understand. I am Margawse."

"It is a pretty name."

"But it has no meaning for you?"

"No, but our time together will be a gem of breath taking beauty held forever in my most secret place. We will be together there."

"That is beautiful. And that you will hold us always together gives me the strength now to part. We should be gone from out beautiful meeting place."

King Arthur gave Margawse a parting embrace, dressed, walked up through the woods, through the gardens, around to the front and joined the group going in as the bells were announcing super. King Arthur went up to his rooms, washed and changed clothes. With his crown on his head, he went down to the great hall, to his place at the table.

"Hail, His Majesty, King Arthur."

"Be seated."

Three fine harpers added to the lively conversation. And there was conversation about the tourney and this included speculations as to what knights were expected to do well.

Said King Arthur to King Ban, "Many of our knights are from small castles and from farms and will not have had the training in tourney skills."

"It takes practice," said King Ban.

"What I have in mind is to take our force to London," said King Arthur. "It has a strong castle. And we can set up our rule there. And so, gain in strength."

It was not late when King Arthur retired to his rooms. He thought about his plans.

King Arthur was up early. He washed, dressed, and was quite ready for the bells which announced breakfast. He went down the stairs which curved past marvelous flying arches. He went to his place at the table.

"Hail, His Majesty, King Arthur."

"Be seated."

Many of those at the table were wearing bright clothes. The men ate quickly. King Arthur ate, then with King Ban and King Bors, went out and around to see the constructions on the lower field. A number of knights and ladies came down to see what was going on.

From there, the three kings went up to the gardens and observed the numbers of knights and ladies who were enjoying the warm, bright morning.

Many knights were busy getting equipment in shape for the festivities. King Arthur was, by Sir Lucan, told about the events of the next day. And the day passed.

At breakfast, the next day, there was an air of excitement. Breakfast was soon over and many rushed from the palace to take part in the parade, or for good places from which they could observe.

There was a blare of melody from a row of brightly polished horns. King Arthur, looking grand in his royal robes, mounted the horse which was behind the horses of King Bors and King Ban. Horsemen with pennants leading the way, the horsemen marched to the lower field. The stands were filled and many horsemen were coming in from distant places. Knights in protective gear lined up for jousting. King Arthur took his place in the ornate shelter. Lords and kings were in front of him, and in front of these, the judges.

In jousting, the less skillful were soon on the sidelines. Sir Kay was one of these. For Camelot, Lord Caradoc and Lord Gornemant were yet to be defeated. For Benwick, Sir Ladinas and Sir Gracian were two of the best. For Gannes, Sir Placidas was gaining praise. The first judge of the tourney was Lord Gwenbaus of Benwick. There were some excellent matches. Then, as the tourney was getting a bit chaotic, King Arthur called a lunch time out. After the noon meal, King Arthur again went to his royal seat. The jousting began again.

The afternoon of the tourney went much like the morning. Sir Bedivere won some important contests. Then, center stage matches between winners became much watched, and the last match between Sir Caradoc and Sir Placidas got a wave of noisy cheers. Sir Caradoc became festival champion and King Arthur was given a gold pendant to present to Sir Caradoc, Gems were then given to Sir Placidas, Sir Gracian, Sir Ladinas, Sir Bleoberis, Sir Aliduc and Sir Gornemant Lord Ricca.

King Arthur had his horse brought up along with those of King Ban and King Bors. The three kings rode to the entrance of the palace. King Arthur dismounted, went to his quarters. The bells rang announcing the evening meal.

On the second day after the tourney, King Arthur went down the stairway to his evening meal.

"Hail His Majesty, King Arthur."

"Be seated. Day after tomorrow, in the morning, first thing, we, you and I, will ride to London. Establish law and order."

While King Arthur ate, there was conversation up and down the tables which seemed, much of it, about the move to London. Most went to bed early. Then, morning.

Breakfast eaten, the knights left the table and some went to see to their horses; some, to get ready what they would wear, or take, on their ride to London. King Arthur went to his quarters and lined up what he would wear, then fixed his pack with things he might find useful to have with him. The day passed.

The day of the trip arrived. King Arthur was up, dressed in his travel clothes; then, set out what the squire was to take. The bells were ringing. The king went down to breakfast.

"Hail His Majesty, King Arthur."

"Be seated."

His breakfast quickly eaten, King Arthur went up the stairs, got himself ready for the journey.

King Arthur went down the stairs, through the hall and out to where his horse was waiting. Horses of Camelot were extended on up the road.

"Have Sir Kay join me here," said the king.

"Who have you with me at the head of the march?" the king asked.

"Sir Aldolf and Sir Segurant," said Sir Kay.

"Very good."

King Arthur rode up the road to the head of the column. Sir Kay rode up.

"King Arthur, we have the column ready to move out."

"Move forward," said King Arthur.

"Move forward," said Sir Kay and the order was repeated up and down the column.

The column moved down the road, moved toward London.

The warriors of Camelot were on the road making good time, and behind them, the companies from Benwick and from Gannes.

King Arthur, following Sir Segurant and Sir Aldolf, rode easily under the sunny sky. There was a slight breeze. On either side were meadows, groves of trees and fields of grain. A black horse moved up to be beside the horse of King Arthur. It was Merlin.

"That forest which, on the right, you see is Bedegraine. And in it are the war bands of eleven kings. They had come to take Bedegraine Castle, but when you were observed on the road, they decided instead, to ambush and destroy you. They know not of Kings Ban and Bors. What you should do, have Kay go back, tell those kings to get off the road, conceal their force in the edge of the forest. Then you set up and organize this side of the brook, which you will come to. The force of the kings is waiting for you, set up on the other side," said Merlin.

"Then, would you inform Sir Kay?"

Merlin rode off.

King Arthur rode forward. He slowed his pace, as the off road travel of King Ban and King Bors would take more time. First on the right, then on both sides, there was forest. King Arthur rode forward with caution. Ahead was a good sized brook. King Arthur called a halt. He called for a camp to be set up.

"But first, arm yourselves. An attack could come at any time," said

166

the king.

The many knights made themselves busy. The area became a hum with activity. Knights set up a tent for the king. The Dragon pennant was put by it.

Merlin rode up to King Arthur's tent. He looked at the wood over the brook.

"I would attack at midnight, keep them busy. Then Benwick and Gannes attack the flank at dawn," said Merlin.

"Very good. Inform King Ban and King Bors," said King Arthur.

King Arthur's staff came to the command tent.

King Arthur explained the plan to them.

Midnight, King Arthur and his men, swords in hand, moved out on foot. The eleven kings had a watch out, so were alerted and ready. Torches were lit. There was a battle under the trees and out into the fields. King Arthur was in front of Lord Cambenet and that lord's men. He felled a number and most of these would never rise again. Sir Ulfin pressed forward and attacked Lord Cambenet and felled him. King Clarence and knights with him rushed over into the gap left by Lord Cambenet and his knights. Sir Brastias led a unit of knights over and engaged them. King Arthur's warriors were achieving wonders; however, because they were outnumbered, they were not making progress. Then, dawn: King Ban and King Bors attacked on the flank. The there was confusion among the warriors of the eleven kings. Sir Melot attacked King Lot and was slain. Sir Kay was defending the command pennant and Griflet was fighting in support of Sir Kay, and several other knights along side of Sir Kay were also defending the Dragon pennant. The knights of the eleven kings were backing up; then, retreating in disorder. King Ban slew one of the eleven kings, and that was said to be King Morganore.

A huge knight attacked King Arthur and the king slew him.

King Arthur pressed forward, moving at a fast pace. Knights were falling under the strokes of Arthur's knights and of the knights of Benwick and of Gannes. The king caught King Cradelment, felled him.

There was Merlin in front on his black horse.

"Enough. Wilt thou never have done?" he said.

The warriors stopped, astonished.

167

"King Arthur, these are your citizens. You will need them," said Merlin.

King Arthur looked back at the overturned tents and pavilions. And at the slain and wounded still on the ground.

"We will care for the wounded. Then we will have breakfast," said King Arthur.

One pavilion still standing belonged to Lady Lionors, daughter of Lord Sevain. She was a healer and King Lot had recruited her to come, with her team of maidens, to care for the wounded. King Arthur went to the pavilion to check on the quality of care. It seemed the wounded, who were being brought in, were in good hands. The king left the tent, walked back to where Sir Kay was seeing to the cooking. The king went over, sat with his staff.

"We fared not badly," said Sir Brastias. "They have at least one less king. King Ban slew Morganore."

Said Lord Baldwin, "And you wounded King Clarence, and he might be dead by now."

"Sadly, we lost Sir Melot. He did well at Lammas, in the lists," said King Arthur.

Breakfast was brought over to the king.

"And," said Lord Baldwin, "Lord Kyner slew Sir Kardens."

"We lost Sir Moris," said Sri Bedivere." But Sir Blyas and Sir Gwinas slew his slayer."

"And, Your majesty, we were, I am certain, all who saw it, impressed by the way you slew Sir Caulang. And felled King Cradelment, who even now might be out of the world of the living. His helm, at least will need the skill of the equal of Weland. Or Gofan. And good to have Sir Ulfin stop Lord Cambenet and his men. And I notice, as I look around, we are all here," said Lord Caradoc.

"And I saw," said Sir Lucan, "Lord Eustace of Benwick and Sir Pynell felled, and they might be dead."

"That would be sad," said Lord Clydno.

"Of our knights," said Lord Baldwin, "Sir Briant and Sir Bellaus looked very strong, and Sir Bleoberis."

"And who impressed you?" said King Arthur to Lord Clydno.

"Sir Morien, Sir Phariance, Sir Ladinas, Sir Lionses, Sir Aliduc. There were so many. And we, us here, set a good way for others to follow."

"You might have included your son, Sir Cynon, as among the strongest," said Sir Brastias.

"Again, who were those kings against us?" said King Arthur.

Sir Lucan ran down the list.

"Kings Lot, Urien, Nentres, Carados, Clarence, Aguisans, Idres, Lares, Belinant, Morganore, and as you know, Your Majesty, King Cradelment."

Said Sir Ulfin, "And the fact that Camelot, with some help from Benwick and Gannes, defeated eleven kings, means we could not recognize, we could not have seen, all the mighty deeds done by our knights."

"That is the big truth," said Sir Naram.

"Yes, there were a lot of knights against us," said Sir Kay, "They say even King Aguisans came with a hundred knights."

"Then that is what we should call him," said King Arthur: "I am going to do some looking at things."

King Arthur walked up to the pavilion where the wounded were being cared for. He greeted Lady Lionors, then went to see King Cradelment who was in much pain. A slash was in his skull and his right shoulder was so cut through that it seemed, his right hand would never hold another thing.

"It pains me to see you so injured," said King Arthur.

"You are a worthy king. It was foolish of us to challenge it," said King Cradelment.

"We will be what help we can to give you comfort," said King Arthur.

King Arthur walked up and down past the rows of wounded. He walked out, down among bushes in a gully. He moved his bowls, returned to the command tent. Sir Aldolf and Sir Segurant the Brown were there. Sir Segurant was saying:

"We had the feeling King Uther was back. We set our strong men up front: Sir Mariet, Sir Emeraw, Sir Morien of Maiden Castle, Sir Gwinas of Bloi, Sir Flanned, Sir Eidiol, Sir Blois of Case, Sir Castlein, Sir Annecains, Sir Ladinas: all good men. I had them right up there. The unfortunate Sir Lardans was one whom we slew."

"Bad luck, get in your way," said Sir Kay.

"Sir Kay, have litters made, the wounded carried to the castle. Have the dead buried. And put out scouts," said King Arthur.

Sir Kay got his details going. He went to the kitchen tent. Squires came back from the castle. They trotted up on their horses with more shovels.

It was mid day. A squire brought lunch to King Arthur. Squires brought lunches to the command tent. Knights lined up for lunch, formed circles at the edge of the woods.

King Arthur called for his horse. He mounted and rode to the pavilion for the wounded. The last of the wounded were being put on litters. Lady Lionors, in clothes covered with blood, looked tired, as did all the ladies who were with her. But Lady Lionors seemed most tired of all. The ladies were getting ready for the walk to the castle.

"If you will, I will take you to the castle," said King Arthur.

"That would be most kind," said Lady Lionors.

The king lifted the beautiful lady to a place in front of him on the horse. They rode through the woods following a path near the flowing brook.

"There is a pool here where we could wash, if you would favour it," said the lady.

"That seems a wise way," said the king.

The king rode down to the brook, helped the lady from the horse. The two walked down to the brook, by a pool, took off their clothes by the pool, washed them and hung them on the limbs of small trees. They then took pleasure in being naked together. They copulated.

Their clothes somewhat dry, King Arthur and Lady Lionors mounted and rode on up the way to the castle. Knights of the castle came to welcome them. King Arthur handed his horse to a groom, entered the castle hall. Lord Sevain walked up, bowed.

"Welcome, King Arthur, to Bedegraine Castle. I am Lord Sevain."

"Thankyou, Lord Sevain. We thank you and your daughter for the aid you are giving to the wounded."

"Thankyou, Your Majesty. We are pleased to have you with us."

"I am pleased to be here. And if you would, have one of my squires inform Sir Kay that I am here."

King Arthur was shown into the hall where knights were drinking ale. All stood when he entered.

The king sat with the men of the castle.

"Your Majesty, we are anxious to hear about the war."

"I can tell you we won. But I am no bard," said King Arthur.

The evening came on. The evening meal was served.

The meal eaten, King Arthur thanked Lord Sevain, called for his horse. He asked to see King Cradelment, was taken to that king, who was in much pain. King Arthur gently touched King Cradelment's smashed shoulder, his head.

"May the spirits of healing be with you," said King Arthur.

He bid farewell to Lady Lionors, left the castle, mounted his horse and went to his tent. He sent for Sir Kay.

"Sir Kay, we set out after breakfast," said the king.

The morning came. Before dawn there was much banging in the kitchen. King Arthur arose, tended to his toilet, washed in the brook. Back at his tent, a squire brought his breakfast to him. Soon, horses were being lined up along the road. Tents, including the kitchen, were dismantled and packed. King Arthur mounted up, rode to the top of the column.

"Forward ho," he said.

The road led to London. After a long ride along the road, King Arthur and his men rode up to the great castle. Lord Brochwael was at the front gate to give him welcome. Sir Kay and Sir Lucan, with the knights and squires of London Castle, were getting knights and equipment organized while King Arthur went with Lord Brochwael to the reception room.

"Your Majesty, you have met your cousin, Lord Glyddiew?"

"How are you, Lord Glyddiew?"

"And this is Lord Gorthmol."

"How are you Sir?"

"Fine thankyou, Your Majesty."

King Arthur discussed with these lords the area which came under the rule of London castle. He asked about its weak areas and its customs.

"In seven days," said King Arthur, "I shall sit on the throne, hear complaints and resolve disputes."

King Arthur's knights and the knights of King Bors and King Ban enjoyed the castle life, met and got to know the women and men of the castle. And each other. Merlin was there and he seemed to enjoy speaking to King Arthur of mysterious things which seemed to relate to the future. Merlin spoke:

"Sweet Apple Tree and a tree of Crimson hue which grow in concealment in the wood of Celidon; though sought for their fruit, it will be in vain until the fierce anguish comes from Aranwynion to the Eagle of Tywi and the wild and long haired ones are made tame."

Then he said:

"A host of flying darts, reeking, will be the gory plain. A host of warriors, vigourous and active will they be. A host, when wounds will be given. A host, when flights will take place. A host, when they will return to the combat."

And he said:

"Wandesborough will attacked, which will keep King Lot busy for a long time."

"That is information worth hearing," said King Arthur.

Merlin said:

"In the field of Urien a bull shall be burned. The mouth of the Usk shall be wet with drying blood. There shall come a beneficent maiden to the City of the Wood. The Petri Mountains shall totter."

Five days had passed when a messenger arrived. He was taken to King Arthur, King Ban, King Bors and to Lord Brochwael, to whom the message was intended. The messenger bowed to the king.

"Your Majesty, a great force under King Saras has attacked your cousin, King Dweyl. We have sent to Devon for Lord Geraint, and for Prince Ermid, it pains us to trouble you."

"It would pain me more if you did not," said King Arthur. "Return and say we will heed the call."

The messenger departed.

"I and my command are at your service, King Arthur," said Lord Brochwael. "We are in this together."

"We will depart after the noon meal," said King Arthur, "Lord, have my staff come quickly: Sir Naram, Lord Caradoc, Sir Brastias, Lord Baldwin, all the others, Sir Kay and Sir Lucan."

"Sirs, I have a report. King Dweyl has been attacked by King Saras."

"And likely by others, Sire. As King Dweyl is the sacred guardian of the Dog of the Parrett, the dog which guards the way to the Land of Arawn," said Lord Caradoc.

"We will leave after the noon meal."

"Sire, we need to have ready our best weapons," said Lord Baldwin.

"Sire, Lord Geraint is in Devon. The more quickly we get there, the less the chance of Lord Geraint being slain before we get there," said Lord Brochwael.

"Let us prepare. That is all," said King Arthur.

All the staff bowed and rushed to get ready.

The Kings, Lord Brochwael, the others, all bowed and rushed off. King Arthur went to his quarters, got his gear ready for the trip. He went to the table for lunch.

"Who does King Saras think he is?" said someone.

"He just thought no one was watching the barn," said another, who was down the table.

"He would have found out there are many eyes on that sacred place," said someone up the table.

King Ban said to King Arthur, "And there will be law in the land in spite of no help from those kings who attacked us."

King Arthur ate quickly, returned to his rooms, armed himself, went down the stairs, out to the horses. He found his horse, mounted, rode up the road where Lord Brochwael, mounted, waited.

After a short wait, the king shouted:

"Forward, ho."

The company moved up the road.

Said Lord Brochwael:

"King Ermid has fast horses. And Geraint. But that is a backward land to which we go."

King Arthur rode in silence. He seemed to be chasing a mysterious dog. He and his horsemen rode past the small, old castle which was on a hill near Yarnborough. They rode on. Then there were horsemen on the right. The flag of King Ermid was recognized. King Arthur called for Sir Kay.

"Line up our chief fighters. Others behind," said the king.

"Hey o," shouted the king. They swooped on the flank of a great body of Picts, who wore little but their strange armour. And their

173

strange tattoos. There was a clang of sword on shield which lasted and lasted. Lord Brochwael rode up to King Arthur. He shouted to the king:

"Geraint has raced ahead. To block the pass.

Kings Ban and Bors had their warriors fill in with King Ermid's line. King Arthur stretched his warriors on a column to the right, forming a right angle.

"Lord Geraint, open the pass," shouted King Arthur. King Arthur's horsemen charged in on the advancing enemy. King Arthur, with Lord Caurdaf, Lord Glyddiew and others, charged up to where Lord Geraint was fighting with horsemen; then, horsemen were running before him. Under Geraint was his fine white, long legged horse. Horsemen on pale horses avoided him. Geraint had pushed as far up as Tone River. King Arthur, with horsemen on death white horses, rushed up, with Lord Geraint's knights, in support of the lord. Geraint was in the lead. White stallions of the Vikings ran ahead of him, and ran ahead of where Lord Caurdaf and Lord Glyddiew the Strong slew those on the right of Lord Geraint. The shins of the white horses which retreated before those three were red with blood. Lord Geraint gave a loud shout of encouragement, while King Arthur was directing the line of battle. Then few were fighting. Then, the last of the enemy warriors fled away.

Sir Cador, in the castle at Langborth, had food quickly on the table for the able warriors. The wounded were carried to rooms, and for aid for these, messengers had gone to King Avalach.

King Arthur was tired. He had rushed like a bear on many groups of fighters. And these, he had cut down. At the table, the beef and ale was most welcome.

"King Bors," said King Arthur, "what flag was that which your warriors trampled?"

"That, King Arthur, was the flag of King Gillomaur of Eire."

"I see. And is that king now dead?"

"I believe he is wounded, King Arthur. And I believe you slew Breidav, King of the Picts."

"I can hope so."

Said Lord Cador, "The largest force against us was that of the Vikings.

King Arthur sat and ate. He spoke:

"I want the battle leaders notified. They should have their wounded cared for, and their slain, they should treat honourably. Tomorrow will be a day for honouring the slain."

King Arthur finished his dinner, had Lord Cador show him a room to which he could retire.

Then it was morning. King Arthur washed, dressed, went to breakfast.

Said Lord Cador, "Sire, I would like to have your sanction on the burial of my father and two of my brothers."

"You have that and gladly," said the king.

Breakfast finished, King Arthur and his staff joined King Ban, King Bors, Lord Brochwael, Lord Glyddiew, Sir Cador, Sir Selyn, Sir Cyndrwyn and Sir Nevyn, and they rode their horses to the head of a long column of horses. Lord Brochwael led the column slowly along the way to Langborth, to a grassy hillock. Druids were called forth, four of them. They lined up where digging was to be according to star formations. Digging was begun.

"I, Lord Brochwael, dedicate this hill to my nephews: King Ermid, Lord Geraint, Sir Kyngar, Sir Iestin, and, especially, to King Dweyl, who fulfilled the sacred mission of guarding, and of keeping sacred, this place which is special to us. Their spirits will surely add power to the guardian stars."

"Now, with the sanction of His Majesty, King Arthur, I take the liberty to give blessings to the burial of these worthy people. My brothers had a life of knowing their duty and of doing their duty, and they did it well. Now as a loyal son should, I will honour my father. And he is a man well worthy of honour. My father is a master of fast ships and fast horses. On his fleet, long shanked horse, accompanied by his sons on fast horses, as it is fitting and proper that he should have been, he raced from his Woodland of Dyvnaint, up through Devon, to swoop like an eagle on the Vikings of King Wulfila and Ossa. My father is an energetic warrior."

"With your leave, Lord Cador, and the blessing of Your Majesty, I would a word of my own," said Lord Caradoc. "One could not have had a better friend than Lord Geraint. Well I knew Lord Geraint. Kind and noble he was. He took us to his blazing campfires, sat us on seats

175

covered with white fur, served us sparkling wine. In battle, unbudging he was. May he be well remembered by the bards."

Sir Cyndrwyn stepped forward.

"I, Sir Cyndrwyn, as a duty of a son, come before you to bid farewell to my father. Duty and responsibility were important to my father. Sedate he was and not a man for excess of show, but he would present what was proper, and was a host most generous and sufficient. As a warrior, he stood firmly for what was right, and he was one of great strength. Most of all, no man can claim he was a lord lacking, in any way of honour."

King Arthur went forward.

"I dedicate this hill to these honourable lords: King Dweyl, King Ermid, Lord Geraint, Sir Iestin, Sir Kyngar. May they continue to guard it and may we remember that it is sacred."

Thank you, Your Majesty, that is most fitting," said Lord Brochwael. "Then, Your Majesty, if you will, I am certain dinner will be ready for us all."

"Forward Ho," said King Arthur.

The long line of horsemen followed King Arthur down the road of soft brown soil. It was an easy ride along the road to the castle. King Arthur, the horsemen, dismounted, went into the hall. As Lord Brochwael had indicated, there was a good meal waiting. It was a sober meal eaten with little conversation. King Arthur gave notice that next day, directly after breakfast, there would be a return to London. There were, however, a good number of wounded who would remain behind.

The next day, after breakfast, King Arthur, at the front of a column of horsemen, set off for London. In a forest, King Arthur brought the column to a halt for lunch. Lunch eaten, King Arthur mounted and led the horsemen into London.

One week passed. It was a work week: much cleaning and repairing was done and this was especially of the battle gear. In the evenings, there was time for the men to be with the ladies in the castle and around London. On the last day of the week King Bors and King Ban, after their supper, went to King Arthur's quarters.

"King Arthur," said King Bors, "it is time that we return to our own lands. There are forces which might try to take advantage of our absence. There are knights who say they would like to stay in this land and serve you. I have given them leave to do so. Providing that it meet with your approval. This would include a cousin of mine, Sir Bleoberis."

"I would be delighted."

The kings bid King Arthur good evening. King Arthur rang for Sir Lucan.

"Sir Lucan, King Bors and King Ban will be departing after breakfast. Sir Kay should know it, and that I would have a proper farewell: mounted, flags presented. And all ready which they need to take with them."

Sir Lucan went to get started on what was needed to be done. The king retired to his bed.

Next morning, breakfast was announced. King Arthur went down to the table. There was excitement in the conversation. Many knights were excited about going home. And many were excited about staying with King Arthur. There was a rush to get on the horses. Knights who were not leaving, all horsed, formed a rank in front of the castle gate, horns blew, flags and pennants were raised. The flags dipped as King Ban and Bors and King Arthur led the ride away from the castle. After a short way, King Arthur's horse stepped aside and King Arthur gave a great wave to King Ban and to King Bors, and to all the horsemen as they rode past him.

Three days passed. King Arthur went down to the evening meal. There was the usual greeting:

"Hail His Majesty, King Arthur."

"Be seated," said the king. "Tomorrow, after breakfast, my horsemen and I will ride to Caer Leon. We expect each man to be ready."

The morning came. King Arthur, Sir Segurant, Sir Aldolf, rode their horses to the head of the column. There was a somewhat confused moving and jumping around of the horses.

"Let us look like experienced horsemen," shouted King Arthur.

The horses quieted down.

"Forward ho," shouted the king.

The column moved off toward Caer Leon. The pace of the march was deliberate. A horseman, another horseman, would stop his horse, have a business behind a clump of bushes, then, ride back in a little further down the column. A lunch break was taken. The night was spent on green hilly fields. The next day, time for dinner, they came in sight of the gold roofed towers of Caer Leon, surrounded, as they were, with green trees.

"Your Majesty, there it is," said Sir Aldolf. "It is a splendid castle: baths, places for bardic and druidic presentations, waters and flowers."

There were pennants flying from the tops of the towers, King Arthur rode forward. There was a blare of welcome from the golden horns. King Arthur rode to the gate of the castle, dismounted. Lord Cador came out of the gate to greet him.

There was the turmoil of dismounting, having the horses secured, being welcomed into the castle. It was not long before King Arthur was seated at the head of a long table with a good dinner set before him.

Days passed. Up at the top of a tower King Arthur looked out at the green, wooded hills, at a peaky mountain behind them. From the hills, thin tails of smoke let him know charcoal burners were at work.

King Arthur descended from the tower, went to his rooms, rang for Sir Lucan.

"Sir Lucan, have Sir Kay see me. We will look at my lands."

"Yes, Your Majesty."

Sir Kay was soon at the door.

"Ah, Sir Kay, come in."

King Arthur motioned Sir Kay to look out the window.

"Out in the country, out there, what do you suppose is going on?"

"Celebrating harvest? Yes, it is Harvest Festival. At Bonmaison, you bet, tomorrow, yes, it would be fun to be there."

"Tomorrow, after dinner, we could ride out, see what we can find."

"That would be great."

"Then, find us clothes a good harvester might wear. We will celebrate the harvest. Go get us some clothes."

The day passed. The next day, cool, but bright and sunny, put the people in the castle in good spirits, and many were taking rides in the country. Dinner over, Sir Kay and the king dressed in the clothes of harvesters, got on two borrowed horses. Sir Kay winked at the porter and out they rode.

King Arthur and Sir Kay rode up the valley of The Usk, stopping here, delaying, there. They passed Radnor.

"Any further south we might be recognized," said Sir Kay.

"Nice to see our old places. But we will go further on," said King Arthur.

Arthur and Sir Kay passed Denbigh, came to a stone bridge over a brook on which a few ducks were swimming. They passed over the bridge on the grassy way and on to a street on which there were stones most of which were covered with mud. A few low stone buildings were on the right and on the left, a frame, barn like building and beyond this, a grassy area where the festival was being celebrated. King Arthur and Sir Kay tied their horses to hitching posts, mingled with the celebrating crowd. There were booths for food, for games, for crafts, and, on a throne made from branches of oak, the Corn Doll, and she was made of wheat sheaves. Around her throne were fruit, vegetables and nuts. From the barn like building came music.

"Who is playing?" asked Sir Kay. He and the king each took a cake.

"Why, who else, but the Ruthin players," said a man - who, like many there, was in costume.

"Who else would it be?" said another man.

"And who might you be?" asked a man.

"I am Kay."

"Good to see you, Kay. Do go peek at our musicians."

Sir Kay and King Arthur looked in at the door of the barn like building. There were a number of young men and pretty girls doing a dance to the music of three pipers. Sir Kay and King Arthur joined in. As the girls outnumbered the boys on the floor, King Arthur and Sir Kay were a welcome addition to the men on the floor. The pipers, to shouts and laughter, played one folk melody after another. A young man entered. King Arthur looked up.

"You could dance better if you did not have a crippled leg," said the young man whom the king recognized as Hueil.

King Arthur rushed at Hueil. Hueil backed out the door. King Arthur attacked him as the two went into the middle of the street. Hueil was knocked into the space in front of bright booths. Further down, away from the road, was a large block of stone. King Arthur slammed Hueil's head down on the block of stone, pulled out the dagger

179

which the Mist Elves had given and with it, cut off Hueil's head. Sir Kay had the horses there at the stone. The king and Sir Kay mounted and rode off.

King Arthur and Sir Kay crossed the brook and rode down the dirt road. After a time on the road, King Arthur took a trail which led into the wooded hills. After a time, the two of them stopped for the night.

"Fortunately, I packed sufficient food," said Sir Kay.

"I was certain you would," said King Arthur.

After a good ride through forests and over hills, the king and Sir Kay rode through the gate at Caer Leon.

King Arthur went to his rooms, washed, dressed, and was quite ready when the horns announced the evening meal. He went down the handsome marble stairs.

"Hail His Majesty, King Arthur."

King Arthur took his seat.

"Tomorrow, after breakfast; I, with my company, will go to Camelot," said the king.

The meal ended except for the continuing of the drinking of ale and the listening to the harpers. The king, along with many others, cut this short and went to his rooms and prepared his belongings for the ride to Camelot. Then, his bed was welcome.

Morning came, King Arthur was up early. He got ready his belongings, washed. There were the horns. The king went down the stairs.

"Hail His Majesty, King Arthur."

"Be seated. I have one announcement, other than to thank Lord Cador for a grand stay here. It is this: There will be a tournament at Samhain. And, that is not long off. So, be ready. It will be at Camelot."

After his breakfast, King Arthur went to his rooms, put on what he wanted to wear, laid out what he wanted to go, took what he wanted to carry, went down and out to his horse. He mounted, waited until the column of riders looked settled.

"Forward ho," said King Arthur.

The company moved forward.

The column wound its way up the river valley, up to a crossing of the Severn, rode over to the Avon, crossed, rode down the valley. The road led, after a time, to Camelot.

The weather turned cool. One day King Arthur looked from his window and saw dark clouds. There were the horns announcing breakfast. He went down the stairs, walked into the hall.

"Hail His Majesty, King Arthur."

"Be seated. We wish all a good morning."

King Arthur ate his breakfast. He went up the stairs to his room. There was a darkness in the room. A patter of rain blew in the window. Merlin entered.

"Good to see you back in your palace."

"Really, I am glad to be back."

"Let you and me take a ride," said Merlin.

"It must have some virtue as the weather, for the ride, is not that which I enjoy the most."

"I like dark, cloudy days," said Merlin.

King Arthur dressed for the rain, rang for Sir Lucan.

"Sir Lucan, have my horse brought to the gate."

King Arthur and Merlin walked down to where their horses were waiting. Merlin and the king mounted and rode toward the wood. They rode through the wood. Merlin pulled up at a round, earth covered hermitage. Beside it was an old grey wagon to which a grey mule was hitched. There was a spatter of rain on the leaves. Drops fell on Merlin and the king. The mule began to move. Merlin and the king followed it. After a spell, the mule stopped, ate vegetation. Merlin and the king climbed on the wagon, ate some of the food which Merlin had put on it. The king and Merlin returned to their horses, followed again the wagon.

Merlin rode through the on and off drizzle. When time came to eat, they sat under the cover over the wagon. They were in rugged, rocky country. There were rock cliffs.

"The rocks relate to the stars," said Merlin. "They hold astral projections. The landscape could look different."

Merlin found a cave. He and King Arthur entered. They came to a chest.

"The contents relate to the Sun to whom we go for aid. Now we can carry the chest to the wagon."

The two carried the chest out and put it in the wagon. The mule began its long journey to Camelot. The rain drizzled on them as they rode through the night. In the middle of the night the wagon pulled up to the gate at Camelot.

"Porter, I am King Arthur and I have a workman with me."

He and Merlin lifted the chest off the wagon.

"May I call for help?" said the porter.

"No, the lifting will do me good," said King Arthur.

He and Merlin carried the chest in, up the stair, in at the king rooms, into the secret compartment.

Said Merlin, "Without the help of the Sun, all the help the porter would have summoned could not have carried that chest."

Merlin executed hand motions over the chest.

"There are times when one or another will deserve a just reward. Now you can give it with often advantage to yourself," said Merlin. "And", said he, "there are other places in Earth where riches are hidden. These can be used when needed."

King Arthur was looking at the curious chest. He turned to speak to Merlin. Merlin was gone.

King Arthur took off his wet clothes, got in his warm, dry bed.

There were the horns. Time for breakfast.

It was time to get the palace and the grounds ready for the tournament. Sir Kay was taking charge and taking a special interest in the kitchen. Eating well would give Camelot knights' strength said Sir Kay. He learned that at Bonmaison. Many of the knights at Camelot were working on strength and timing.

"Camelot is not back in the sticks and I do not want people to think that it is. Or should be," said Sir Ozana to Sir Aliduc. Sir Bleoberis and Sir Lionses of Payarne were also on the field working with targets. All the while, workmen were making preparations for the crowd which was expected. Cleaners and taylors were being patronized, as many wanted to look their best in the evenings. People from far and wide were gathering at the palace. In two days there would be the Druidic rituals. It was close to time for a number of beings to go to the Underworld. This needed to be included in King Arthur's plans.

The last day of October, there was the blare of the horns. King Arthur went down the marble stairs. Arches were hung with black drapes. The flags and hangings from a number of King Arthur's lands were displayed. The king went in to his place at the breakfast table.

"Hail His Majesty, King Arthur."

"Be seated."

While the king ate, there was much conversation around the table; much, about the tournament. King Arthur went up to his rooms. Sir Lucan appeared.

"Your Majesty, Lady Lionors asks leave to speak with you."

"Have her come in."

The lady entered.

"King Arthur, thankyou for seeing me."

"It is good to see you, Lady Lionors."

"My father and I have come to celebrate Samhain. But it is a secret word with you I wanted. I am going to have your son."

"You are beautiful and loving, and would make a king a fine wife. But your true path is as a healer."

"True. But I truly need a path away from my castle."

King Arthur rang for Sir Lucan.

"Sir Lucan, I would speak with Lord Brychan.

Sir Lucan left the room. Shortly, Lord Brychan was at the door.

"Your Majesty?"

"Come in Lord Brychan. Lord Brychan, I wish you to have a daughter. She is a healer who has done me much service and I am certain you will find her a person of value. She will have a son and he and his mother of worldly goods, will have sufficient."

"Your Majesty, she will be a true daughter to me."

"And this is your daughter, Lady Lionors."

"Your Majesty, may all good things come to you," said Lady Lionors.

"Come, I will introduce you to your family," said Lord Brychan.

The two bowed to King Arthur, departed.

King Arthur went to where his new chest had been put, opened it. There he saw the full chest: discs of bright gold, bright diamonds and other bright stones. It was obvious, he could be generous in his gifts to Lady Lionors.

King Arthur went from his rooms, across an arch, which was part of a web of beautiful, white arches, to where, from a balcony, he could see a landscape dressed in its fall colour. In the distance was the mysterious, dark forest. Beautiful rolling green hills led away from his palace. Here and there, near the castle, were drops between hills which seemed to hold ancient creations: left overs from long past. The king walked on his balcony taking great pleasure in the beauties of his landscape. The horns were announcing lunch. The king went down to the hall.

"Hail His Majesty, King Arthur."

"Be seated."

The tables were filled with many visitors. The event at the beautiful palace inspired people to dress up in their fine clothes. King Arthur looked up and down the table, saw his many friends looking their best.

King Arthur finished what he wanted to eat, went to the reception room, took his seat on the throne. Knight after knight entered, came to the throne, bowed, wished him well. Druid Dubric, the arch druid, entered.

"If it please Your Majesty, we might give our presence to the passing to the Underworld."

King Arthur rose up, walked with the druid to where the porter stood at the gate.

"Sir, have our horses brought forward," said the king.

He had not long to wait. He and the druid mounted, rode over a grassy slope, down a grassy terrace, over a grass covered dipping field, down a grassy terrace, over a field, down a terrace, up a valley between two tree covered hills. Where the valley narrowed and rose was a building made of old grey logs. It had a large front entrance and a round thatch roof. To the right of the house trickled a small brook. On either side of the house were hawthorns, and from these hung long, pale cloths. King Arthur and the druid dismounted, went into the building. It was dark inside. There was the sound of the trickling brook. In the rear, a floor of flat stones led out a wide exit and down.

Following King Arthur and Dubric, there entered a large druid in white. He carried a double bladed axe and this he gave to Druid Dubric. Into the building came two women in white gowns, and they were leading pale ox. This they took to the large druid in the white robe.

Druid Dubric, who was also in a white robe, handed the large axe to King Arthur.

"The druid would like you to hand him the axe."

King Arthur handed the axe to the large druid.

The ox was led out the rear entrance. King Arthur observed sheaves of grain and dried flowers hanging from the walls. There was the sound of the ox being slain. The large druid came in, handed the axe, now bloody, to Druid Dubric. Druid Dubric handed it to King Arthur.

Two women dressed in white gowns, came in the entrance leading a hog. The large druid was handed the axe by the king. The hog was led out the rear entrance, was slain. The large druid came in, handed the bloody axe to Druid Dubric. Two women in white gowns entered. And they were leading a white ram. Druid Dubric handed the axe to King Arthur and King Arthur, to the large druid. The ram was taken out the exit in the rear, followed by the large druid in his white robe. There was the sound of the axe striking the ram. Then, coming in by the rear exit was a woman leading a white mule. She wore a mist white gown and her bare feet were covered with blood. She went to King Arthur.

"Great Lord over sacred things, I have a request."

"This is not the time nor the place for making a request," said Druid Dubric. "You should return to your land."

"None the less," said King Arthur, "I will hear the request in seven days time. It is then I will be on my throne hearing the problems of my people. It is then I will hear your request."

The woman turned, led her mule out. She left, leaving the way she had come in.

"Your Majesty, I see her as ill news. I had wished you would tell her to go out the way she had come in," said Druid Dubric.

"However, I will hear all who come before my throne to speak," said the king.

The large druid and the women who had brought in the ox, the hog and the ram formed a rank and bowed to King Arthur. The king and Druid Dubric left the house, mounted their horses, rode to the hill, up the hill and to the gate of Camelot. They dismounted, walked in to where many knights and ladies were walking about, laughing and engaging each other in lively conversation. The horns were announcing the evening meal. King Arthur went to the table.

The large crowd stood, greeted the king. The king ate, listened to the lively conversation.

"Many have been working hard on their skills," said Lord Brochwael to King Arthur. "But when I was young, we had no time for spending on this sort of thing."

"An orderly land can give much pleasure," said King Arthur.

A harper then filled the hall with song.

"One thing I notice," said Lord Baldwin. "The ladies are wearing more bright clothes than in former times; and some, made in strange cuts."

"It is the building," said Sir Bedivere. "The white, twisting pillars and curves of arches create a desire to look good beside them."

"That makes sense," said Lord Caradoc.

The harper changed songs. People gave attention to what he was doing.

King Arthur went to his rooms, lay on his bed and thought about the coming tournament.

King Arthur was up early. He took care of his toilet, washed, dressed in bright clothes of white, gold and blue. He looked out his window. It was a grey day. Fog concealed the ground below him. The horns were blowing. King Arthur went down to breakfast.

"Hail His Majesty, King Arthur."

The table was filled with joyful, jubilant knights. King Arthur ate quickly, went up to his room, put on what he wanted to wear as he overlooked the matches and pageantry which the day would offer. He walked to the curving, white stairs, down and out to his horse. His staff was already mounted, their horses lined up behind his. He waited for the line to fill with horses and their riders. The bright shields and shining helms made a bright display. King Arthur looked down the line of horses.

"Forward ho," shouted the king.

King Arthur led the column of lords and knights to the field, and this was decorated with banners and bright hangings. King Arthur, followed by the shining column, made a complete circle of the field, stopped by the bright stand where he would sit. On the stand, he was joined by Lord Brochwael and his lady, by Lord Brychan and his lady, by Lord Do, and by a good number of their daughters and daughters in law. The stands filled with many other women, and these wore the brightest of garments. The stands also held a number of men: many of these were the young or the elderly. Town people were around the field, and many others of them, on nearby knolls.

While the lists were being set up, costumed musicians, with pipes, horns and percussion instruments, walked here and there entertaining. Lord Caradoc walked to them, told them to make their exit. The palace horn blowers rode to the center of the field, blew their horns. Two riders rushed toward each other with lances and the tournament was begun.

At first, there were so many knights competing that few but the score keepers could have known much as to who was doing well, but in the afternoon, many of the less skillful would be off the field.

"Sire, it is good to get those who are out of practice off the field. In spite of protective gear, this game is still quite dangerous," said Lord Brochwael.

King Arthur noticed Sir Kay was still on the field even though he certainly had but little time for practice. And there was Sir Bedivere still on the field.

The sun informed all that it was noon. Horses were brought for Lord Do, for Lord Brochwael and for his lady, for Lord Brychan and his lady, and King Arthur's horse was brought to the stands. The king left the field, the column of horsemen following him.

King Arthur left his horse with the porter, went in the palace, up to his rooms. He went down to lunch. There was an enthusiastic cheer as he went to the table.

After his lunch, the king went to his rooms, changed clothes, went down the stairs and returned to his horse. He led the column of horses around to the tournament field.

The king turned his horse over to a squire, took his seat in the stands. There were less knights seeking for victories in jousts; many more were on the sidelines observing, and this included Sir Kay.

The sun went down. King Arthur's horse was brought to the stands. The king mounted and led the column of horses, and the walking host, back to the palace.

King Arthur went to his rooms, changed into clothes which would be right for the evening. He went down to the table. There was a great cheer.

"Be seated," said the king.

There was laughter to the sound of harp music. Food eaten, there was beer. Four pipers and three clowns replaced the harpers.

King Arthur went to his rooms.

The next day came grey and cloudy. King Arthur arose and prepared for breakfast. There were the horns.

King Arthur went down the stair, went to the table. There was a great cheer for him. The crowd seemed not to miss the sun. There was laughter and it seemed, joy.

"The cool wind will keep their gear cool. They can not object to that," said Lord Gornemant.

King Arthur ate, went up to his rooms, put on his festival clothes, went down to his horse. He led a column of horsemen which was much shorter than the one of the previous day. The king circled the field, took his place in the stand. A cool breeze was blowing. One after another horseman hit the dirt. Lunchtime came. King Arthur led the company to the palace.

Lunch over, King Arthur led the horsemen to the tournament field. King Arthur saw that Sir Bedivere was still on the field. And Lord Caradoc was also among the contenders. Beside King Arthur was Lord Brochwael.

"Sire, I am, as I suspect you know, ruling Langborth. Cador is a splendid battle leader, but I have much experience with rules and regulations. Our grandfather was called a great warrior, but I believe his chief strength was in his ability to keep order. His name got to mean regulation. He was not called King, but only Theoderic, and far and wide, that meant law. I am certain you will inherit that. King Arthur will have that meaning.

I intend, under your authority, to have a coronation, New Years Day, and I would be honoured if you would be there."

"Thankyou, King Brochwael. I certainly intend to be there."

There, Lord Caradoc was one of the contenders. However, Sir Bedivere was now watching from the side lines. King Arthur watched the skillful jousters. Jousters still on the field were down to a score. The sun set. Horns came to the center of the field to announce the event. King Arthur's horse had been brought around and stood patiently waiting below him. The king mounted, rode from the field, and the staff, then the other horsemen followed.

King Arthur went to his rooms, changed to clothes that were right for dinner, went down to the table. There was a great cheer for him when he entered the hall. Three harpers played throughout the dinner; then, when the mead replaced the meat, the three clowns with the four musicians supplied loud music. King Arthur went up to his rooms.

In the morning, King Arthur got up and his room was dark. He washed in the twilight and there was a patter of rain. He went to the window. Gusts of rain swished down. There were the horns.

King Arthur went down to the table. It was raining.

"Hail His Majesty, King Arthur."

"Be seated."

The knights seemed happy and lively. But there was rain. It was raining.

"I thought the rain might dampen their spirits," said King Arthur.

"No, my lord," said Lord Gornemant, "There is joy because you are seated there, a crown on your head, so that they feel secure in their lives. When they sow, they can depend on a harvest."

King Arthur sat, listened to the conversation. The rain came down. King Arthur returned to his room.

All morning it rained. King Arthur went down to lunch. During lunch there was a steady rain. Finished eating, King Arthur returned to his room. He rang for Sir Lucan.

"Yes Sire."

"Sir Lucan, I need a squire to go to a tailor. I need twenty bags the size of my fist and one, double that size."

"Yes, Sire."

It was an all day rain. It rained through the afternoon. At the evening meal the knights were cheerful, and there was entertainment, but when the clowns and musicians came in, King Arthur retired to his room.

Morning came. Another dark day. King Arthur tended to his toilet, washed, dressed in fine clothes. There were the horns. King Arthur went to the stairway, went down to breakfast. A great cheer went up when he reached the table.

189

"Be seated," said the king.

The day was brighter, but there were yet spatterings of rain. King Arthur ate, returned to his room. He watched the sky. He went to his chest, filled each of the bags with small discs of gold. He rang for Sir Lucan.

"Sir Lucan, I would speak with Druid Dubric."

"Yes Sire."

King Arthur looked out his window. It was not raining. The sky was lighter.

"Yes, Your Majesty."

"Druid Dubric, after lunch I want you here dressed in fine clothes and with a fine looking case which you can easily carry."

"Yes Sire."

The druid left the room. King Arthur watched the lightening sky. There were the horns.

King Arthur went down the stair, went to the table. There was a great cheer.

"Be seated. Now hear this, we will take a ride to the tournament field."

There were loud cheers from a host of voices.

King Arthur ate his lunch, went to his rooms, waited by his window. Druid Dubric was there in robes of white and gold accented with blue.

"Come in, Druid Dubric."

King Arthur took the handsome, green and gold case, opened it, put in the twenty bags and closed it. He returned it to the druid.

"Take a seat beside me when we get to the stands," said the king.

He and the druid went down the curving white stair, which went under the high white arch. The king went out to his horse. He mounted, led the horsemen around to the tournament field. He took his place in the stands. The arch druid took a place down and to the left of King Arthur. On the field, twenty knights had their horses trot up and down the length of the field. Three horsemen, their shields covered in black, black cloth on their helms hiding their faces, had their horses do turns and zigzags.

The twenty knights took places in the lists, each knight trying his skill against one knight then another. The judges called a halt. They escorted a knight to the king.

"Your Majesty," said one of the knights with a black shield, "We are pleased to present to you the knight who has shown himself to be first in the skill of jousting: Sir Caradoc." The horns blew.

"Come forward, Lord Caradoc," said King Arthur.

Lord Caradoc went up dismounted, walked up and bowed to the king. Druid Dubric handed King Arthur a sack from his case. The king presented it to Lord Caradoc. Lord Caradoc bowed, went back to his horse.

The second knight with a black shield came forward on his horse, and riding on his right was a horsed knight.

"Sire, we are pleased to present a second knight who has excelled in jousting: Sir Fergus, son of Roch." There was a call from the horns.

"Come forward, Sir Fergus, said King Arthur.

Sir Fergus rode forward, dismounted, walked up and bowed to the king. The arch druid handed King Arthur a sack. King Arthur presented it to Sir Fergus. Sir Fergus bowed, returned to his horse.

The third knight with a black shield rode up, and to his right rode a knight. They stopped before the king.

"Sire, we are pleased to present to King Arthur a third knight who has shown great skill in jousting: Sir Briant." There was a call from the horns.

"Come forward, Sir Briant," said the king.

Sir Briant rode forward, dismounted, walked up to the king.

The arch druid handed King Arthur a sack. The king presented it to Sir Briant. Sir Briant bowed, returned to his horse.

"Have those other fine jousters come before me and say who they are," said the king.

The knights rode up, formed a rank before the king. Right to left, they called out their names: "Lord Gornemant, Sire." "Lord Glyddiew, Sire." "Sir Bleoberis, Sire." "Sir Aliduc, Sire." "Sir Blyas, Sire." "Sir Cynon, Sire." "Sir Caurdaf, Sire." "Sir Hervy, Sire." "Sir Nevyn, Sire." "Sir Gracian, Sire." "Sir Blois, Sire." "Sir Placidas, Sire." "Sir Ladinas, Sire." "Sir Guy, Sire." "Sir Emeraw, Sire." "Sir Flanned, Sire." "Sir Ozana, Sire."

"Come forward in that order and be honoured," said King Arthur. The horns gave a call.

As each went forward, he received from the king a bag of gold discs. After the last sack had been given, the horns gave a call. King Arthur called for his horse. He led the column of horsemen to the front of Camelot. The king handed his horse to a squire, walked up to his rooms. There was a joyful noise in the halls below him. The evening meal held a loud joy. Many who had not won a gift felt that they had done quite well.

Rain came up in the night. In the morning there was a grey drizzle. The day was filled with an off and on drizzle. In the halls the celebrating went on. In the night the rain stopped. In the morning there was a cool breeze. The sky was filled with grey clouds. Many knights took advantage of the clear weather. Directly after breakfast many of them set out for their homes. King Arthur, in his reception room, accepted farewell after farewell. Some of the knights made their departure after their lunch. The evening meal, to King Arthur, seemed quiet, but it was only that if it were compared to those loud festival meals. After the meat had been eaten, the harpers were there playing. King Arthur went up to his room.

King Arthur woke to a grey day. A fine drizzle was falling. He attended to his toilet, washed and dressed in what seemed appropriate. There were the horns. He went down the white marble stairs to breakfast. There were the cheers when he got to the table.

"Be seated," said the king.

The hot food tasted good on the chilly morning.

"This is exactly what I would have ordered," said King Arthur to Lord Baldwin.

"It tastes good to me," said the lord.

"And I appreciate your efforts. Every object was always where it should be," said the king.

"It was a group effort," said the lord. "The food we enjoy. That is in part do to Sir Kay."

"I can see that," said King Arthur.

King Arthur ate, went to his room put on what his throne called for. He went down the stair, into the reception room. He had with him the large sack of gold discs. He sat on the throne.

Lord Brychan entered bowed.

"Your Majesty, I and my family thank you for a wonderful stay."

"I am glad it gave you pleasure. I have this for you."

He gave Lord Brychan the sack of gold.

"I am most grateful, Your Majesty."

Behind the throne were Lord Clydno, Lord Caradoc, Lord Gornemant and Druid Dubric, and these were standing stiff and stern looking. There were nods of approval all around when Lord Brychan went out.

As he departed, a woman entered the throne room. She was barefoot and wore a wet, very thin gown.

"Where have you been staying?" said King Arthur.

"In the woods yonder, Your Majesty."

"Why did you not stay at the castle, and the porter, or, I am certain, any other knight would have seen you had a warm garment. Why did you not ask?"

"Because I come as a beggar. But I do not come to beg for clothes, nor to beg for food. To beg for one thing only have I come: for a knight to rescue my lady from an awful tyrant. Already he has slain many knights who have tried to defend her. Sixty, I believe, he has slain."

"Damsel, I will accept that task," said King Arthur.

"Your Majesty, what you mean to say is that you intend to send some worthy knight with this woman?" Druid Dubric asked.

"Not at all. I intend to go myself,"

Lord Gornemant gave a slight negative shake to his head.

Lord Clydno gave a slight negative shake to his head.

"Your Majesty, if I may speak as one of your advisors, and I am certain your other advisors will concur. I do not advise you to go with this woman. As we know, as a rule, it is the duty of a king to sit on his throne and, as we say, rule. If there are missions which it is felt important that one should do, that is what knights are for. However, I have grave misgivings about the wisdom of anybody going off with this woman. Who came to us out of death, her feet wet with the blood of death, to disturb our sacred ritual."

"I like this woman," said Lord Caradoc. "She has done her duty with grace and good will. It would be a shame if she were left holding the bag."

"Druid Dubric," said the king, "the damsel might have felt this mission was her sacred duty, and what better time to speak of it than when we were engaged with sacred things. And as to the mission, I would never send a knight on a mission which I would not myself go on. And as I have never had the experience of going out, knight errant, as I intend to send knights out, I should get for myself that experience. And as I intend to rule this land, it might be wise to learn more about it, to learn what people away from Camelot are doing. When they have no thought that Camelot is with them.

However, I am accustomed to rugged country women who pull their own weight. I expect to depart directly after breakfast tomorrow. You must be rested, fed and ready to travel. Travel is tough and I do not need a castle garden flower who will wilt from starvation when I most need her. Your horse should be fed also. If you seem not to be rested and fed, I might change my mind, send with you some eager squire who greatly desires to be dubbed a knight, but has as yet to have his first fight. Lord Caradoc, take charge of this damsel and see she gets fed and is rested."

"Yes, Your Majesty."

King Arthur got from his throne, went to his rooms. He rang for Lord Baldwin.

"Ah, Lord Baldwin. I am going to take a task, knight errant. I intend to have Lord Caradoc take charge of the kingdoms and I am certain the staff will give him much help. In going, I intend to look like a country knight: my old helm, my old clothes. And I need my shield covered. My first choice is goatskin. Have a tailor cover it with goatskin."

"Your father used a goatskin covered shield as I recall."

"Good reason for me to have one."

Lord Baldwin took the shield.

"Your Majesty."

He bowed, departed.

King Arthur rang for Sir Lucan.

"Your Majesty?"

"Sir Lucan, a damsel has come to tell me of a problem. I decided to solve it myself. I am having Lord Caradoc look after things and I am certain you and others of the staff will be a big help. I would like to see Sir Kay, and Lady and Lord Kyner."

In a short time, Lady and Lord Kyner were in King Arthur's

rooms.

"Hello, good to see you," said King Arthur.

Sir Kay came in.

"I want to tell you," said the king, "a damsel has come with a problem and I intend to solve it for her."

"It sounds like something I should be doing," said Sir Kay.

"No, I would like to do it. But I want a good bit of food which will travel well. On my horse first thing tomorrow."

"Use good, sound reasoning," said Lord Kyner.

King Arthur told of his first seeing the damsel, and of her request in the throne room.

"You might gain strength from the experience," said Lord Kyner. "But I advise, get back as soon as you can. You should stay the one that people expect to hear."

There were the horns announcing lunch.

"That seems good advice. Sir Kay, after lunch, I would want to see Sir Ulfin, Sir Brastias and Sir Naram, and yourself in my rooms."

The four of them left the rooms. King Arthur, with Sir Kay and Lord Kyner, went to the hall.

Lunch was eaten without much conversation. It seemed, there was little attention to the thinly clad woman who entered and went directly to the throne room. The king went to his rooms. He waited but a short time, Sir Kay, with Sir Ulfin, Sir Brastias and Sir Naram entered.

"Lords, I have decided to go with a woman to solve her problem," said King Arthur.

The king told his knights the events of the damsel.

"And," said the king, "I am leaving Lord Caradoc in charge, and I trust days will go just as if I were on my throne."

Sir Baldwin was at the entrance and with him was Sir Lucan and two squires.

"Come in. I am just now explaining the situation," said the king.

Sir Baldwin and the staff discussed what would be needed on the journey. The squires worked on this and that.

"I want to avoid a new look. I do not want to sparkle," said the king.

"How about this covering, cloths with wild onion, for your helm," said Lord Baldwin.

A squire entered with the goatskin covered shield. King Arthur and his staff smiled when they saw it. There was the sound of the horns. The king and those with him went down the stair and to the hall for dinner. There was a cheer for the king.

"Be seated. I have a statement I want you to hear. Fro a time I will be on a journey. While I am gone, Lord Caradoc will speak for me. All will do what Lord Caradoc says to do."

King Arthur ate. Up and down the table there was much conversation. There was speculation as to where King Arthur was going and why.

King Arthur finished eating, went to his room. He got to bed early.

The morning, he was up, took care of his toilet, washed. He looked out the window. It was clear. There were the horns.

King Arthur went down the stairs, in to his breakfast. There was a great cheer for the king and much attention was given to him as he ate. There was concern for him expressed, as some had seen the young woman.

King Arthur went up and dressed in his good sturdy clothes he had worn at Bonmaison. He made a last stop at his toilet, went down the stair, through the hall, out to the gate. The damsel stood waiting.

"At a distance, I thought you had sent your squire after all. Some stout country boy," said the damsel.

"That somewhat tells who I am," said King Arthur.

The damsel got on a mule. The king mounted.

"We are off," said the damsel.

The two took the way up a valley, around the hills, to Langborth. There they took a break. They relieved themselves on some nettles, went down to the water and washed. King Arthur got out food and they relaxed in the shade of an oak.

"Tell me," said the damsel, "that eager country lad with little experience, which you threatened to thrust on me: were you speaking of yourself?"

"That is somewhat true. You have found me out."

They both laughed at that.

"But that could be serious," said the damsel.

"I am from the country," said King Arthur, "where we were troubled with raiding Picts and Vikings, but it was not our custom for a lord to go himself to solve these difficulties, or to send out a single knight champion; but, for protection, to do things together, the warriors, as they came of age. Camelot will have different customs: as the knight errant. I am a new king and your request for a knight errant is the first such request I have had. And I have recently come of age."

"It is all very strange. I mean, why Camelot? Well, let us mount up. We will follow on up the Parrett," said the damsel.

The two of them kept close to the bank of the river. They followed it as the river wound in and out through the valleys. The sun sank behind the trees. King Arthur and the damsel dismounted. They took off their clothes, washed in the river. "We could climb that hill, if you have the energy."

"What hill is that?" said King Arthur.

"I believe it is called Burrow Mump. Come."

They walked over, up a rise.

"See? That would be Glastonbury up there."

"You do know the area?" said King Arthur.

They hurried down the hill, to where the horse and the mule waited. It was quite dark. King Arthur got out food for them. They sat and ate.

"Well, I am not tired," said the damsel.

"And I feel fresh."

"And can your horse keep moving onward?"

"That it can."

"Then, let us ride on a way, your horse can follow the mule. The mule knows what it's about."

King Arthur rode on for what seemed hour after hour. The river lapped and murmured beside them. The blanket of stars swung overhead, the formations slowly changing place. On and on they followed the river.

"You should rest," said the damsel.

The mule came to a stop; the horse, behind it. The damsel and King Arthur dismounted. Each of them got blankets and these they combined. They got undressed, got under the blankets.

"First time?" the damsel asked.

"Second. If I get the question."

"Gone to bed with a woman. Country girl when you were young?"

"Yes. That is, I am still young."

"Yes."

The damsel laughed.

"But I do know one thing. Your father was a famous fighter and he gave you one ninth of his power."

"That is why Caradoc is one of my advisors. He knows everything."

"Did you love her?"

King Arthur slept.

King Arthur woke. It was light. The river was murmuring beside him. He got up. The damsel opened her eyes. King Arthur grabbed her hand, pulled her up.

"Hey," she said.

Together they ran into the river. They took their time with washing. Suddenly a woman came riding over a grassy hill. Her dress looked costly. Then over the hill rode a man with a drawn sword. King Arthur grabbed his sword, jumped on his horse, rode between the woman and the man with the sword. The sun came up. King Arthur's wet body looked bright in the sunlight. King Arthur rushed at the man, swung his sword. The man somewhat blocked the swing, fell from his horse. He had a badly cut arm. The king jumped from his horse, raised his sword.

"I surrender," shouted the man.

"Surrender to this woman," said King Arthur.

"I do not want him. Do with him what you will." He has already slain the companion, the knight, whom I was with."

"What is your story?" asked King Arthur of the man who had attacked him.

"I have loved this lady for many years. She went off with another knight. I decided, if I could not have her, no man would."

"How are you called?" asked the king.

"I am Sir Wasteland."

"I demand, on your honour, you agree to put yourself under the authority of the lord at Camelot."

"Where is that?"

"In Lyonesse."

"Where is that?"

Said the damsel, "Follow the Parrett, when you get to Glastonbury, go south to Butleigh, then south."

The knight got up, picked up his sword and walked back over the hill. The damsel had been getting food together.

The lady in the fine dress dismounted. "Blessings come to you. Are you not a river demon?" she asked.

"I am a wandering knight," said the king.

"You certainly come from the water. You are the Knight of the Parrett."

"So be it," said the king.

The damsel had slipped on her very thin, sheer white gown. King Arthur slipped on clothes and sat beside her.

"Would company to your home be helpful?" asked the king.

"I would take pleasure in the company. Especially, as I would like you to see our castle, which is very fine. Although the lord over it makes all comply with his foolish wishes, like swear his lady is Beauty Over All."

"Will you share breakfast?" asked the damsel.

"No, thankyou, but my castle is not far."

King Arthur and the damsel sat and ate. The king finished his portion.

"Shall we go?" he said.

"I am not going," said the damsel.

"But we said we would take her home."

"Whether you go is up to you. But I will not ride my mule to their castle. Tell them I went back to Waterland."

"Ah, the Parrett. But I will come back."

"As I said, it is up to you."

King Arthur dressed for the ride, mounted his horse and rode with the mounted lady. The two rode through the valley, around a couple of round hills, and there on a round hill was the castle. The courtyard at the front dropped into the valley, and in it were men and women dressed in bright colours. As King Arthur rode toward them he could see that there was a jolly engagement in horseplay among many of those present. And much of the horseplay seemed lewd. In the meadow beyond there were tents set up. It looked like a festival in progress. There were groups of men and women singing. When they saw King Arthur, many stopped what they were doing and jeered at him.

"Go back where you came from," shouted some.

"And I will take your reputation for rudeness with me," said King Arthur.

"He is the man come out of the Parrett to save us," said the woman.

"Save yourself before it is too late," shouted a knight.

From the castle and into the park rode the lord and lady and in front of them was a small horse on which was a bird in a golden cage. In charge of the horse, to its rear and goading it, was a dwarf. The lady had a hard, stern look. The lord was in full fighting gear. As soon as he saw King Arthur, he rode to him to give him battle. It was a furious battle. The lord's sword clanged past King Arthur's shield, cut through the edge of his helmet and sliced down his face. King Arthur increased his vigourous attack, cut off the lord's sword arm. The lord fell from his horse.

"Do not slay me," he cried.

"How are you called?" called the king.

"I am Lord Merciless Lion."

"He has taken from those you see and made them swear to be his slaves," said the woman whom the king had saved.

"You must swear to release all those you have taken and to return all their property," said the king.

"Oh, I do," said the lord.

Women came up and carried the lord into the castle. The lady whom King Arthur had saved led the king to the castle, helped him dismount, took him to a room of the castle, had women there fix the king's wound.

The king rested. He was given good food.

"The hospitality has been good, but I must get back to the Parrett," said the king.

"Of course you must," said the women who had been giving care. "That is the way with water spirits."

They gave King Arthur a package of food. He walked to his horse, mounted, rode back to the Parrett.

"Oh lord," said the damsel.

"I am sorry," said the king.

"It is not to me you owe anything at all. I do not tell you what to do. It is to the task to which you are pledged. You came that close. That is a bad cut. I should take you to Glastonbury."

"I will not go back," said the king.

"And I will not go forward. Until I feel you are ready."

The damsel cried.

"I brought you some food," said the king.

They sat and ate.

"I was afraid you would not like it. Then I would really have been defeated."

"I know. This gives us an answer. You know what it is?"

"Yes. Yes I know," said the king.

The damsel found herbs in the wood, made lotions and washed King Arthur's wound. King Arthur worked on his helmet and his other equipment. At night the damsel was extra careful not to bank into the king's face.

In the morning the woman whom King Arthur saved was there with food.

"Thankyou," said the damsel.

"All are most appreciative of their freedom," said the woman.

"Though none have come to tell me so," said the king. He smiled.

"They are afraid. I told them you were not a demon. They said they were certain I was right. Only their concept of what a demon was might not be the same as mine."

The woman sat while King Arthur and the damsel ate. She said:

"I would like to know about the Water World. I wonder, is there a feeling of great freedom?"

King Arthur smiled.

"Yes and no," he said.

The damsel gave the suggestion of a laugh. The three thought for a minute. They all laughed. The Parrett Knight and the damsel finished eating. The woman took the container, returned to her castle.

"I like the woman," said the damsel.

"She is very human," said the Parrett Knight.

The two of them laughed.

"There is a freedom in not being human," said the damsel.

"They have no thought of how we should be," said the Parrett Knight.

"We can be like this. Be water demons," said the damsel.

"Now are we in Somerset?"

"No, it is quite different. It is difficult to get to Somerset from here. Notice, the weather is different. This is Logres."

The Parrett King and the damsel walked together in the woods. They washed in the river. They ate some food Sir Kay had sent with them. In the evening, the woman from the castle was there with a supper.

"What is the castle called?" the damsel asked.

"It is Clausuel; and people say it is King Lear's, though I know of no one who has seen him,"

"How are you called?" asked the Parrett Knight.

"I am Lady Montgibel, daughter of Lord Gorlois."

The damsel sucked in her breath, caught the knight's eye. They exchanged a quick smile.

"Though I never knew him," said the lady.

She sat with them while they ate.

"How will your castle be ruled?" asked the Parrett Knight.

"No one seems in command now. I believe we will need to decide on someone," said the lady.

"That would be wise," said the Parrett Knight.

Seven day passed. The woman of the castle sat with them at their evening meal. Said the damsel:

"Directly following breakfast we will go on a journey. It would help if we had a weeks good meals to go with us. We have enjoyed our time spent with you and am thankful for all you have given us."

"It has been appreciated," said King Arthur.

"I will really miss you," said the woman. "And if, I want to say, I enjoyed seeing the sun come up. And the river. And so many things."

"Yes, life is good and we are glad for you," said the damsel.

She went back toward her castle.

"She should not have needed to thank us for life itself," said the

202

damsel.

King Arthur nodded. The two of them wrapped in their blankets, which were by the river. The sound of the river entered their sleep.

The two got up early, jumped in the river, swam, washed, washed each other. There was the woman of the castle. With her was the dwarf with the horse and on the horse were the packages of food and the golden cage in which was the Thrush.

King Arthur gave a questioning look at it all.

"Well, you won it," said the dwarf.

The four sat by the river and had breakfast. They got up.

"Will you come back?" said the woman.

"One can never tell," said King Arthur.

He and the damsel dressed and packed. They mounted their beasts.

"Were you not interested to know whom the lady was with whom you travelled?" asked the Thrush.

Said King Arthur, "I presumed if she wanted me to know she would tell me."

"Well I will tell you," said the Thrush. "It is Beauty Sans Villainy, heir of Lord Valsin, who is now dead."

"How old are you?" asked King Arthur.

"Going on seventeen."

"I too. I am seventeen," said King Arthur.

The three rode through the morning along a trail by the river. Under shady trees they stopped, got out food, sat near the water and the Thrush sang beautiful music while they ate.

After eating, King Arthur and Beauty went and found some weeds which they could piss on:

"We are ready," said Beauty when she and King Arthur got back to the fire area.

They mounted and rode along the path by the river. All afternoon they rode along the path. The sun drifted down the sky. At sundown, the sunset silhouetted a castle on a nearby hill.

"I know that castle," said Beauty. "The lord there is a nice person."

"Would he welcome company?"

"Oh yes. I think so."

"Because it is time we began planning for the night," said King Arthur.

Beauty led the company up a winding road to the castle. She got to the gate. She called to the porter:

"Hello, this is Beauty here, Lord Valsin's daughter. I have with me a lord and a dwarf.

"Hi Beauty, always good to see you. You all come in."

The gate opened. Beauty, King Arthur and the dwarf entered. Inside the castle, the lord and lady came to meet them.

"Hello Beauty, and would this be the Knight of the Parrett?"

"Then you have heard of me."

"Oh yes. By now, people all up and down the valley have heard of you. Beauty, are you two together?"

"Oh, yes. Yes."

"Very good."

Dinner was brought in. At the table were a few knights, a few ladies. They spoke of the wicked and greedy Merciless Lion and of the correct conduct of lords.

"I am interested in these opinions," said King Arthur. "Myself, I am a young knight, still learning."

"Beauty, we like your choice," said the lord.

The butler showed Beauty and King Arthur to a room. Beauty ordered hot water. It was brought and Beauty cared for the king's healing wound.

The castle was old and resembled, in some ways, Ludlow castle.

"I'm not familiar with this kind of toilet," said Beauty.

King Arthur helped Beauty with the toilet. The two had a laugh over that. They crawled into their fine bed, got as close to one another as they could.

In the morning, Beauty and King Arthur were awakened by the beautiful song of the Thrush.

"It is time for the greatest knight in the world to get up and do great things," said the Thrush.

"Listen to that. The bird is poking fun at me,"

Beauty laughed. "It got one thing right. It is time to get up."

The two of them got up, used the toilet, washed.

The butler entered, said, "It is time for breakfast."

King Arthur and Beauty dressed and went to the hall where breakfast was to be served.

"I am glad Lord Caradoc and his family got me ready," said Beauty.

"That is what advisors are for," said King Arthur.

Beauty and King Arthur sat and enjoyed breakfast with the lord and lady and people of the castle.

"We thank you for a most enjoyable stay," said King Arthur.

"Thank you for the courtesy of a visit," said the lord. "And do me the honour of picking up a package from the porter when you head out."

The two both thanked the lord for his thoughtfulness. They went to their room, got things together, got the dwarf and his charge, set out on the road. At the gate King Arthur secured the package which the porter gave him. They took the road down the hill, then up the river valley. The sun climbed up the sky. Noon came and King Arthur called a halt for lunch. Beauty said that before eating she was going to do a good weave with wild onions on King Arthur's helmet. And she did.

"Now that broken place is not obvious," said Beauty.

The road wound up away from the river. Up ahead, on a long hill, was a castle.

"There it is," said Beauty.

She and King Arthur rode toward it. It was up the hill above them.

Coming toward them on a very large horse was a huge knight. His face seemed more beast than human and his breath seemed a smoke. And he roared so that the trees, the rocks, the very Earth seemed to shake and vibrate. Beauty, on her horse, fled up the trail toward the castle.

"Let me out. Let me out," said the Thrush.

"No, you and I are going to set the example for bravery that you and I sing about," said King Arthur.

The monster knight slowed as he got closer to King Arthur.

"He is scared," said the Thrush.

The monster advanced, swung his sword at King Arthur. It clanged off the king's shield, but the force knocked King Arthur from his horse. King Arthur jumped behind the monster, crippled the monster's horse.

205

The monster lept off, came at the king with an axe which it held in its left hand. Again King Arthur deflected the blow with his shield, gave the monster a cut on the leg, ran behind the monster, stabbed it in the back so that smoky blood poured out. The monster turned to face King Arthur, moved back and forth, raised and lowered the axe and sword. King Arthur, moved, changed position, changed position again. The monster swung his sword as the king stepped quickly out of the way, stabbed the monster in the side. The monster screamed, swung the sword again at King Arthur. King Arthur cut off the sword arm. The monster roared, ran toward the woods, which was below the road. It fell, knocked down trees with its axe arm, then threshed around knocking down more trees while its hot blood boiled out and smoked.

Down the trail from the castle rushed four horsemen with pikes.

"Hello there, can we be of help?" called a horseman.

"Yes, thankyou. Good to see you. I could use an escort to the castle. And the mule should carry the bird and be encouraged to go to the castle."

"But we came to help with the monster knight," said another of the four.

"That has all been taken care of. He lies over among those trees."

The horsemen rode to the trees.

"Yeow, look at this."

The horsemen rode back to King Arthur, put the Thrush on the mule, started it moving toward the castle.

When the horsemen and King Arthur reached the castle, there was a great cheer. The gate was opened and people on all sides cheered.

"Knight of the Parrett tore up the Monster Knight," shouted one of the horsemen.

People cheered.

A very blond queen came forward with a huge bunch of flowers, and by her side was Beauty, and the queen gave the flowers to King Arthur.

"Why did you send those knights?" said King Arthur.

"In my judgement you were overmatched," said Beauty. "And I hoped to give you some chance."

"Had they come a bit sooner, they could have messed up the one thing I had come all the way from Camelot to do."

"I certainly could not have gone back to Camelot and tried to explain to Lord Gornemant and to Lord What's His Name and Caradoc how I had not done everything I could do to get you back to Camelot alive."

"But it was my choice."

"Yes and you are king. But be sure when I decide a thing needs to be done, I intend to do it, let you put on three crowns."

"Oh."

"But my duty was to bring a knight for this good lady. I have done it. Lady Blondhair, this is the Knight of the Parrett."

"You are the champion who saved our land and nothing is held back from the things which we would give," said the queen.

She dismounted, took King Arthur's hand as he dismounted. She led the king into the castle, up to her rooms. Two damsels prepared bath water for King Arthur, got out fine clothes for him to wear.

The queen entered and she had silvery blond hair and ice blue eyes. She walked with King Arthur to the hall where supper was to be served. All stood when the two entered and gave a great cheer. The mood was festive. Musicians and entertainers entered and the entertainment was directed at King Arthur and the queen.

Said a knight, "They could hardly be praised more were they the sun and moon."

The Thrush, in its golden house, was brought in and the house put on a golden table. The dwarf entered the hall, went up to the Thrush.

"Here I am, ready to care for you."

"No, you ran off and left me. We have gone our separate ways. I have given myself to the best knight in the world. He stood and faced danger with me," said the Thrush.

The dwarf went bawling from the room.

King Arthur seemed tired, so a fine bed was made in a hall for him and the Thrush brought to sing sweetly while he was going to sleep.

Morning came, four damsels came to take King Arthur to where there was a toilet, to get a pool ready for his bath, and they had fine clothes for him to put on. Lady Blondhair came to the bath and she and King Arthur went together to the hall where knights and ladies were gathered for breakfast. There was a cheer and all stood to greet Lady Blondhair and King Arthur when the two entered. King Arthur and the lady sat and ate in the midst of cheerful conversation.

Breakfast eaten, Lady Blondhair was impatient to see the slain warrior. She called for horses to be brought for her and the company. Horses brought, she mounted and she and King Arthur led the company down the road from the castle, down the hill to the grove of trees in which the monster knight lay. There was an awful smell about the dead body, and the body looked grotesque. King Arthur noticed what he had thought was a battle axe was the monster's left arm, which ended in huge sharp claws. And the helm was of horn, and had certainly never been off.

"Oh boy," said Lady Blondhair.

She looked up and down the huge monster. "How did you ever do it?"

"He was cautious."

"Yes, Yes, you look different from knights one sees everyday. You are from Camelot?"

"Yes. Yes, I am from there."

"And not from some water world beneath the Parrett?"

"No."

"I've seen enough," said Lady Blondhair.

She turned her horse around.

King Arthur was turning his horse around when he saw a rider coming down the Parrett valley. As she got closer she was heard to be shouting. There came the words, "Hail. Stop. Wait." She rode up threw herself on the ground by Lady Blondhair's horse.

"I will not rise up until the Knight of the Parrett comes and agrees to go with me to rescue my lady."

On their horses, the knights and ladies from Lady Blondhair's castle gathered around her. One shouted, "Oh yes, the Knight of the Parett can do anything."

It seemed numbers of the knights and ladies felt that the Knight of the Parrett should ride away then and there and solve the woman's problem: that it would be easy for him. Seeing where the opinions lay, Lady Blondhair kept her peace.

"But there is our Yule Tournament. It would be a disaster if you were not part of it. Promise you will be here for it," said Lady Blondhair.

"I will do my best to be here," said King Arthur.

"It will be so marvelous," said Lady Blondhair. She then turned to the woman who was on the ground.

"How did you hear of the Knight of the Parrett?"

"Everybody in the river basin knows of the Knight of the Parrett," said she.

She then told of her problem.

"My lord, King Belnain, was killed at a tournament. His seneschal took charge as ruler of the land, and he was so powerful that the king's lords supported him. They were afraid not to. The one thing that would have secured the seneschal's rule was to wed the king's only child, but she will not have him. She, with her mother, has shut herself up in a tower, a castle, and the seneschal can not get in. So, at risk to myself, I went out of the tower and have come for help."

"We have a tournament which I said I would try to be here for. And I want to be rested for that. So. After the tournament, I will agree to go with you and see about the seneschal. How is that?"

"Then you will stay at my castle," said Lady Blondhair.

The damsel from the Isle of Maidens nodded, but did not seem all that pleased.

"I'll tell you what," said Lady Blondhair. "I'll give a kiss to the winner of the tournament."

Among the knights, there was then much joyful conversation. The damsel remounted and the knights and ladies rode back to the castle.

At the castle, there was relaxed, good humoured conversation until time for lunch. At lunch the Thrush was glad to supply song. King Arthur noticed that the dwarf, though glum faced, was back in company with the Thrush.

The afternoon passed. King Arthur walked around the cool castle that under the grey sky, seemed not to get warm. The evening meal was a happy event. Beside the song of the Thrush, there were harpers.

"I would like to have Beauty fix my cut after we eat," King Arthur said to Lady Blondhair.

The company finished eating. A damsel came to King Arthur and took him to a chamber. He and the damsel went inside. Beauty was there.

"First, let's get your clothes off," said Beauty.

She slipped out of her robe. She and the damsel helped King

Arthur out of his clothes. Beauty put King Arthur's head in her lap. The damsel left.

"Going to fight some seneschal is not exactly going to take care of your kingdom."

"Go back and sit on my throne? I would never have a reputation at all."

"I do not believe that."

Beauty gently rubbed an herb salve all around King Arthur's cut forehead.

"What you could do. Go as the king you are and make demands."

Beauty kept rubbing in herbs.

"If I messed that up, the kingdom messed up. If a wandering knight messed up, it would be soon forgotten."

Beauty looked for other scrapes and bruises. Rubbed King Arthur with salve.

"My mistress. Pretty is she not?"

"She is. Pleasures on her surface. Nice."

"Can she be a queen?"

"Oh yes. I do not see her as mine. But I might wed some lady like that. Someday. Someday."

"But right now, the thing is to get your forehead healed."

"Your mistress did well with that. The tournament was a sharp move."

"So, you will be with me to go toward good health."

Beauty worked more with the hot salve.

"Same time tomorrow," said Beauty.

The two got dressed.

For King Arthur, it had been a long day. He went to bed.

In the morning, there was the song of the Thrush. It was a cold, grey morning. King Arthur washed, used a near by toilet, dressed and went to breakfast. There were many more women than men. The dwarf entered the hall with the Thrush. It was an enjoyable breakfast. While the company ate, the Thrush sang beautiful songs.

King Arthur finished eating, walked out of the hall, out of the castle and to the gate. He called for his horse, mounted. Beauty rode up beside him.

"Do you especially need solitude?" she asked.

"No."

They rode together down the hill, rode to the grove where the monster was.

"Look. Where the blood has touched all the plants have died," said Beauty.

The two rode on up the river. They found a secluded pool, took off their clothes and washed in the water. And they enjoyed the loving sharing of their bodies. Then it was time to ride back to the castle, to dress for lunch. At the table, all stood as beautiful, very blond, Lady Blondhair entered, took her seat. At lunch the Thrush sang and three harpers supplied music also. King Arthur got many questions to most of which he smiled and gave cryptic answers. Only two there, if one excludes the Thrush, knew that he did not come to them directly out of the Water World of the Parrett, and one of these, Lady Blondhair, was not all that sure that he did not.

By evening knights and ladies were arriving for the tournament, as its first day December sixth, was not that far off.

The evening meal was full of lively conversation. Not only was the Knight of the Parrett an attraction, but the kiss from Lady Blondhair also drew much conversation, as many were now thinking of it as the fore runner to a wedding; or, at least, to a copulation. And it was asked:

"What if the Knight of the Parrett got the kiss?" And: "What if he did not?"

Each day, morning and evening, more knights and ladies came to the castle. It was a cheerful gathering. The ladies of the castle were much pleased with the numbers of young, handsome knights. And some of them felt that they had a real chance of winning the kiss for themselves.

"The Knight of the Parrett," said one, looks good and stout, but, at the same time, rather young."

As the days passed, more and more knights arrived, and more of these were interested in seeing the Knight of the Parrett, or the Parrett Knight. There were many things knights wanted to discuss in conversations with the Knight of the Parrett. And Lady Blondhair often came to enjoy his company. Standing with him, they made a handsome couple. And every where Lady Blondhair went, so striking was her beauty, many people would turn and look. And the Thrush was a marvel which many thought, the greatest wonder of all; as, certainly, they had never known a bird to sing so well.

The castle was hung with bright cloths and other decorations, and bright fires were lit on the hearths. It was a handsome castle and it held many fine ornaments and furnishings. Lady Blondhair was like a splendid ornament.

It was thought that the knight who would kiss Lady Blondhair would be the one to marry her. Especially this thought went around because the lady opened the door to a bedroom which displayed a marvelous white bed. The whiteness of the bed glistened like snow under a white, very bright light. And the bed was trimmed with bright gems. The bed was under a dome formed by high arches. In the center of the dome was the statue of a falcon, and from its beak hung a gold chain to which was attached a large carbuncle. And this stone gave off a light. The hawk was on a golden table and above it, on the ceiling, gems formed pictures of beasts and birds. And the room held in it a sweet smell of perfume.

Lady Blondhair invited King Arthur into her magical bedroom. There she informed him that she would, for love, let him enter into her, that he would not need to do well in the tournament to gain her favour. King Arthur and the lady went down to the evening meal with the perfume of the bedroom in their heads.

The table was quite filled with loud talking knights and ladies, so that it gave competition to the harpers and entertainers.

After he had eaten, King Arthur went to where Beauty was waiting. Beauty went over King Arthur's body with ointment.

"It's looking good," she said.

King Arthur bid her good night and went to his bed.

Morning came, King Arthur was up early, washed and early at the breakfast table. Then he was one of many horsemen joined in a parade, the horsemen behind musicians, and men with pennants and decorative colours.

The parade marched to and around the tournament field and the musicians and other entertainers did a couple of flourishes while the knights in the lists got themselves lined up.

In the field, in its center, were decorated grandstands filled with ladies and in its center was the section for the lords and ladies of the castle. Lady Blondhair, in most beautiful robes, was seated there.

King Arthur, in his first match, was unexceptional. He deflected a lance correctly off his shield, but his own lance missed its target. This was not the magical touch which many had expected, as many had thought the Knight of the Parrett was from some Otherworld.

The fact that the Knight of the Parrett won more than he lost mattered little to the crowd when he lost a match to Lord Doldays and Lord Doldays said the Knight of the Parrett was a very average sort of knight and certainly not worthy of a kiss from the beautiful Lady Blondhair.

Some knight suggested that perhaps in the Water World of the Parrett they might not, as a regular thing, use lances.

"Well it seems not all of them use them well," said Lord Doldays.

"The fact is, he did it as a favour to me," said Lady Blondhair. "I wanted him to let some other knights win some."

King Arthur finished eating, went to where his bed was. Later in the evening Lady Blondhair sent for him. He was taken up to Lady Blondhair's room.

"Why did you say I acted dishonourably with those other knights?" said the Parrett Knight.

"I just knew you were better than all those."

"I am just a knight who does his best. To say I am not doing my best is to say I am a bad knight. You want me to be a bad knight. I will be a bad knight. This is a bad knight."

He gave Lady Blondhair a slap. She fell and cried as if her heart would break. The Parrett Knight went off in a huff, went to bed.

The Parrett Knight looked up. Beauty was kneeling by his side.

"Arthur, don't destroy my mistress."

"I did not much hurt her."

"Let me explain. Lady is in a different world than you and I. Hers is a play world filled with playthings. Very fragile playthings. I love my mistress. When she is broken, I bleed inside. Would you go love her?"

King Arthur kissed Beauty, went to Lady's room.

"Lady?"

He went in, lifted Lady in his arms, held her like a child.

Lady said, "It hurt me."

"I know. I'm sorry," said King Arthur.

He rocked Lady gently, kissed her lips, her eyes. Lady slept and he laid her down gently, went back to his bed. Beauty came to him, kissed his lips, went back to her bed.

King Arthur was awakened by daylight. He got up, took care of his toilet, washed. Beauty was there.

"Shall we wear these?" she said.

She helped King Arthur into this, into that.

"Now wait here, I am putting on more clothes."

She was back fully dressed. She said:

"Let us go to breakfast."

The two walked down the stairs. She said:

"This is a game. You do the best you can, but you do not need to win. You do not need to be a winner to enjoy a game, and to help someone else enjoy winning."

"I will do my best."

"I know you will."

Beauty kissed King Arthur. They went in, sat at the table. An elder lord was seated on the other side of Beauty. Beauty introduced the gentleman as Lord Valfort.

"Congratulations on a good day yesterday. I could see you were not entirely happy with it, but I thought you did well," said the lord.

"Thankyou. You mean, for a young knight like myself?"

"For any knight. You won more than you lost. There are many good knights who would be quite happy with that."

"Except I made mistakes. And these lances take the places of weapons of war, and one mistake against one of those, I would be dead."

"I would say yes and no. For a farmer who spends much of his time with a plow and a hoe, a lance might be a valued weapon. But, again, it would be best if he were not on a horse. For a warrior, my opinion, the weapon he should have in his hand is his sword. It is the most noble of weapons."

"Good to be reminded of that. Yes, the sword."

Beauty caught King Arthur's eye and the two smiled.

"So one does the best with the game. Thinks what is going to do the job," said Lord Valfort. "And, in my opinion, a generous congratulation wins more battles than a well placed lance."

Beauty and King Arthur finished eating. They bid good morning to Lord Valfort and left the table.

"So, enjoy yourself," said Beauty.

She went off to be with her lady. On her lady's face she put ointment and powder to cure and hide any mark of violence left over from the day before.

King Arthur got himself together, went out to his horse. He joined with other knights in the parade to the field below the castle where the second day of the tournament was to be held. Musicians and dancers did rounds in the center of the field; then, what the crowd was waiting for: knights began matching themselves, one against another. By mid morning, it was seen, the Knight of the Parrett was the best knight: he was then winning match after match. Then, there was only himself and Lord Doldays left. Then the two were meeting. The first: it went to the Knight of the Parrett: the second: it went to the Knight of the Parrett: the third: it went to the Knight of the Parrett, and in this, Lord Doldays was injured and needed to be helped from the field.

It was mid day. The judges decided that the Knight of the Parrett had, no doubt, won the tournament. He was declared the winner. The horns blew. Maidens holding bright colours escorted the Knight of the Parrett to Lady Blondhair. She warmly kissed his lips.

King Arthur said he thought Lord Doldays deserved an honour for his fine showing the day before. Lord Doldays, at Lady Blondhair's request, was brought up and praised for his victories.

"I see a bright future for the Knight of the Parrett," said Lord Doldays.

Beauty and Lord Valfort exchanged smiles.

The Knight of the Parrett joined the parade to the castle. King Arthur dismounted, went in with the crowd of horsemen, went up and washed and dressed for lunch. Beauty came and got him and they went down to the hall together.

"I'll be leaving for Isle Fort tomorrow morning," said King Arthur.

"Is there a chance, you will return," Beauty asked.

"I will return if I am able."

"The good news should not make me cry. But it does," said

Beauty.

"The Thrush gave me your name, as you heard. I take it to mean, you will be waiting for the reason? So will I," said King Arthur.

After lunch many knights and lords and ladies and their companies were saying their farewells to Lady Blondhair and were leaving the castle. Beauty and King Arthur, in warm robes walked here and there in the cold castle gardens.

"I'll see that the damsel from Isle Fort is ready to travel," said Beauty.

The two went in to dinner. It was a quiet meal, but Lady Blondhair looked happy. Two harpers played and the Thrush sang sweetly.

After the meal, Beauty took King Arthur to her room. She and King Arthur undressed and Beauty washed King Arthur in her pool, then put robes on him and herself and she took him to the room of the marvelous bed. Two unclothed damsels helped King Arthur, then Lady Blondhair, out of their clothes. The light glistened not only on the mass of silvery blond hair on the lady's head, but on the good amount of blond hair on the lady's arms, on her legs, and the good mass of blond hair on her stomach. The damsels rubbed a quantity of scented oils into their bodies.

Lady and King Arthur let the damsels instruct them; then, in a liquid bliss, further instruction was hardly heard at all.

King Arthur felt a hand on his shoulder.

"It is morning."

It was Beauty.

King Arthur got up gently off the flaxen haired lady, went with Beauty to her room.

"Your connection to Camelot has already drifted away from her thoughts. For her, you will ever be the Magical Prince of the Water World of the Parrett; a prince out of the Dream World," said Beauty.

"She is my dream princess," said King Arthur.

Beauty washed King Arthur in her pool, and they got dressed.

"I'll get Lady up," said Beauty.

Then Beauty and Lady were there and the three of them went to breakfast.

The damsel from Isle Fort was at the table.

"I have all waiting at the gate," said the damsel.

"The dwarf and the Thrush insisted on going on the trip, so they will be there also."

King Arthur bid farewell to the lords and ladies at the table, to Lord Valfort. He then kissed both of Lady's hands, then went to the gate with Beauty and the damsel. At the gate, King Arthur and Beauty held each other in a long embrace. King Arthur mounted and his party was off.

The party rode up the river valley. They stopped for lunch under some trees by the river and ate food Beauty had packed. After eating, a long ride took them to a small castle and there they were made welcome. They dined and were given a bed. The damsel snuggled her body around King Arthur.

"I still smell Lady's perfume on you," said the damsel.

"It is unusual," said King Arthur.

"I like it," said the damsel.

Morning: King Arthur and the damsel arose, washed, dined with the people of the castle, thanked their host, then were off again. And the dwarf kept up with them. The group stopped, had lunch. The damsel was tall, slim, athletic and good humoured.

"How am I as a travelling companion?" she asked.

"Fine. You feel good in bed."

"They both laughed.

In late afternoon, King Arthur and his companions came to another fortified homestead. The lord was quite taken with the Thrush and the Thrush, pleased, gave marvelous song at the evening meal. After eating, while others were entertained by the Thrush, King Arthur and the damsel worked lovingly with each other's bodies.

King Arthur and his company were up early for breakfast. Then after, they rode down to the river and there they took card of their toilet and washed. They traveled through the morning; then, on the banks of the river, all thanked Beauty again for the goodness of the food she had fixed. In the evening, the group was entertained at a fine fortified homestead. The Thrush again provided song while King Arthur and the damsel cared lovingly for each other's bodies. The two of them held up just short of copulation.

Morning came. Again, King Arthur and his group arose early, had breakfast, then went to the river where they made their toilet and washed.

Then, mounted, they rode up the trail.

"Halt. Stop scoundrel."

King Arthur turned his horse, saw a large knight riding hard up the trail toward them.

"They been saying 'Parrett Knight is better than you.' I said, 'Here, I must be the best. I will cut off his right hand so you will see who is best.' "

"Some other time. Now, he is on a sacred mission, do not get in his way," said the damsel.

"Who asked you?" said the knight.

He drew his sword, attacked King Arthur. His sword banged furiously on King Arthur's shield, his shield banged into King Arthur's side. King Arthur's sword sliced through his shoulder. He fell. King Arthur looked around. The damsel had a long knife in her hand: a slender sword.

"Do not look so stunned. Just say to yourself, 'I am not travelling with Beauty. I am not travelling with Beauty'."

"I can defend myself," said King Arthur in a huff.

"That is not what I call a certainty."

They rode in silence for a while.

"Do not be silly. Let us stop for lunch," said the damsel.

She laughed at King Arthur. Then he laughed at himself.

They sat and ate.

"One word, if I may. When one sees a gentle person, one sometimes fails to see the strength," King Arthur said.

"Beauty. And I should look at you to see what needs patching up. Most women are healers when they need to be."

"Tonight you can see what you think. - And the squabble I had with Beauty was much the same thing."

"It was? I did not know about that."

"That was before you came. What I came here for."

"Good for Beauty."

"Yes, always," said King Arthur.

The damsel smiled. She went to a clump of weeds, pissed on it.

"Could you use help with anything?" she said.

"Perhaps later."

The group mounted, turned up a valley on a woodland trail. The trail came out on meadows and not far off, on a grassy hill, was a castle. Toward the castle they rode. They had ridden a way over the meadow when four damsels rode from the castle, rode up to them and invited them to the castle. King Arthur and the damsel were delighted with the offer, so all rode to the castle.

At the castle, King Arthur and his group were made most welcome. The castle was owned by a Lady Noble. Lady Noble was a healer known throughout the area as one of the best. And she, first off, looked at King Arthur's cuts, she told King Arthur that they were serious and that he was fortunate she caught them in time. Neither the damsel nor King Arthur himself had realized, before they saw them, how bad the injuries were. The damsel and the lady said that until the injuries were healed, he could not go anywhere.

King Arthur, for some days, was confined to bed where he was cared for by Lady Noble and the damsel, and they had help from other ladies of the castle. Yule came and King Arthur was able to go into the big hall where the dancing and music was. A dozen musicians played for the dancing and for various games, and entertainments often featured the song of the Thrush. And the Yule fires and decorations were most pleasing.

Lady Noble came and sat beside King Arthur.

"That was a good slash that caught your skull."

"Better swordsman than that fellow down in the woods. And he might still be living. But his fighting days, one can be sure, are gone. Unless it is against Old Man Death, the one who waits for us all."

"The healer did a really very good job."

"Beauty. She has gentle hands like yourself. In fact, she is every way gentle."

"And you love her. But you will not wed her?"

"If I could go back to plowing the fields. And to raising a few hogs. Then yes. But I have that which I must do, as does she. So that is my life story."

"We knew you were the Knight of the Parrett because of the Thrush. But we thought you would be richer looking, bright weapons, well fitting garment."

The damsel came, sat on the other side of King Arthur.

219

She said, "And here he is, just a youth in old clothes. With a working knight's every day sword. Kept sharp enough to pass any seneschal's inspection."

"I did not say it, but yes," said Lady Noble.

"Yes, I am still learning," said King Arthur.

"Well," said Lady Noble, "I hope we all get you back home, so when your father dies, you will be there with your experience. Do make him mind you, damsel."

"So, happy Yule, Sir Parrett," said Lady Noble. She gave King Arthur a kiss.

"Happy Yule," said the damsel.

She gave King Arthur a warm kiss.

"A most happy Yule to both of you. The Yule celebration is a big spirit lifter. I have always celebrated Yule and not being at a celebration would have made me sad. So here it is. Happy Yule," said King Arthur.

King Arthur sat a while longer enjoying the festivities. Then he retired to his bed. Lady Noble - and the damsel rubbed salve on his wounds. The damsel undressed, lay beside him. She spread her legs, wrapped them around him, kissed him hard on the lips.

"I know it's right. I know it's right. – Oh thankyou, thankyou thankyou forever."

King Arthur pulled the damsel close to him and slept.

The morning came. King Arthur and the damsel arose, washed and went to the toilets, dressed and washed for breakfast. She sat next to King Arthur. Lady Noble looked at her and smiled. The damsel caught Lady Noble's eye and the two had a smile together.

"I feel so - different," the damsel said to King Arthur. It was still Yule celebration. King Arthur and the damsel, in the great hall, together enjoyed the music and the Yule celebration.

"Tomorrow, first thing, we will go see what we can do for your lady," said King Arthur.

"Maybe we can work some bargain," said the damsel.

"If you would rather, an impressive looking, fifty year lord, I can get you one."

"No, certainly not."

"Because my bargains are do what I tell you or face trouble. But cheer up. We will see what can be done."

The two of them went to tell Lady Noble their plans and to thank her for the tremendous help she had been. Then it was time for lunch. Then the afternoon fled past. Then, the Yule celebrations at dinner. All joined in the singing.

King Arthur and the damsel went to bed early and before it got late, King Arthur was deep inside the damsel.

Morning. King Arthur and the damsel were up. Their toilet needs cared for, they washed, dressed and went to breakfast. This eaten, they made their rounds, expressed thanks and said their farewells. Aside, King Arthur told Lady Noble that she could count on Camelot should she ever need a friend.

King Arthur and his party rode across the meadow and into the forest. Through the forest they rode until the sun reached mid day. At this point, they stopped in a grove and had lunch.

After lunch they remounted, rode a forest way to a castle on the lands of Lady Flor of Mont. This castle was ruled by a Lord Andois, and he treated the damsel and her friends in a most hospitable way. He explained that when the father of Flor was at war with King Marioch and Lord Cite Fort, with the help of Lord Andois, he won. The father of Flor also had the help of some foreign lords. These he rewarded, but he overlooked Lord Andois. So, Lord Andois said he was not going to take her side against the seneschal, who had usurped controle.

King Arthur and his group were taken to a hall where, with a company of knights and ladies, they were served an excellent dinner. After eating, they were taken to a high domed parlour in which was planted a garden and in the garden flowers were in bloom. The damsel sat next to him.

"I am home now. Tomorrow, if I may, I will take you to my lady and she can explain her problem. One thing: This is not a land ruled by a princess who has her head in a world of dreams. This is a land where there are many lords, and each has his own way of seeing things. After I introduce you to my lady, you will be somebody. I will not. More than each of these other damsels whom you see around the waters and flowers. So: I am one of them. Take care. Keep your wits at your finger tips. One question: Will I ever know more about who you are?"

"I believe you will. As it is only in this time that my identity needs

221

to be hidden. But if there is a strong wish to know, you might go to the Princess of Dreams. It might take asking more than once."

"Tonight I will be very lonesome."

"And you have become a special part of me."

The damsel drifted away among the other damsels and the flowers. Then it was time for bed. King Arthur was shown to a fine bed in a room where his belongings had been put.

It was morning. A knight came in.

"Sir, breakfast is being served."

King Arthur got up, got himself ready, went down to breakfast. After he had eaten, the damsel came to his place at the table and said she was ready to set out for the tower. A horse was brought for the dwarf and King Arthur's horse, made ready, and they set out; Lord Andois and four of his knights providing an escort. Lord Andois and his knights rode with King Arthur for what seemed about seven miles, then they turned back.

King Arthur rode on. He and the dwarf came to a wide marsh where marsh grasses stuck their tops above water. A road wound its way through the marsh and King Arthur set out on the road. Ahead of him was a castle and a fortified gateway. When King Arthur got closer, he saw some knights guarding the gate. King Arthur rode up to the gate.

"Open the gate. I have business on the other side," he said.

"Sir Knight, who are you? I do not recognize you."

"I am known as the Knight of the Parrett."

"We do not permit stranger knights to pass. And we are especially to be on the alert for knights with funny names like yours," said the knight.

"There is nothing so funny about my name that it should deny me courtesy and hospitality."

"My friend, turn around and go back. You can not go this way. Surely good sense will tell you that."

"My good knight, I have not come this far just to turn around and go back."

"Since you came this far and alone, you must be one of the great magical hero's that bards sing about. If you are, there are nine of us; you, with a lance, will be able to knock over the whole line of us, one at a time. Then you can keep going. If not, if you fall from your horse, you become our prisoner."

The knight offered King Arthur a lance.

"You have become rather good with the lance. Give it a try. Dwarf, cut up some of this cloth. Stick it in Parrett's ears. Take a deep breath, check all your gear," said the Thrush.

The Thrush then whistled a song ever so beautiful. King Arthur checked everything as the Thrush had said. Then he rode toward the first in line. The first in line started forward, but by the time he reached King Arthur he was fast asleep, easily toppled from his horse. The others in the line laughed; then, they too fell asleep and were easily pushed from their horses. King Arthur and the dwarf rode on.

"I will go see how they are doing," said King Arthur.

He turned his horse and rode back. The gatemen were still asleep. King Arthur sat and waited.

"Good morning," said King Arthur.

"Oh, you're still here," said the chief gateman.

"Yes, I wanted to introduce myself. In spite of my funny name, I am not all that funny. I am going from place to place searching for contests where I can, in fair play, test my skills. I have avoided revealing exactly who I am because, for one thing, I am expected at tournaments, and if people got word I was way up here, it might be more difficult to bring people to the tournaments."

"I would say, there concern would be justified," said the chief gateman.

"To what tournament?" said a second gateman.

"For one, May Day at Camelot."

"We have some stout lads here. Might be a good tournament to attend," said the chief gateman.

Lord Andois rode up and with him, a half dozen knights and a half dozen damsels.

"Good morning Lord," said the chief gateman." We have a young knight here looking for contests."

"I have met him. He won the tournament at Castle Damours. Defeated Lord Doldays three times on the final day."

"Did he now?" said a gateman.

"And lost to him twice the day before," said King Arthur.

"Can't win them all," said the chief gateman.

"Yes, you can have contests here," said Lord Andois.

"And he can stay at my place. Say, who is that dwarf fellow?" said the chief gateman.

"Came across him on my way. Seems like a good fellow, but I don't know his name."

"Better watch him. Might be a magician," said the gateman.

"Most of them are," said King Arthur. "And I should get to know the ruler of this land."

"That is a complex problem," said the chief gateman.

"Yes, that is complicated," said a knight.

"We must be on the watch for rules," said a knight.

The Knight of the Parrett was invited to stay with the chief gateman. In the day, King Arthur found the dwarf and he too was invited. The dwarf had little to say and little to do but feed his bird.

"The reason no one knows his name," said a gateman, "is that nobody cares."

Sir Parrett, as King Arthur was often called, had much to say about the farming, the farm equipment, and about the horses. And he was interested in what Lord Andois was doing with his inside garden. The damsels there said the Knight of the Parrett needed to take the Thrush to sing for their lady. So eight damsels went with King Arthur to get the dwarf and the Thrush, and the company rode toward the tower where the royal ladies were.

As the group rode forward, King Arthur noticed the damsel who had brought him there was crying. He rode over, put a hand on her back.

"Hey there, you are supposed to be the tough one."

"It was a mask."

"So, why the tears?"

"I should never have brought you, a young knight, into this place. It is full of death traps. And none of us were dying."

"The world is dangerous. We do the best we can, then leave. Cheer up. I have a few wits. Another thing, if you need her, Beauty will help you. And she will be happy to help."

"Those words are a wonderful gift."

They were still some distance from the queen's tower and there on their left was a tall mount. On the mount was a fortified stone structure. From it, a knight rode toward them.

"Here comes the seneschal's standard bearer. He is very cruel. He is considered the strongest knight in the land. He wants to destroy every knight who comes here," said the damsel.

The seneschal's knight rode up.

"So you are the strange knight come looking for the contests."

"I am the Knight of the Parrett."

"Here I am, ready with all weapons I need."

"Very good. I suggest tomorrow morning in front of the lady of the land, so she can judge who is a worthy head banger."

"I will accept that," said the standard bearer.

The standard bearer went back to his hill.

The damsels, the dwarf and the Knight of the Parrett rode on through a valley which wound around hills. To the front, on a round, medium sized hill, was a large tower which looked ancient. It was built of large stones which had been skillfully fitted together. The group rode up to it.

"Hail," shouted a damsel.

From the wall on the roof she was answered.

"We have come, do let us in."

A small heavy door was opened and the dwarf, the damsels and King Arthur entered. Inside were a dozen damsels whom King Arthur thought all must have been between thirteen and fifteen. The gathering of the damsels, to all in the gathering, meant a party. And they were thrilled with the dwarf and the Thrush. The Thrush sang to them and, in great joy, they sang to the Thrush. Princess Flor and the queen came down the stair and the queen looked so sombre that the music failed to cheer.

The Knight of the Parrett walked over and greeted the queen.

"How do you do, Lady. I am the warrior which you sent for."

"The Knight of the Parrett. You look like a stout warrior. You look rather young."

"True. For what age is worth, I am not rich in that."

"But I hear you are an honoured knight in Lyonesse."

"Thankyou."

"And they say, King Arthur is a mighty king there. Do you know

King Arthur?"

"Indeed, I am his best friend."

"Well, that is something."

"So what is this all about? Can you rule this country?" asked the knight.

"I will rule the country," said Princess Flor. "Rule it with justice, which that seneschal knows nothing of. And no one gave him the right to rule."

"Where is that man?" the knight asked.

"Tomorrow one will be here who can put you on the right road to find him. He stays hidden a long way from this place, then sends out tyrants with whom he communicates but never sees," said the queen.

"Tomorrow, I have a contest with the lands standard bearer. After that, I am at your service."

"As the guide does not come every day, and likes not to wait, we hope you will be ready," said the queen.

"You can be certain, I spent many days on this trip to see that guide, he can wait a bit, should there be the need, for me. And should he not, I can be a bad tempered knight."

"Dear Sir, you are our last hope and so many things could go bad. So we gently hold our little hope and say, 'Give this bad tempered knight health, strength and love,'" said the princess.

"But if the guide leaves, the wait would be a year.

But sit down with us for your lunch. The damsels will take you to wash," said the queen.

The damsels took the Parrett Knight to where there was water for washing and a place where he could make his toilet. A number of damsels were there engaged in the same operations.

The knight was taken back, up the stairs, to the table and given a seat, joining Princess Flor and the queen. The Thrush was nearby, and while damsels carried in food, it sang a soothing song.

"In some ways, I am reminded of Ludlow Castle," said the knight.

"I hope in a good way," said the queen.

"Oh yes. Everything in those years was good. If I may, on this ride, I will leave the dwarf with you, as I ride at a speed which might be too much for him."

"We will be glad to have him," said the queen.

The Parrett Knight finished lunch, bid farewell to the princess, and to the queen and left the tower. He rode back to the chief gateman's place. There, he put his gear in order, then explained to the chief gateman what the challenge was. The chief said the knight needed supporters who would have lances when they were needed.

The day passed. Morning came. After the Parrett Knight had eaten, he went to his horse, and three gatemen were mounted and ready to travel. The knight mounted and the four rode toward Fearless Keep, the name of the tower where Queen Isle Fort resided. When they got to the tower, they found, at the bottom of the hill, the Standard Bearer there and waiting for them. The Knight of the Parrett got set and he and the Standard Bearer charged against each other. The struck each other down at the first pass without knowing who had acquitted himself the better. The standard bearer drew his sword so the Knight of the Parrett was quick to follow his example. The battle was fierce, but the Knight of the Parrett forced his challenger backward, then the challenger fell.

"I surrender. I declare you the better knight," said the standard bearer.

"I will accept your surrender if you swear allegiance to Queen Isle Fort."

"I will do that."

The standard bearer went to where the queen and Princess Flor of Mont were watching from the tower.

"I have come to swear allegiance to you," said the standard bearer.

The door to the tower was opened and the knights went inside. Damsels took the standard bearer to wash him. The queen and Princess Flor took the Knight of the Parrett to their own room. They washed him and put him in fine clothes. They then escorted him to a room where a large table was, and they joined the other knights and damsels. Many conversations mixed together and formed a happy sounding hum. Food was brought in and the room got quiet while people ate.

Knights bid good day to the people of the castle, went out to their horses. The queen and the princess took the Knight of the Parrett to their room took his clothes off and put him in the queen's bed. The queen and the princess rubbed the knight with sweet oils until he

227

slept. The sun had gone down when the queen woke the Knight of the Parrett.

"The varlet has come," she said.

She and the princess got their knight up, helped him with his toilet, washed him, helped him dress and took him to their table and there, damsels had food ready for him. He ate. The queen and the princess led him down the stairs to where his horse had been gotten ready. On the horse had been packed a good supply of food and wine. The Parrett Knight mounted his horse. Princess Flor handed him his helmet, and this, she had decorated with gold and silver.

The varlet stood beside the horse.

"Come," he said.

He led the way to a secluded grove, which was in a gully. In it was a long necked, horned beast. This, the varlet mounted: and he, on the beast, led the way, by a narrow path, to a moon lit landscape. Over the moon lit fields the two of them travelled many a mile. In front of them, in a plot of ground, was a blooming tree.

"We may go no farther in this way," said the varlet, "but pick a flower from the tree and secure it in your clothing."

The knight picked a large, scarlet flower, put it in a secure place.

"You will see knights and ladies at a tournament. They will invite you to take part, and this you may do. However, if you take part, you will receive a wound which can never, in your world, be cured."

The varlet went into the dark shadows.

The Knight of the Parrett sat beneath the tree and the wonderful smell of the flowers drifted over him. Then there they were. Knights and damsels rode onto the field. Then further on, there was a tournament. A knight looked toward the tree.

"Why, there is Arthur."

Another looked around.

"Arthur come and join us, help us defeat – "

A damsel rode up.

"Come, Arthur, it will be fun, join our knights over here."

She rode off a way. Another shouted:

"Where are you Arthur, we need you," shouted a knight.

The Knight of the Parrett saw them riding, saw pennants flying. The temptation was great. He stood up, walked to his horse. Then he saw an ancient druid walk to an old stone wall, and in niches in the wall there were skulls. The druid rang a silver bell. The tournament vanished.

The sun came up. There was a path, vague though it was, which seemed to lead forward from the way he faced. He saddled his horse and rode on. He came to a stone on which there was a cross carved deep in the stone. And there, the path divided: one, went on one side of the stone; the other, on the other. He rode down the path to the right.

A long way the Knight of the Parrett rode, and the way led into hilly country. A hysterical woman he saw running down the side of a high hill. When she got to the bottom and had calmed, she shouted to the knight she saw.

"Sire, a serpent has roughly carried away a friend of mine and I am afraid he is dead."

"Damsel, where is this serpent?" the Parrett Knight asked.

The damsel pointed, so the Knight of the Parrett rode quickly off in that direction. He had not gone far when he saw a serpent which held a knight in its mouth. He attacked the serpent and slew it, but the dying serpent, flailing around, struck him with its tail and knocked him into a lake and poisoned him with its venom. He crawled out of the lake and, ill though he was, he climbed on his horse and rode on. However, a short time later, the illness caused him to pass out.

The Knight of the Parrett woke and he saw the lady who was on the hill side and a knight. The knight, who said he was the one being carried off by the snake, said, "I interrupted a fisherman stealing your gear." Then, when he saw that the Knight of the Parrett was not dead, but ill; he took him home, and there he learned it was the knight who saved his life. The lady gave the Knight of the Parrett some food and some healing teas while her lord told about the journey ahead.

"The way is dangerous," he said. "It is a two day's journey through lawless lands. At the end of that time, you will come to dark waters which there is no way out of. Beyond the waters is a round hill, and on the hill, the dark shape of a castle, its walls and towers ending in tall spikes. Over the waters; a tall arch goes to the castle, but it is so narrow that no horse may walk over it. And over the center of the bridge is a wheel which sweeps all which is under it into the dark waters. So that is the end of the journey. When one comes to the bridge, one may turn around and start back for home."

"But," said the Knight of the Parrett, "there are those who go to that castle."

"There are those who have gone there by magic, but who knows if any have ever returned."

"But you must stay here today while I make you teas of herbs which will make you strong for the journey," said Sir Amorous' lady.

The Knight of the Parrett spent the day at the fortified homestead, walking over the grounds with the knight, being shown the herb garden by his lady; then, at evening, eating with them what the land produced.

"And here I am," said Sir Amorous," some scrapes and bruises and a few puncture wounds, but none the worse. The toxin went down the hill away."

The Knight of the Parrett got to bed early, then was up early to pack his gear for the journey. He was given food to eat along the way. Then it was time for breakfast. Sir Amorous said he would ride with him some of the way.

After breakfast, the two knights got on their horses and were off. The first day was a ride through plots of thorns and scrubby trees. There was a stop for lunch, a stop for supper, then sleep by the side of the road. Morning came: there was breakfast, a ride through dried grasses and leafless bushes; then, lunch. Mid afternoon, away in the misty distance, the faint shapes of spires could be seen.

"That is my signal to return," said Sir Amorous. He turned his horse around.

The Knight of the Parrett rode on. He had a lonesome supper, then rode on. The moon rose and lit a bare dirt path. It seemed to go on and on. The Knight of the Parrett got sleepy. He dismounted and slept.

Then it was morning. The Knight of the Parrett ate the last of his food. Then he looked in front of him. The castle rose up dark and horrid. He mounted and rode forward. There was the high arch of the bridge. The Knight of the Parrett rode up to its base. There seemed no way to cross it. It was like a thin silvery rainbow. Then, at its center, there seemed a circle of darkness. However, the dark circle seemed to have shifting lights and darks. So it was turning. And Queen Isle Fort was being ruled by something on the other side of that dark circle: the dark wheel.

"One thing." Said King Arthur, "Queen Isle Fort would not have sent a knight here if he would have no way to get past that wheel."

King Arthur thought of everything he had, everything he could think, which might be his key. He thought, the tournament, the place of skulls, and from there, he got a scarlet flower. He rode on through brambles and rough stalks. There was no path here. Here and there, there were the screams of beasts. Out of the bushes a huge naked woman jumped on King Arthur and knocked him from his horse. She was covered with bristles and her muscles were as hard as ropes. She had King Arthur around the neck and he could not pry her hands loose, so he pulled out his dagger, stabbed her one, two, three times, in the stomach. Then her hands fell away.

King Arthur walked forward to the arch. There was the end of it in a pile of gravel. He got the flower from his shirt, hung it from his neck.

He went to the arc, stepped on its thin width, but could feel he could not walk on it, so he began to crawl. The span shook and a wind blew so that it was hard not to get blown off.

There in front of him was the wheel. King Arthur took the flower in his hand, went forward. He went through what seemed a rainbow made of mist; then, down the slope to a ledge of rock. He walked over the flat rock, walked past some knights and ladies. And these made no indication that they even saw him. King Arthur walked down a stair. There on a great throne was a savage looking king. The king grabbed a sword and shield and attacked King Arthur. A good fighter though he was, he was not a match for King Arthur and King Arthur split his skull. A knight came to King Arthur. He pointed to a bell over the throne: a little silver bell. King Arthur got it and gave it to the knight. The knight rang the bell. All around King Arthur began to crumble and fade. Not far from him was a druid ringing a silver bell. And there was the old stone wall, the skulls in the niches of the wall. He walked back down a path. There was the naked woman with muscles like ropes and with blood spilled out onto the path. There was his horse.

"Sir Knight, would you like to have breakfast with me?"

"Yes," King Arthur would.

"Yes, it would be much appreciated."

The two had breakfast together. King Arthur told the druid his story. After they had eaten, the druid said:

"Come."

He took King Arthur down a path to what looked like ruins to an old castle. Stones were scattered and in piles, and on a heap of stones was the man he slew.

"I slew him," said King Arthur.

"I thought you had. We should take him to the queen."

The druid got a couple of horses and some food and they began their journey to Fearless Keep, the home of the queen.

The two took their time on the road, as they had many things to discuss. Then they rode up to the keep and the people there were wild with joy. Then the word got out and more and more came to honour the queen and the princess.

"It will be a glorious burial. I trust you can stay," said the queen.

"As I have said, I have some places where I need to be," said the Knight of the Parrett.

"We can load you down with riches."

"Again, no. Too many riches makes a man lazy. But I will let you give me a good supper and a good breakfast."

The Knight of the Parrett and the druid went in the keep, were washed, and they enjoyed an excellent meal, and the standard bearer was there also, and the dwarf.

After dinner and festivities, the Knight of the Parrett was getting weary, so a number of damsels washed him and, by instruction, put him to bed in the queen's bed, and the queen and the princess, shortly after, got in bed with him.

In the morning, King Arthur was helped with his toilet and washed and dressed, and he was taken to the queen's table. Breakfast was enjoyed.

"Would you permit a damsel to ride with you?" asked the queen.

"Certainly."

King Arthur went out to where his horse stood waiting; his and two other horses. On one of these was the golden house of the bird.

"Hey, I am ready," said the damsel.

"It will be a cold ride," said King Arthur.

"I know," said the damsel.

A glum looking dwarf sat on his horse.

"Now Dwarf, cheer up. We won," said King Arthur.

They started off.

"I am dying to hear how you solved our mysterious situation. It saved the country from untellable misery. The only thing it lacked: the young golden hero did not marry the young princess he saved."

"I can not marry everybody."

"And likely you have a lady back home."

"And I just saved a golden lady of another land."

"Yes, of course."

They rode on.

"Tell me how you found and slew our enemy."

King Arthur told the damsel the story.

King Arthur had lunch with the chief gateman and the two of them talked of Camelot, and King Arthur said again he intended to be there for the May tournament.

Soon after lunch, he rode to the castle of Lord Andois, and there he had dinner. He decided to spend the night there so that he could discuss political problems with the lord while his damsel had what she thought might be her last fling with her girl friends. The Thrush and the crowd of damsels entertained each other.

King Arthur told Lord Andois that any time he could visit Camelot, he could be certain of a royal welcome.

First thing in the morning King Arthur and his group were on the road. The weather was cold, so they hurried along. The nights were much pleasure for King Arthur and the damsel. Physically, the two of them fit well together and the damsel was a fun person to be with. Then one breakfast, King Arthur and the damsel discussed their futures.

"I believe it is here our paths should part," said the damsel. "I should ride up to Lady Nobles. I can learn useful thing there. Especially useful if I should have a baby."

"And I hope you do. And I never asked, but – ?"

"My name. It is Gwyl."

The two gave each other big hugs and the damsel jumped on her horse and rode up the trail. King Arthur packed up, then he and the dwarf set out toward the city of Lady Blondhair.

King Arthur did some hard riding between cold nights, then he and the dwarf rode up the hill toward Damours Castle. Before he got to the castle, people had streamed out to see him and there was a shout, "The Knight of the Parrett."

Before King Arthur reached the gate, Beauty and Lady Blondhair ran out to greet him and themselves to help him off his horse, Lady Blondhair, crying, threw herself into King Arthur's arms.

"The Prince of the Parrett," she said, "I was afraid."

Beauty took King Arthur in her arms.

"Funny time to cry," she said.

Tears ran down her cheeks.

"Can you stay?" said Lady Blondhair.

"I can stay three days."

"Come get washed, you and the dwarf, and we will have food gotten together," said Beauty.

She and Lady Blondhair, when they all had gotten into the castle, took King Arthur to the lady's room and got him ready for his lunch.

While he ate, he told the story of his adventures.

"You had trouble right off," said Beauty.

"An example: one selfish knight thinking to take for himself some other person's reward for hard work or wise choice," said King Arthur. "Even though the result of the trouble was obtained through the injustice, it had its rewards. We needed to spend time with Lady Noble, a person whom I find, worth knowing. The damsel is with her now."

King Arthur went on, telling of his adventures.

"And an example: the friends with whom you travel can be of great value: can save a mission. It is known, my work with a lance is not always of the best. When I was faced with the need to knock down nine in a row, my friend Sir Thrush sang a song so sweet that they fell from their saddles. Merlin could not have done it better."

"Merlin. That worrier over muddles of oak twigs. Give him ass ears. Merlin," said the Thrush.

"Merlin is a friend of mine." Said King Arthur.

"Merlin is a friend of mine too. Except when I am forced to listen to a bunch of nonsense about how great he is," said the Thrush.

"Then, let me get on with my adventure."

King Arthur talked for a long time about the character of the country of Queen Isle Fort. He spoke of the garden of Lord Andois. The conversation went on up to the dinner hour.

"A gift you can give me," said King Arthur. "A good home for Sir Thrush and the dwarf, should they desire it, as I am not going from here directly to Camelot."

"It would be a gift to us if they would consent to stay," said Lady Blondhair.

"The king will be off to find a queen," said the Thrush.

"I knew you would need a queen. But still – ," said Beauty.

"Your last battle, Beauty will be at that place.

The last ship you see, Beauty will be on it. The last song you hear, Beauty will be singing it," said the Thrush.

"At my time of greatest need, you will be there," said King Arthur.

"And likely, of mine," said Beauty.

Lady Blondhair wiped away her tears.

"Well, at least there is time for supper first," she said.

The four of them went to the hall where supper was ready. The crowd stood and cheered as they came in. King Arthur noticed there were many more damsels than knights. The food was most enjoyable. There were harpers. The Thrush enjoyed these, so the harp music was augmented by beautiful song from the Thrush.

Beauty and Lady did not stay in the room where the music was, but took King Arthur to Lady's rooms where the sound of the music floated through the sound of the water falling into the pool. Lady and the two damsels took King Arthur's clothes as they themselves undressed. Beauty gave King Arthur a big hug and went to her rooms.

The damsels and Lady washed King Arthur and rubbed scented oils over his body, and King Arthur washed them and rubbed scented oils into their bodies. Lady took King Arthur into her as much as she could.

"A magical prince to flood magic into my body makes this the top of magical kingdoms," she said.

The castle was very beautiful: white curving walls, spires, statues, falling waters and pools, and music echoing from the walls. And beautiful art in this place and that. And the wind sang through the pillars and spires.

A couple of damsels came in. They were unclothed. They woke Lady, got her up and into the pool, got King Arthur up, took him into the pool. Lady and King Arthur washed each other and played in the water. The damsels took Lady and King Arthur from the pool and dressed them for breakfast.

Lady, with King Arthur, went to the breakfast table. The company at the table stood and cheered. They sat and ate.

"I want to borrow your prince after breakfast," said Beauty.

King Arthur finished eating and he and Beauty went off to her room.

"We will take time together in my pool," said Beauty.

Undressed, the two hugged and kissed; then, on a ledge, lay in each other's arms. They talked together.

"We never spoke, I wonder, about whether I should put my member up in you."

"No need. Some, who feel some lack, use it as a way to touch another's spirit. But that goes such a little way," said Beauty.

"So little people can do. But you and I," said King Arthur.

"Yes, of course, we found it." said Beauty.

King Arthur and Beauty spent the morning with each other. Lunch time came. The two joined the company for lunch. In the afternoon, Beauty took King Arthur to a neglected part of the city where they could be alone. Below them flowed the river. It flowed from distant mountains, misty in the distance. The two stood holding each other.

"I will be going that way," said King Arthur.

"It will be a long journey. You will be further and further away. It will be lonesome," said Beauty.

Supper time came. The two went to the table, joined the company for dinner.

Dinner over, King Arthur again joined Lady on her wonderful, white bed. He and Lady spoke of elfin kings and enchanted cities. Lady was beautiful with her flaxen hair and ice blue eyes. And King Arthur was the prince of her dreams. In his most gentle way, King Arthur stimulated Lady's bottom. Time and time again he unloaded his member as high up as he could put it and drew her in to his body.

Morning came. The two damsels were there to help King Arthur and Lady get it started. King Arthur kissed Lady's nipples, kissed her lips. Lady needed one more penetration. Then it was to the toilets for King Arthur and Lady, then to wash and dress for breakfast.

"That gives me a feeling of floating," said Lady.

"It was beautiful," said King Arthur.

Lady and King Arthur went down to the breakfast table. The people stood and cheered. Beauty was there. King Arthur touched her cheek as he passed.

Breakfast over, Beauty went over, greeted Lady, led King Arthur away.

"We could walk to the river," said Beauty.

She took King Arthur to her room, put a warm wrap around him, one around herself. They walked down and out the gate. They walked down the path toward the river. Then there it was. It looked cold, bright and mysterious. King Arthur ran his fingers through Beauty's hair, watched the shadows on the surface of the water.

"As I watch the water, I wonder if I have ever done anything else. If my real self is not somewhere under the water," said King Arthur.

"The real Knight of the Parrett," said Beauty.

There were bells ringing.

"Time to go back," said King Arthur.

He and Beauty walked up the curving road.

King Arthur and Beauty walked up to the castle, through the gate, into the dining hall. King Arthur took his place to the right of Lady.

Lunch over, Beauty stepped over, took King Arthur's arm, took him up a stair to a high tower. The two of them looked down at the river valley. The air was cold. King Arthur looked at the river.

"Where do you suppose the Monster Knight came from?" he asked.

"I think he came from the river."

"So he would have been the real Knight of the Parrett," said King Arthur.

"It would be a strange world," said Beauty.

"And I wonder about this world. It occurs to me, I don't know your name."

"Silly."

Beauty started crying.

"You know my name."

She put her arms around King Arthur, put her head on his chest, cried.

"Silly," she said.

She pulled King Arthur to her, cried on his chest.

"I'll take you down," said King Arthur.

He took Beauty to the stair, helped her down and to her room. He undressed her, then himself, and put her in bed. He got in beside her, pulled her close.

The two sat together through the afternoon. A damsel in a white robe entered, said that dinner would soon be served. King Arthur and Beauty got up, washed each other and dressed. Together they went to the table.

The company at the table considered this an occasion for joy. Happy laughter and conversation competed with sounds from the harpers and the song of the Thrush. The food was fine. King Arthur enjoyed all on his plate. He took Beauty's arm and stood up.

"We are going to your room, Lady," said King Arthur.

The two went up the stairs to a very pretty room in which was a comfortable looking bed. Lady went into the room behind them, took off her clothes. King Arthur and Beauty took off their clothes, sat side by side facing Lady and leaned back against soft pillows. The three chatted about this and that.

Said Lady, "Now are you going to sleep with Beauty tonight?"

"No Lady, he is going to sleep with you," said Beauty.

The three sat and talked for a while. Beauty sat on King Arthur, kissed him, picked up her clothes and went away. Lady lay King Arthur down, kissed his face, his lips.

"You a bit worried about that long, cold trip ahead of you?"

"Perhaps a bit. But Lady, that is not what I was thinking about. Have you had something important, something big, that you knew, but you did not know what it was?"

"If there is only one thing, you are indeed fortunate. Now I am going to pull my legs out of the way, so you get my port to our liking. Then we become one flesh."

Morning. Damsels, unclothed, came in, got Lady and King Arthur up, to the toilet, then into the pool. They were washed; then, dressed in splendid clothes.

"There. You look like the prince I know you are," said Lady. "Now let us go get Beauty."

Beauty was up and dressed. Beauty kissed King Arthur and Lady, and the three went down to breakfast. King Arthur noticed how impressive Lady Blondhair looked. She was tall and straight and in command. Her head did seem, in the stars.

King Arthur and Beauty excused themselves from the table.

"I am riding with you down the road a way," said Beauty.

The two put on winter clothes.

"My shield and helmet look great," said King Arthur.

Beauty smiled at King Arthur.

A great company was gathered outside with pennants flying. King Arthur, with Beauty, went out, went up to Lady Blondhair.

"Thankyou most beautiful, most gracious, lady for your generous care which was all ways lovely."

Lady, in her magnificent robe, walked down and kissed King Arthur's lips.

King Arthur and Beauty mounted the horses which were standing there ready. Trumpets blared. There was a shout:

"Hail, Prince of the Parrett."

King Arthur returned the salute. He and Beauty rode down the way from the castle. King Arthur looked back. There was the castle, tall and white, its spires, twisting and reaching toward the sky. And round domes and globes, as part of its structure, at a distance, made it seem as if it were made of soap bubbles.

The two rode on a way.

"I have not seen a great variety of places, so this journey will add much to my knowledge," said King Arthur.

He and Beauty rode side by side in silence.

They rode up the valley in a trail near the river. Miles passed.

"Beauty, what is love?"

"It is a feeling like the one you and I have for Lady. She is beautiful, giving, loving."

"Yes."

The two rode on in silence.

"Beauty, is there a word for you and me? I mean, you and me?"

"No."

Beauty thought on it.

"No, I don't think so."

They rode on a way. Beauty slowed.

"Arthur, do not look back, but ride on. You will always be the distant star. Ride away. It's the only way."

King Arthur took her at her word. It was her gift to him. He rode forward on a trail now most rugged and around him were scrub covered, rocky hills. When the Sun was high, he stopped for some of the food which Lady had made certain was packed for him. Up the valley were misty blue peaks of distant mountains. King Arthur sat on a rock in a bare, rocky space near the river. While he ate, he looked at the far away mountains.

After eating, King Arthur retrieved his horse from the grass plot where he had been left, and he mounted and rode on. The hills to his left, across the river, got higher and rockier. To his right, in the distance, over high rocky hills, was a castle. King Arthur followed the trail by the river until he came to a path which led more in the direction where the castle would be found. He rode over a rough, rocky trail until, at sundown, he rode up to the old castle; the castle, surrounded by a high stone wall; the wall, of old assorted stones. King Arthur rode up to the gate, identified himself as the Knight of the Goatskin Shield. He was admitted.

The castle was on the basic lines of a square. It was built, the central part, of huge timbers in between which were rocks and all, plastered in with mortar. In the center of the great hall was a fire on a great hearth. The smoke curled through the opening in the roof.

And elderly lord stood up, welcomed the arriving knight, mumbled who he was.

"Glad to know you. I am called Sir Goatskin Shield."

"Goatskin Shield. That sounds familiar. But that would have been a long long ago. Sit. There is mead and meat enough for a wandering knight."

"Thankyou. It will be most welcome."

King Arthur sat with a half dozen other warriors who were also at the table in front of the fire. King Arthur enjoyed the meat and mead.

"A wandering knight. You needed to be a bit on the lookout for this Knight of the Parrett, this monster knight out of the Parrett River."

Said another knight, "He rode up and down through the Parrett River valley slaying warriors and creating havoc and I hear he slew half a hundred knights at Amorous City, the city of Lady Blondhair."

"The Knight of the Parrett is now dead and can be seen, as long as Mother Earth and Father Time allow, below the castle at Amorous City, in a grove of trees near the river.

"And you have seen him yourself?" asked the lord.

"I slew him."

"You did?" said the lord. "How did you ever manage to do it?"

"As a swordsman, I believe I am better than most. And I had Lady Luck with me. A couple of things went my way. All in all, I had a good day."

"I will say you did," said the lord.

"Now I am on my way up river. As far as you know, what am I likely to find?"

"A castle here and there," said the lord. "As you get farther up, you will find them better fortified. And with good reason. There are lawless bodies of warriors who roam the hills. Then, there are outlandish creatures which are most dangerous: beasts and monsters, some, quite large. Then, in that direction, way in the distance, is a ferocious ogre who has about him a collection of monstrous warriors who are nearly as large as himself. But, as I say, they are a long way away and there would be little reason to bother about them."

The other knights talked about beasts and rascals which they had come across. Said one:

"Up river, I know of a female monster, a good way from here, but the news comes down that she is very dangerous. A number of good knights are said to have been slain by her. The call her, I think it is, Cantrig the Greedy."

Another knight said, "They say she is a terrible hag who eats people."

"That situation needs to be fixed," said King Arthur.

"Best just let her alone," said a knight.

"That's one way not to get eaten," said another.

The knights laughed.

"Now where is she to be found?" King Arthur asked.

A knight gave a location up river. "But that is not certain to be right," the knight said.

"She would whip three or four knights," said a knight.

"Yes, but one has bears and lions before one gets there. And gangs of rascals," said a knight.

As King Arthur looked sleepy, the lord showed him a place where he might make his bed.

Morning came. King Arthur got up, found where the toilets were done. He washed with the wash bucket which had been provided, which was out in the shed where the toilet was made. He went in to breakfast with the other knights.

"And down that way, we would have had our hogs," said King Arthur.

"We got em," said a knight.

"Down that way," said another.

The knights laughed. The fire crackled and smoke curled up toward the chimney.

King Arthur got up, thanked his host for a most pleasant stay.

"It reminded me of home," said King Arthur.

"It was good to have you. Come back again," said the lord.

The lord insisted on augmenting King Arthur's food supply. King Arthur went out into the cold air. His horse had been brought around. He fixed his provisions, mounted and, with a salute to his host, rode off. There was a grey light from a grey sky, grey from horizon to horizon. The air was cold, it froze King Arthur's fingers. He wrapped his right hand with a fold of his coat, grabbed the reins. The road swung down toward the river. King Arthur followed it at a moderate pace. In front of him, stretched across the sky, were smoke like clouds of a darker grey than the grey sky. The road dipped into the valley, which curved to the right and widened. In front of King Arthur was a brook and this, King Arthur crossed over. On either side, beyond the flat, rocky fields, were rising patches of woods and to the front, at a great distance, blue mountains. The valley divided. To the left, it narrowed as it followed the river. To the right, the rocky flat lands were bordered, on the left, by the high rocky hills which ran along the river; then, on the right, some distance away, by low wooded hills. The brook flowed near the hills on its left. King Arthur came to a vague trail that, from the river road, branched off to the right. The trail went to the right of the high rocky hill which was in front of King Arthur. The river road went to the hills left. The trail King Arthur took climbed up the right side of the rocky hill. It then dipped before another climp. Here, in the dip, King Arthur pulled up. There seemed to be vegetation which his horse could eat, and it was time for his own lunch. He dismounted, walked off the road, pissed on a bush. He got out some oats, gave it to his horse, got out his own food, sat and ate.

His lunch eaten, King Arthur mounted and set out on the rough trail. He rode down a grade, rode up a higher hill, and this was covered with boulders. On its top were scrubby pines. Through the afternoon he rode up and down through scrubby pines. He took a path to the left. It went down a slope. It was getting dark. King Arthur dismounted, walked away to some weeds, took care of his toilet needs, returned, gave his horse some oats, then got out food for himself. He ate, then mounted and rode on further down the trail which bent left and sloped down. The moon came up. Moonlight on the dry, frost covered stalks showed the way. The moonlight was far spread and lit up the frosty branches of trees left, below the path, and right, above the path. The way became flat. King Arthur stopped, dismounted, made his bed for the night.

Morning. King Arthur woke, packed away his blankets, ate, mounted his horse and was again on the trail.

King Arthur rode through the cold air. To the left were low mountains, which were on his side of the river. To the right, from the trail, the land rose to be a string of hills. King Arthur rode the rocky trail which bent this way, then that. The way dipped, then rose to the top of a low hill. To the left, near the river, was a long, boat shaped mountain, high fore and aft and low midships. It was time for lunch. King Arthur dismounted.

Lunch over, King Arthur mounted and was back on what was the suggestion of a path. To the left scattered trees multiplied, became a woodland. To the right were clusters of trees between rocky rises. To the front, the pale grey peaks of mountains could be seen. The way dipped to rocky flats. On the left, the woodland became groves of trees.

It seemed the flat lands, to the left, dropped down to the river. After a long ride across the flat lands, King Arthur stopped at a grove of trees. It was dusk. King Arthur ate, made certain his horse had food, made his bed at the edge of the grove of trees.

King Arthur woke early. He was stiff and cold from his night on the cold ground. The eastern sky was tinged with faint pink streaks on its pale grey field. The king got up, fixed his bedding and secured it on his horse. He got some of his food and this, he sat and ate. In the trees he took care of his toilet needs; then, back at his horse, he mounted and was again on the trail and headed toward the distant mountains. In front of him were rocky hills. The path went along the top of the hill he was on, curved left and down toward a grove of shrubby trees; then, at the trees, dropped to a valley below the line of hills which he had been on. The way was down the steep hillside.

King Arthur lost the trace of a path, made his way through the brush-filled valley. He crossed a small brook, which was flowing over a gravely bed, then rode up the gradual climb up a flat covered with dry stalks of tall plants, rode to where, on his right, scraggly pines covered the top of a hill. The hill fell away, on his right, to ragged cliffs in front of which were boulders, and he found himself riding around tall pinnacles of rock, around jagged boulders. When he got to the bottom of the hill, to the right front was a boulder covered field, and this he crossed. Then on his right were high cliffs as the boulder covered field dipped down, sloped down to a boulder filled brook. King Arthur stopped, dismounted, took his horse down to the water. He then got out food and had lunch. He fed oats to his horse. He mounted and rode forward.

He followed a path as it swung around the mountain's rugged side, rode into a flat area filled with rocks and underbrush. In the center of the area was a rugged boulder around which the ground was bare, and around the boulder were skulls, bones and tattered garments. King Arthur hid his horse in a clump of tall shrubs, went near the rock and crawled under a patch of briars. He observed that there were also, scattered about, swords and helms. King Arthur watched the area. Long he waited. The only living thing he saw, three vultures flying in circles high above.

Late afternoon, the boulder lifted, moved to one side. A hideous head stuck up out of the hole which the boulder had covered. It had round eyes, a beak like nose and a mouth which reached from ear to ear. She sprung out of the hole, a naked woman. She was larger than a normal man and had muscles which stood out like iron bands and her fingers ended in claws. She saw King Arthur, rushed toward him. King Arthur moved quickly into a defensive position. She grabbed King Arthur's left arm, which was like being grabbed by a jaw of iron. Quick as a wink her lion like mouth moved to bite King Arthur's head. An inch away from his face, King Arthur's fist met her nose. He grabbed a foot, raised it up, kicked inside her knee on her other leg. When she fell backward, King Arthur kicked her head. He gave the head three more kicks, drew his sword and cut her head off.

King Arthur went to the hole out of which this woman with the lion like mouth had come. Beside it was the boulder, and on this, a spider web had been carved. The hole was a tunnel. It was a stone wall around a circular stair. King Arthur went down the stair. First, he noticed the bad smell. He came to a room behind pillars of stone. In the room were rustics in farm clothes: five men, four women, six young children of which four seemed to be girls. King Arthur released them from the cell. He sent them up the stairs in front of him.

"She would have eaten us," said a man.

"We were her food," said a woman. "And when I was captured, she was attacked by three warriors, she ripped them all apart, then ate them."

"You can go home now," said King Arthur.

"What may we call you?" said a man.

"I am Knight of the Goatskin Shield. And are your dwellings near? I could use feed for my horse."

"We are a great distance off, but we do have food," said the man. "We can hardly believe she is dead."

King Arthur went to his horse, mounted.

"A long distance, best if I go on, send back help. Your village: where is it?" King Arthur asked.

It was a small fishing village up the river, or so the rustics seemed to say. King Arthur turned his horse toward the river. He crossed the valley, then by the time he got up into the mountains, it was dark. He came to a small mountain stream, and there he brought his horse to a stop. He saw that his horse had food and water, then got food for himself. He found a place for his bedding and there slept.

It was morning. King Arthur filled his water containers, had his breakfast, attended to his toilet, secured his bedding, mounted and was off through the mountains and toward the river. All morning he climbed the rising way, then stopped for lunch. The afternoon, the ride was down, then on another climb. Then, in the dusk, there was another brook. It was there he made his bed for the night. In the morning he was again on his way toward the river. By lunchtime, he could see the river below him. After his lunch, he rode toward the river and was on the banks of the river at sundown. It was there he made his camp for the night. Morning came. After breakfast, King Arthur began a ride up the river. There was a trail and by lunchtime, a good distance had been travelled. He ate his lunch; then, before sundown, there were a few round, thatch and wattle dwellings on high ground, back from the river. King Arthur rode up to the dwellings and dismounted.

King Arthur told of finding and of killing the female monster. This pleased the people of the village, as they were, a few days back, missing a couple women and a couple children and would go look for them. They were glad to give food to King Arthur and to his horse, and they offered a place to stay, but the Knight of the Goatskin Shield needed to move on. King Arthur asked about the other people who lived in the area and learned, there was a Lord Neton a good distance away. And there were monsters. Then, way beyond the blue mountains, there was a great, awful ogre. King Arthur thanked them, mounted and rod on. Near the village he rode past some cows, but saw no horses. By moonlight he followed the trail until he came to a brook. There he stopped for the night.

Morning, King Arthur ate his breakfast, secured his bedding and was off. By midmorning he came in sight of another village, which was up in high fields not far from the river. He rode to that village, introduced himself as Goatskin Shield, told about the monster woman and got a supply of food and oats. He then rode on. He had his lunch on the river bank, followed the river through the afternoon; then, at evening, he found a few trees on a hill near the river which seemed to him a good place for his camp. He spent the night there.

In the morning, after his breakfast, he rode through the river valley, had his lunch on a little hill, then rode on.

At sundown, on a mountain, a great distance away, King Arthur saw a castle. In the dusk he rode in the direction of the castle, then stopped for the night, stopped on a hill, in a little grove of trees. He took his horse to the bottom of the hill where there was a little brook. He got water, fixed supper and ate - up under the trees.

Morning. The sky was clear and there was a cold breeze. King Arthur hurried his breakfast. He stowed his bedding, set out toward where he had seen a castle. He rode up and down wooded hills, up a valley which climbed between hills, up a high hill, and it was time for his lunch. The castle, under a blue sky, looked as far away as ever. He watched it as he ate.

Lunch over, King Arthur set out again toward the castle. On a hill, at the edge of a wood, he passed by a couple of wood cutter's shacks, rode down and followed a trail around a hill. He was then riding past fields which had been cultivated. In the fields were a good number of large, slaty stones. There were scattered groves of trees; then, in a grove, a smithy and some cottages. These picked up the late afternoon sunlight, and the sun shown on the castle. It was a large castle, now only a few hills away. King Arthur stopped in a woods, relieved himself, then looked at the road ahead. In the valley below were a few houses, and beyond them, a bridge over a brook. "Now what did Sir Thrush say?" King Arthur asked his horse.

King Arthur mounted, rode down the hill, past the houses, over the bridge, up a wooded hill. He rode down the hill, up a higher hill and below this were cottages. Beyond these, large gates to a castle. King Arthur rode down hill, rode past the cottages and up to the castle gate.

There was a porter. He called down:

"May I ask, whom have I the pleasure of addressing."

"I am Knight of the Goatskin Shield."

The porter went off. He returned, said:

"Will you not come in Sir."

King Arthur was taken to a lords reception room.

"Good Evening, Sir. I am Lord Neton, and you Sir?"

"I am Sir Goatskin Shield."

"Very good. And have you a mission?"

"The mission I had has been completed. I am now a knight errant seeking adventure. I hope I find you and your land well and the times enjoyable for all."

"Likely it would be all that," said the lord, a tall, clean shaven man, "Except that up in the hills behind us is a lake, and in the lake is a monster called an avrank. The avrank slays our farmers, steals out women, and not only that, but causes the lake to overflow, so that it floods homes and, also, our market places. But enough of my troubles, now is the time to get you fed and rested."

The lord stood, led King Arthur to a fine dining hall. A number of knights sat at the long table, mugs of drink in front of them.

"Sirs, we have with us Sir Goatskin Shield."

The knights stood, greeted the arriving knight. Food and drink were brought out for him.

King Arthur ate.

"Back to the avrank," said King Arthur to his host, who had taken the seat to King Arthur's right.

"Why has not the avrank been stopped from doing this?"

The reason, none can stand a chance with him in the water, and if more than two or three knights go to fight him, that is where he will be. And he in not likely to come from the lake if he sees danger to himself unless there is an unclothed female he desires. And I mean, he has an eye for beauty. If there is no danger, any woman, clothed or unclothed. But he will only face danger to get a beauty. And what happens to the captured women, who knows? But we never see them more. There may be some place under the lake where they still live; as, way beyond those mountains to our north, there are blue lakes which are the gate to other lands, or so I have been told. But this lake, called Barfog, as is the avrank, little we know about it."

"Tell me of the times Barfog has been lured out of the lake to fight," said King Arthur.

"Many years ago," said the lord, "it was seen that Barfog would come out to fight a knight in order to steal a beautiful woman. He always slew the knight, stole the woman. Then, when there was a most beautiful woman, and she, unclothed; he came out to fight two knights, and slew them both. Then, if the woman was beautiful, he would fight three knights. Of course, the maiden is always bound, so

248

she would be a secured prize. Being you are a knight errant looking for adventure, I was tempted to mention the avrank. However, you are only one knight, and it is winter, and I do not expect any of our maidens to stand out bare in the cold."

"The thing is to get the avrank out of the lake," said King Arthur. "I will challenge it should it come out of the water. However, I will think more about it after I have rested."

King Arthur was shown to a place where he could make his bed. He retired for the evening.

Morning. King Arthur woke, followed knights to the area where the wash room was. He made his toilet, then washed. He went down to the hall for breakfast. He had just completed eating when a young girl came up to him.

"Sir, I am Lord Neton's youngest daughter. Would I be satisfactory as a lure for the avrank?"

"I am certain you could lure anything with a heart."

"Then I am at your service."

"Then let us plan for tomorrow before sunrise."

She was young. King Arthur guessed twelve or thirteen, but obviously a woman.

"You looked like a knight I could trust."

"I did slay the Monster Knight of the Parrett."

"I will be ready. Today I will be with you. Come, I will show you the palace."

King Arthur walked with the maiden all over the fantastic structure with its curves and twists. They investigated balcony after balcony, tower after tower. They told each other of pretty things and fantastic things. King Arthur thought of the Thrush.

"And for much of this journey," said King Arthur. "And the Thrush could sing songs so beautiful that those who heard would fall asleep."

He told of the line of knights at Isle Fort.

"I have heard of such a Thrush. Was his name Hob?"

"That I know not."

The two climbed the highest tower. The maiden looked at the tall mountains. She told her knight.

"Way up there, beyond the blue peaks you see, it the fantastic land of the ogre. They say he is very dreadful."

"So I have heard."

King Arthur looked long at the mountains in that direction. The longer he looked, the more mysterious the misty blue mountains looked.

The maiden put her hand on his neck.

"They are very beautiful," she said.

The two went down from the tower, went to the gardens and enjoyed the pools and waterfalls.

"I would not need to own pools and gardens," she said. "I could find pools and gardens on the hills."

"No. I spend so much time with them, people think I need them."

She looked at the water falling in the pool.

"Would you rather go have lunch with the knights?"

"I would not."

"Then they will bring us lunch by the pool."

It was not long before lunch was brought and put on a rock slab table. They sat side by side and enjoyed the close touching.

"I suppose I should feel like I am competing, but I am too happy just to be here," said the maiden.

"I could have said the same thing," said King Arthur.

The dishes were cleared away. The maiden got up, took King Arthur all around the castle grounds. Then it was time for the evening meal. King Arthur was the honoured guest, so the maiden bid him goodnight.

King Arthur went into the hall where dinner was served. All at the table cheered him.

"You look so relaxed and confident, Sir," said Lord Neton. "That helps me have hope and somewhat eases the great sadness I feel because of my daughter's insisting on being the one to go out. I was ready to blame the weather and send no one."

"All blessings to my beautiful companion," said King Arthur.

All cheered and drank.

King Arthur sat and thought. He thought about the Thrush and the things it might have said but did not. He finished eating, thanked his host, retired to his bed.

Before dawn the butler came into the sleeping area.

"Sir, kitchen wants you to know you may eat when you are

ready."

King Arthur got quickly up. He went to where the toilet was, took care of that, washed. He went to the stair, went down and to the hall where the lord was waiting at the table. Breakfast was brought to him. He had a small breakfast, went to his area and dressed in what he would need for the battle; then it was down the stairs, out and to the gate. There was his horse waiting. There was his maiden and she was mounted.

"I'm naked under my coat."

"Beautiful," said King Arthur.

The two rode off. They rode around hill upon hill, with rise after rise, to higher ground. Over a long low hill, there was the lake. It looked huge.

The maiden dismounted, took a pipe from her coat pocket, took off her coat, folded it, put it on the ground. King Arthur was standing near her. She jumped in his arms. The two hugged each other and kissed.

The maiden sat on her coat, which was on the top of the mound. She picked up the pipe, played the most beautiful music. The sun shown bright on the water. The music went on and on.

An awful head, which was covered with long black hair, stuck up out of the water. The maiden rose to her feet, continued to play. The avrank edged closer to the shore. The music was beautiful. Closer came the avrank.

Suddenly the avrank, a stone headed spear in his hand, rushed at King Arthur, suddenly thrust out his spear. King Arthur ducked just in time, stabbed with his sword. The avrank thrust four quick jabs in a row. King Arthur jabbed his sword at the hand that had reached for his shield. Again he blocked a spear thrust. The music rose and fell. King Arthur stabbed at the arm without the spear. He blocked three spear thrusts, stabbed the avrank in the groin, backed off, blocked a spear thrust. The avrank tried to turn and hit King Arthur with his tail. King Arthur stepped in quickly and gave the avrank a cut on the arm without the spear, then blocked a spear thrust. The two fighters circled. King Arthur blocked two quick spear thrusts, stabbed the avrank's wounded arm.

"Temptress," screamed the avrank.

He swung his tail, hit the maiden in the head. She fell. King Arthur stabbed the avrank in the groin, blocked a spear thrust, gave a deep stab in the avrank's belly, backed off quickly. He blocked a spear thrust, faked a stab, blocked a series of nine spear thrusts, moved in and stabbed the avrank in the belly. The avrank fell. King Arthur chopped off the avrank's spear hand, then split the beast's skull.

King Arthur went quickly to the maiden. Her neck was broken, she was dead. He put her coat around her and with her in his arms, mounted and took the long ride to the palace gate. Her four sisters came out and met them. They took their sister from King Arthur.

"She loved you very much," said one.

"And I, her."

King Arthur got his belongings ready for travel. He went down to the hall for lunch.

"Lord Neton, I would do anything to bring her back," he said.

"Yes, I know," said the lord. "And I would give you another daughter, but I know none of the others would be good for you. As wives."

"I belonged to the one who is gone," said King Arthur. "I will be departing early in the morning. And I thank you for all you have given me.

King Arthur ate his lunch, then went up in the highest tower, looked at the mountains. The cloud formations made the mountains look like they held strange caverns.

King Arthur went down to the hall for supper.

"It was a mighty victory," said a knight. "You are certainly a great champion. We are so sorry for your loss."

That was all that was said.

King Arthur got to bed early.

He was up before sunrise. He got his belongings together, went to the hall where breakfast was being brought out. He ate quickly, bid goodbye to the knights, to Lord Neton. He went out to his horse. It was well supplied with provisions. There were also, at the gate, four white horses. Four young ladies in cloaks, came out, each gave King Arthur a hug.

"We are going to bury our sister."

"In the way she was born: And, as we were born."

"Goodbye dear beautiful ladies."

King Arthur rode toward Lake Barfog, then into a rising valley. It was a long ride up the valley. King Arthur stopped at a brook, had lunch. Patches of white cloud floated overhead. Lunch over, King Arthur mounted, took a trail around a hill. There were some round, wattle sided dwellings at the bottom of the hill. The way rose, then dipped into another valley. In the valley were a dozen round dwellings and the old grey boards of an enclosure. These, King Arthur avoided, took a path up the side of a hill. The way went down, then up a steep climb. It reached a hilltop and here, King Arthur stopped for the night. There were brambles and brown stalks which the horse found edible.

Morning came. To the front, in the far distance, were the tall peaks of mountains. King Arthur took a way down the hill, then up a hump covered with clumpy grass. From there, the way led to a valley and around a pile of rocks which were on the bottom and on the last third of a low hill, then up a rocky hill. In front of him were jagged hills, hills in irregular shapes. Below him was a brook. He rode down and dismounted. He fixed his lunch, fed his horse.

King Arthur remounted, followed the valley through which the brook flowed, past wooded hills; some, with steep, sparsely wooded sides; some, with sides covered with sheer rock cliffs. The brook came down a fall of rocks, became hidden behind great arches and half arches. King Arthur stopped for the night.

Morning light revealed a dusting of snow.

King Arthur shook the snow off his blankets, fixed his breakfast. He washed in the falling water. He packed his horse, led it out of the gully where the brook was, mounted and rode through the dip between hills. The going was slow as to avoid underbrush, the ride needed to go up onto slippery hillsides. Where the brook turned King Arthur halted for lunch. After eating, then attending to his toilet, King Arthur mounted. He rode up a hill sparsely covered with bushes and small trees. The snow was then mostly melted on the hill. From the top, he could see the tall, blue mountains. He rode down the hillside to a dip, then the way rose again; then, ran up and down along the hill top. He rode down into a tree filled valley, then up another long climb, up and down out of the valley; then back and forth on the top of a long hill with many tops; then, the sun went down. King Arthur came to a spring where the water flowed out of the ground. He made his camp for the night.

Dawn came. King Arthur went down the valley, made his toilet, came back, washed in the stream from the spring, made certain his horse had food, then fixed breakfast.

Breakfast over, King Arthur mounted, rode down the dip, then up a hillock on which there were brambles and then, stalky plants growing up from around brown rocks. Overhead, the sky was filled with long, pale grey clouds. King Arthur rode down the slope, rode up a long, wooded hill. From the top, he could see mountains; some, oddly shaped, or lopsided. He rode toward those mountains. He rode down the slope to a brook. Here he stopped, got out food for lunch.

Lunch over, King Arthur rode up the side of the wooded hill, up to a thinly wooded top, and this became the rise and fall of a rocky surface, then there were huge jagged rocks, then huge rocks on rocks, great blocks of rock. King Arthur was riding over rock hills. He rode down to a valley, rode through the valley to a large brook. He stopped, dismounted, made his camp.

With the early light King Arthur was up. He made his toilet, washed, fed his horse, had breakfast. He mounted, made his way up the valley, then through an aisle between rock cliffs, around great mounds of rock, tall pillars of rock, up rock hills, around rock streets. He stopped for lunch, fed his horse. He mounted, rode again through the rocky valley. The valley twisted and twisted around rocky mountains. He came to a large brook. Here he camped for the night.

Morning light, King Arthur took care of morning needs, had breakfast, mounted and headed up the valley following the stream. He rode past tall pinnacles of rock, rocks as tall as trees, rode between tall rock walls, rode under arches of rock. The ground sloped up, so King Arthur was riding on a flat mountain over cliffs. With higher peaks rising on either side, King Arthur kept to the twisting turning valley. He stopped for lunch. While he ate he listened to the harsh cries of wild birds.

King Arthur mounted, rode carefully around ruts and gullies. The horse's hoofs caused echoes as the sound bounced against the cliffs. Ahead, the way led around a mountain which had a peak which rose to a point. The way rose up and around mountains which had become tall. King Arthur was on a hump on the mountain side. Water flowed over a rock and there King Arthur made his camp. He got out food for himself and for his horse. He got in his blankets and slept.

Morning, King Arthur got up, got his breakfast ready. As he ate, he watched a lone hawk circle high above. He got food and water for his horse. He mounted and rode down a slope to where it connected to the rise of the next mountain, and this, through the low shrubs, he made his way around. He stopped for lunch. Then mounted, he rode down into a valley, then up a mountain side. High above were the peaks of mountains. He rode over the low humps of a mountain. He rode down to a little brook. The sun was setting. King Arthur made his camp.

Morning: King Arthur packed his things, had breakfast, mounted and set out up the side of a mountain. He circled the mountain, looked below. There below, on a lower hill, was a square fort, and it was surrounded by a wooden wall. King Arthur turned to ride in that direction. He got to a level place, stopped for lunch. He fed and gave water to his horse. He mounted, rode down to the valley, rode up the hill to the gate of the fortification. From where he sat on his horse, he could see the tall, misty blue mountains in front of him. Their shadowy summits pierced the air. On one near peak were arches and towers of blue mist: a city which seemed half cloud. Then, the hill he was on: to the left was the gate to the wall, which was made of stout logs, horizontal between vertical supports. Outside the wall were fields of grass. King Arthur rode up to the gate and dismounted.

King Arthur stepped to the gate, said in a loud voice, "Hello there, is there a porter?"

"What do you want?" said a gruff voice.

"I want a porter here at the gate to greet me."

"I am porter here. I am Glewlwyd Mighty Grasp. Who are you?"

"I am Knight of Goatskin Shield."

"Oh."

There was a wait. The gate swung open.

"Come in."

King Arthur walked behind the huge, broad shouldered porter to the door to a great hall. The walls were of large logs and large timbers stretched across the ceiling. From these hung lamps which gave a good light. A hearth was at each end of the room, and in each hearth burned a fire. In the enter of the room was a huge, beautiful round table around which sat half a hundred monstrous warriors, and in the seat in front of the fire on King Arthur's right was a huge warrior whose great head sat a head above all others.

Light flickered on the rough cut rafters, which were covered with smoke. It flickered on the grotesque faces, on the mugs of ale which were on the table in front of each warrior. King Arthur stepped toward the huge warrior,

"Lord – ."

"Who are you?" interrupted a voice from the great head and the voice filled the room, echoed off the walls and rafters, so it seemed, all the air produced the voice, the great room itself and not only the head.

"I am Knight of Goatskin Shield."

"I only know of one Knight of Goatskin Shield and he is dead."

"I am another."

"I know. – What brings you here?"

The room seemed to tremble and shake with the voice.

"I was looking for the club wielding ogre."

"Then you are in the right place. I am Ogrevran. And there in the corner is my club. A sword is a good thing. But a club is greater. And it always has been. What business had you with the ogre?"

"Curiosity."

"It is good to be curious. Sit over there. It is certain you would welcome food."

"Thankyou, I have come a long way. – Such a time it was to get here, Lord, this land seems at the very end of the earth."

"It might seem so, King Arthur. It might seem so. There are, however, lands farther on in the dim distance. There is the castle at Sidi in the gloom of a haunted twilight, a luminous dark, shadows to life, living things to shadow. It is a revolving castle. Difficult it is to speak with the sentries.

There is the Castle of Rigomer, Castle of the Strong Door, the Royal Castle. Twilight and darkness are there. Then it is very dark. Bright wine is served by the host. And memory drifts away into the past.

There is Caer Pedryvan. The four cornered castle. Castle of the active door where sparkling wine is quaffed. There twilight blends with jet black darkness. Before the portals of the cold palace, horns of light burn.

There is Caer Vandwyd. Lady Silverwheel is there. At the Castle On High, castle of the Perfect Ones.

There is Caer Colur. And gloomy it is. Three hundred sentries stand on its wall. And difficult it is, the conversation with the sentinel.

There is Caer Wydyr. A glass castle. The door, as hard as diamond. The pearl rimmed cauldron is there. Warmed by the breath of nine maidens.

There is Ochren Castle. On the shelving side of a hill. A squat castle of huge dark stones. Under an – ever abiding canopy of dark clouds. Which hover close above it. Ochren Castle is beaten by the rains, and the thunders – rumble on and on. And the lightnings' strike, strike mostly Ochren Castle, as if for that edifice harbouring a particular anger.

And then there is, at Zazamank, the last castle of Zazamank. A towering ruin, slumbering in perpetual gloom. On the rim of a deep – gorge. And the valleys far below. So hidden in fog that shapes with in it can not be distinguished, but what they are is of little concern, because this is the land of uncompleted journeys. And every shape there would be always – a little further on. And that, King Arthur, is the last castle. Of Zazamank."

And the echoes of Ogrevran's rumbling voice seemed to go on and on, bouncing from rafter to rafter, wall to wall.

Three tall beautiful women entered the room. One, with food for King Arthur; then, one with very bright, very blond, hair, served wine to King Arthur.

"Here are my daughters: Gwinhwyfach, Guinhwyvare and Lenomie. Daughters, this is Sir Goatskin Shield."

The three exchanged greetings with King Arthur.

They went back to their jobs of bringing food and drinks to the warriors.

"With pretty girls to look at, introduction to us would be useless words," said a warrior.

"Not at all," said King Arthur.

"Sir Goatskin Shield, the warrior who did not want to waste words is Echel Bighip. I will continue. Next to Echel is Wythneint of Elei. Then you see Lord Manannan son of King Lear. Then Gwyn Godyvrion. And next to him, Lugh Longspear; next, Gwyn son of Nudd, who is King of the Tylwyth Teg and Lord of the Unknown. Next is Cysgaint son of Banon. Next, Maelgwyn and then Llyr Lluyddawg. Next, Menwaed of Arllechwed. Then, Lud Ilurugog. Then, Mael Hir. Then, Goronwy son of Echel. Then, Cadiereith son of Porthfaur. Next, Seithwedd Saidi. Next, Mened. Next, Cubert son of Daere. Next, Corvil Bervach. Next, Luber Beuthach. Next, Dalldav son of Cunyn Cov. Next, Gallgoid. Next, Drwst. Next, Sinnoch ap Seithfed. Next, Wadu. Next, Garwyli son of Gwythawg Gwyr. Next, Sarahnon son of Glythfyr. Next, Gusg of Achen. Next, Drudwas son of Tryffin. Next, Nerth son of Cadarn. Next, King Dunarth. Next, Teregud son of Iaen. Next, Isgawyn son of Banon. This here is Sir Goatskin Shield. There, consider yourself introduced.

"I must remark on this marvelous table. The craftsmen whom you had here to make it had a touch of magic in their hands."

Said Ogrevran, "This was not made here. This was your fathers and - he said he had hoped to fill all onehundredfifty seats, each with a worthy warrior. He was not able to do this and as he had come near his end, he gave me the table saying he hoped I would fill the table, as it deserved to be filled. As you might expect, from the many empty seats, I have fallen short from what the two of us had wished. Less than a dozen of my warriors are not here in their seats. One, the porter owns one of these."

"The amazing thing: it is here. I never knew my father."

"I know," said Ogrevran in his great, rumbley voice.

"I saw a marvelous city ahead of me as I reached here. I suppose they have tournaments?"

"Hel no," said Echel.

"That city is Ramsay," said Ogrevran. "No, they have no tournaments in Ramsay. It is not that sort of city."

"Tournaments. Men here do not care for that sort of thing," said a warrior.

"If it sport we need, we find a man's sport here in the hills," said a warrior.

"However, my daughters went to the tournament at Camelot. They stayed hidden in the crowd," said Ogrevran. "They do that sort of thing."

Warriors laughed.

Ogrevran's daughters entered with ale, filled mugs all around.

King Arthur followed a couple of warriors and as he suspected, they led the way to a room with a rock trough. Here they, then King Arthur pissed. He returned to his seat.

"I hope you can be with us for a bit. That you do not need to rush off," said Ogrevran.

"I have put myself into a duty to be seen a good way from here."

"Not an individual settling of differences I hope. That sort of thing usually comes to no good," said a warrior.

"Not at all. A public event."

"Yes, of course. You are a person of wide interest. Let me hazard a guess. People want to see you unhorse knights with your stick?" said a warrior with a chuckle.

"Only right in part. I doubt if any whom I expect to be there have ever seen me unhorse a knight with a stick."

"But it is a tournament?" said the warrior.

"It is. But tournaments are not my favourite place for showing my skills. I am out of the country. Learned more skills with the plow than with the lance."

"And skills of far greater value," said Ogrevran.

There were many nods of agreement.

There was a hum of conversation about the value of tournaments and of their substitutes. Glewlwyd Mighty Grasp came in and a warrior went out to replace him at the gate.

"Tournaments can be fun," said a warrior. "We take some practice among other activities. You might come and see what we do, and any criticism, we will take it as coming from a ploughman."

"I would enjoy it," said King Arthur.

"Down in the south, life is too soft. Even with practice most of those warriors down there, too weak to get good. They set up pavilions at road crossings where they can sit with their lances and say, 'Sir Knight, wouldst thou joust?' They hope I will say, 'Hel no.' But I joust. One got knocked off, wanted to continue the confrontation with swords. I said, 'Pardon, your weapon of choice was the lance.' I hit him a few times with my lance, rode on," said a warrior.

"He was just as glad, that is certain," said a warrior.

"When is that tournament?" said Ogrevran.

"May Day."

"May Day? This is February."

"Yes, Lord Ogrevran, but this is a long way away, and good as my horse is, and he is good, I can not praise him enough, but a horse can only do so much. The other choice, walk to Lord Neton's. But you know how long that would take."

"You tell me you have come all this way on a horse?"

"Yes, this is the same horse I started with."

"And I must say you gave that horse Hel," said Glewlwyd Mighty Grasp.

"Did you not know you could sail?" said Ogrevran.

"Yes, you and your horse and a good many warriors too, if you so desired."

"I did not know, and I am still in the dark."

"Your shield is your ship. Be sure you will sail back. I have one also. But how did you get from Somerset to Logres. That must have taken weeks?"

"As I recall, it took at most, two days."

"You did not decide, on some whim, to step into Logres? My guess is, someone was with you who wanted you in Logres?"

"Yes, I was with a damsel."

"And she worked a bit of flim flam, it seems. Was she pretty?"

"She was perfect."

"Good answer. She was herself. And that was enough. Did she tell you her name?"

"No, but I was told."

"Is it a thing you would share?"

"I was told it was Beauty."

"Now, that is what we call a pet name. It is what a mother calls a child when the name a father has given is too long, or too difficult to say. I suspect, in any real sense, it is not her name at all."

"It was, she got that thought from me."

"And where did you go, if that was not on some secret mission?"

"To Castle Damour."

"Ah, to the Great Lady herself. There are few I would dip a knee to. She is one."

"Oh. I could have been louder with thank yous."

"Yes, she can be most generous," said Ogrevran.

Ogrevran's daughters came in with food for the evening meal. While the warriors ate, there was a rumble and roar of conversation. King Arthur enjoyed the well prepared meal. Glewlwyd had admired King Arthur's horse.

"One thing", said Lord Manannan," the horse will get to sail home."

The conversation drifted to horses. Ogrevran's daughters put wood on the fires. Smoke and sparks shot up toward the roof. As King Arthur looked sleepy, Ogrevran had Guinhwyvare, his daughter with the bright pale blond hair, show him a place where he could sleep.

"Thankyou Guinhwyvare."

King Arthur saw his belongings were there. He was soon asleep.

Morning came. King Arthur went to the area where the men were washing, taking care of their toilet. He joined in with others, went to the round table for breakfast. The daughters of Ogrevran were there to serve the food. Guinhwyvare, as she served food to King Arthur, said:

"After breakfast we often watch the warriors get their morning exercise."

King Arthur, the other men, finished eating. The warriors began leaving the table. King Arthur left the table, walked through the courtyard, out the gate. He walked left; then, down to a field where a number of warriors were on their horses. And their horses, running around the field. Guinhwyvare was at the edge of the field seated on a low stone wall. King Arthur walked over, sat beside her.

"You should not need to serve us," said King Arthur. "There are many, I am certain, who would be delighted to serve at that table."

"I do it because it gives me pleasure. I enjoy serving at that table."

The two of them sat and watched the horses running.

"Glewlwyd said thou hadst an impressively fine horse," said Guinhwyvare.

"Black is my steed and brave beneath me. No water will make him fear. No man will make him swerve."

Guinhwyvare replied, "Green ist my steed, the tint of leaves. No disgrace like his who boasts and fails. He is no man who fulfills not his word. In the forefront of the fray, no man holds out but Kay the Tall."

"It is I that will ride and will stand and walk heavily on the brink of the ebb. I am the man to hold out against Kay."

"Pshaw young man, it is strange to hear thee. Unless thou be other than thou lookest, thou wouldst not, one of a hundred, hold out against Kay."

"Guinhwyvare of the bright face do not insult me. Small though I be, I would hold out against a hundred myself."

"Pshaw, young man. After scanning long thy looks, me thought I have seen thee before."

"Guinhwyvare of the smiling face, tell me, if thou know it, where thou saw me before?"

"At Arthur's long table perhaps."

"Guinhwyvare of facetious speech, it is a woman's nature to banter. It is there thou didst see me."

"So what hast thou been doing with thy time since departing from Camelot?"

"Beauty and I came up the Parrett River – ."

"Does she live up to her name?"

"In every way. She kept me in line. She tried to keep me in line. Praise Fortune, she kept bad judgement from ruining my mission."

"What was that?"

"Someone was needed to destroy a monster knight."

"And you did. How did Beauty keep thee in line? That might be of some use to know."

"Logic. Good sense. And by being stubborn."

"Not by lovings, by kisses."

"No, not Beauty."

"Hast thou promised to return to her: to see her again."

"No. But she was told she would see me again."

"And by whom?"

"A bird."

"Now thou art making a serious question into a joke."

"No, on my honour, it was a bird. And I believe the bird is still with Lady Blondhair. Thou may go and ask it."

"I am sorry. It was that it sounded strange. So after thou slew the monster knight, what?"

"I was needed to turn around a bad situation in Isle Fort."

"Was Beauty involved in this duty?"

"No. Another messenger came and got me."

"A temptress?"

"No. She had not that in mind when she chose to get me. Though now I think of it. She got me there. And I was needed. It was a hard job."

"Was the damsel pretty?"

"Yes. But seeing her, thou wouldst not consider her a threat. But she looked good."

"How was she called?

"Let me think, Gwyl."

"Strange. Then did another damsel whisk thou away?"

"No. I just by chance came upon a monster."

"What sort?"

"An Avrank."

"You slew it?" "I did."

"Let us return to the hall, as I have duties," said Guinhwyvare.

The two made a leisurely walk to the gate, to the huge main structure. Horses were being put up, warriors were coming up. King Arthur went in with them and to the table. The warriors chatted together. Lunch was brought out.

King Arthur enjoyed his lunch.

Said Ogrevran, "I suppose you were pressed into being company for one or more of my daughters."

"I had the pleasure."

"Not more than one I hope."

"I was with Guinhwyvare."

"Ah. I hope she was taken by your charms."

"She said I boast too much."

"Boast. I – like a man that boasts. Usually the men that boast are men that will give things a try. If they make their boast good, splendid. If not, – they are good for a laugh."

"What did you tell her you had done, or could do?" said warrior.

"I told her I could stand up to a hundred men."

"Good, said Ogrevran. "Of course, an extravagant boast - is not to

263

be taken as an exact fact. It is a man's way of saying he is a stout armed fellow. Knocking down a man, or perhaps two, – that is his boast – his hundred. – But women don't know that. They expect you to line up a hundred warriors, charge into them, knock them all over."

Said Sir Wythneint, "Of course there are men, then there are men. Women are impressed by numbers. Coins in a purse. But men. There are some men, a hundred like them should be of no trouble at all. The others, one is more than enough to wrestle with."

Ogrevran's daughters brought food and drink to the table.

"So that's the way women think," said Echel.

Warriors laughed. They concentrated on eating

"I would like to see the horse that you spoke highly of," said Guinhwyvare.

"I will be glad to show him to you."

There was a rumble of talking around the table.

"It is often," said a warrior, "finds fault because she is trying to convince herself. She feels herself slipping away to a wedding."

King Arthur finished eating, walked out into the courtyard. Guinhwyvare joined him there. She had across a shoulder, a bow and arrows. The two walked around the building, called for their horses. Stable men brought out two horses.

"I do like thy horse," said Guinhwyvare.

"Yours, not only is it finely built, but she actually has a green colour to her. Where could such an animal be found?"

"She comes from Ramsay. Shall we be off?"

She put a bow and arrow in her hand, lept up on her horse. King Arthur mounted the black stallion. The two rode out the gate, rode down the hill, rode on paths around the hill. Guinhwyvare put an arrow to her bow. Riding at top speed, she put the arrow into the trunk of a tree, head high.

"Not every warrior could have done that," she said.

"That was well done," said King Arthur.

The two rode together through the afternoon enjoying the movement of the horses. King Arthur noticed that not only her horse, but Guinhwyvare had an athletic grace, a grace which had power in it. King Arthur and Guinhwyvare rode together through the fields. With the sun sinking low, they rode up the hill, through the gate. They dismounted, left their horses and walked through the courtyard.

"That was fun," said Guinhwyvare.

King Arthur went to the washing area, washed and got ready for the evening meal. He moved here and there among the warriors greeting this one, that one. The warriors went to the table. Food was brought in. There was a rumble of conversation.

"Lord Ogrevran, it has been wonderful being here. I really should resume the burden of looking after my lands," said King Arthur.

"Who is looking after them now?"

"Lord Caradoc."

"Caradoc Shortarm. Good man. I am certain they are well looked after."

"I would ask a favour. When I am ready to depart, unlock for me the secrets of my shield that I might sail instead of needing to ride."

"It is hardly a secret, King Arthur. Guinhwyvare, in a few seconds, can explain all that. And I would ask a favour. Guinhwyvare would like to visit the people at Hayonwye. I am too busy for that. Unless I get pushed into it. Also, she wants to see some unicorns. You could tell Caradoc Shortarm I slowed you up, and certainly he will be understanding."

"I will be delighted to have company."

"Then that's settled."

Then the warriors wanted to know about King Arthur's travels. He gave a much edited edition. He spoke much on the different landscapes. Glewlwyd was then at the table, another warrior having replaced him at the gate.

King Arthur, getting sleepy, begged to be excused, and went to his bed. As he lay in bed he could hear the voice of Ogrevran rumbling and thundering in the hall below, swelling and fading in and out among the other sounds in the castle.

Morning: Arthur rose before the sun, got up and went to the washroom, took care of his toilet and washed. He went out to the courtyard. In the east, the sky was pale pink. He watched it get brighter. The warriors were going in for breakfast. King Arthur went in to the table. He enjoyed his breakfast, got up:

"Lords and noble warriors, I have taken much pleasure in being part of this company. And Lord Ogrevran, thankyou for having me as a welcome visitor. You have been most gracious and I do hope to return."

"You would be most welcome."

King Arthur went to his bed, collected his belongings, took them out to the courtyard. There were two horses in the courtyard: King Arthur's and another. There were also a number of huge boxes. Guinhwyvare came out. She wore beautiful clothes and these, showed much of her body. And she was beautiful. She showed King Arthur how to turn the shield into the form of a boat. The shield took a shape and size to hold two horses and all the belongings which were waiting there.

"Now I want to see where the avrank was," said Guinhwyvare.

King Arthur told the ship where to go. The ship lifted, sailed up into the clouds.

"This is how birds must feel," said King Arthur.

The ship flew down, set on the lake, on the great body of calm water. The ground showed the signs of the battle that had been fought there. A farmer came, looked with wonder and surprise at the ship. King Arthur and Guinhwyvare jumped from the ship to the shore, walked up to the farmer.

"Where is the avrank?" King Arthur asked.

"Sir, Lord Neton tied it with ropes, had his oxen drag it up into the hills."

"Look, here is where thy horse was standing. And another horse was here," said Guinhwyvare. "Thy horse must have stomped there. Well. That is that."

She put her hand on the rail of the boat, jumped and landed inside. King Arthur did the same.

"Let us sail across the lake," said Guinhwyvare.

"Across the lake," said King Arthur.

The boat sailed over the water. The water reflected the bright sky. The breeze was cold as it blew off the water.

"A bit chilly. But beautiful. Let us be off to the Unicorn Island," said Guinhwyvare.

"Can you direct us there?"

"I can."

Guinhwyvare told the ship how to sail. It went up into the clouds, flew for a way; then, down. Below was a beautiful shoreline. A great field was in front of a woodland. There was a dead lion and a couple of dead wolves. Guinhwyvare dipped down to look at the lion. A unicorn sped from the woodland, lept at the ship. Guinhwyvare pulled the ship out of the way.

"We do not want a dead unicorn," she said, "because they are so beautiful."

Three more unicorns ran from the wood. Guinhwyvare sailed away.

Take us to Hayonwye," said Guinhwyvare.

"Hayonwye," said King Arthur.

The boat went up, sailed through the clouds, then down, down on the Wye, sailed to the shore.

"Let us get the horses and ride to the castle gate," said Guinyvare.

The two of them mounted, rode down the road, up to the beautiful castle, in at the gate.

"It is the King. And Guinyvare," shouted the gateman. He came out and bowed. Lord Brychan and his lady came out. Gwladys was there. And other young women: Elyned was there and Pystyl and Lionors. They all came up and gave hugs.

It was an hour past noon, so those in the castle had already begun lunch. Places were quickly set for King Arthur and Guinyvare.

"We were having a bit of a family get together and you two coming makes it just perfect," said Lady Erduduyl. All at the table, at the same time, had to tell King Arthur about their families. King Arthur had to tell about his trip.

"I really must get to Camelot. They might be getting worried," said King Arthur.

"I can understand that. We were all getting worried, and I know that there are things you will be wanting to get your attention on," said Lord Brychan.

"You see, I am soon to have a child," said Gwladys.

"Yes I saw," said King Arthur.

"And of course," said Lady Lionors.

"All blessings come to you. Come to you both," said King Arthur.

King Arthur finished lunch, gave hugs to all the women, and a special hug and thankyou to Guinyvare. He went out, called for his horse, mounted, rode down the road and around to his boat. He shaped the boat so his horse could ride on. King Arthur rode his horse on, dismounted and sailed his ship to Camelot, put it down on a field which was not far from the palace. He got his horse, all other things, off the boat, turned the boat back into his shield, packed all his things on his horse, rode over the fields, up the road to Camelot.

THE DARK SHIP

Sir Bedivere returned from the
Margin of the lake, past where
Sir Lucan lay fading into death,
To where lay his mortally wounded sire,
King Arthur.

"Sire," he said, "I beheld a marvelous thing.
I flung Excalibur, as you commanded,
Far out into the lake; but, before it touched
The water's surface, a white hand rose up,
Grabbed it by the hilt, three times
The sword it waved; then,
Sword and hand together
Vanished beneath the water."

"It is well," said the king," but your dawdling
Has wasted precious time. Make haste,
Assist me to yonder brook. I go to Avalon."

Sir Bedivere looked up. He beheld
Even a greater marvel than he had
Witnessed at the lake. Up the brook,
Which flowed close at hand, drifted a
Coal black barque. A gentle breeze
Filled a single black sail.
And in the barque stood three
Blacked robed queens, black robed
and black hooded. And these,
the Queen of Northgalis,
the Queen of Out Islands,
And Morgan the Fay.

Sir Bedivere carried his king
to the place which the dark ship approached,
The three queens reached down,
Gently lifted the king from Sir Bedivere,
Lay him down between them,
Then over King Arthur lay
a sky blue cloth.
The ship sailed on, sailed up the brook.

"Sire, what am I to do?"
Called Sir Bedivere after the departing ship
"Of all the fellowship, there is none left but me."

There was a cry in the heart of the sky.

Whether spirit or bird, Bedivere knew not,
But more answer, there was none.

The ship sailed on, sailed up the brook,
and was seen no more.

   While they sailed Morgan sang, sang until her emotion flooded
over. Song changed to a flood of crying,
   "I was scared Hob might not know," she said.
   "I knew you would be here. – Whom have you with you?"
   "This is the Queen of Out Islands. And this, the Queen of Norga-
lis."
   "Then, this was the word you could not say."
   "Yes. – I am your sister, Morgan."
   "Where will our bodies be?"
   "They will take them to Glastonbury. – They will think I am
Guinyvare. – You and I will have our secrets, – Arthur, just the two of
us."

   Below the rocky cliff, where the brook flows out of the rocks,
were found boards from an old boat. And the bodies.